REBEL

FAITH MORGAN

REBEL

HODDER &
STOUGHTON

First published in Great Britain in 2021 by Hodder & Stoughton
An Hachette UK company

1

Copyright © Faith Morgan 2021

The right of Faith Morgan to be identified as the Author of the Work has
been asserted by her in accordance with the Copyright, Designs and
Patents Act 1988.

This book is a work of non-fiction based on the life, experiences and recollections
of the author. In some cases names of people or places have been changed to protect
the privacy of others. The author has stated to the publishers that, except in such
respects, the contents of this book are accurate and true according to their memory
of events.

A CIP catalogue record for this title is available from the British Library

Hardback ISBN 9781529347593
Trade Paperback ISBN 9781529347609
eBook ISBN 9781529347616

Typeset in BEMBO by Manipal Technologies Limited.

Printed and bound in Great Britain by Clays Ltd, Elcograf S.p.A.

Hodder & Stoughton policy is to use papers that are natural, renewable
and recyclable products and made from wood grown in sustainable
forests. The logging and manufacturing processes are expected to
conform to the environmental regulations of the country of origin.

Hodder & Stoughton Ltd
Carmelite House
50 Victoria Embankment
London EC4Y 0DZ

www.hodder.co.uk

For mum.
Thank you for giving me your blessing to write this book. You are the bravest woman I know. I love you!

Contents

Preface

THE CAR, SURREY, 2019

'Mum . . . is it true? Were you in a sex cult?' Driving my fifteen-year-old son to school one beautiful spring morning in 2019, I am hit with the question I dread being asked. It is unexpected. He has found the papers in the box marked 'loft'. We have just moved, and there are packing crates everywhere. The box is filled with media reports. Court statements . . . my teenage diary. He wants facts: what happened to me? Was it full of paedophiles? How did I escape? 'Were you raped, Mum?'

I answer without thinking, 'Oh no, Jude, not raped . . .' but then he asks me to tell him what happened, and as I describe it, I realise. 'You were a child, Mum. He was forty. He groomed you and you were raped.' We are outside the school now. 'Love you, Mum,' he says before getting out of the car. I'm working from home that day, so I drive back to the house, shaking. I go up to the loft and look at the box. It is time to remember.

It is strange leafing through the letters, diaries and yellowing magazine interviews featuring my teenage face, the defiance unmistakable, daring anyone who looked into my eyes to feel my anger at what had happened to me, to children like me. Looking into that face is like opening the door to a world I put behind me long ago. That defiance faded, because it had to, in order for me to go on to live, to love.

And here I am, twenty-five years on, a wife and mother, sitting in my attic in the home counties. My two beautiful children are almost adults: Jude, and Theo, who is eighteen, and had discovered my secret a year or so before Jude. I had talked about it a little. It was the summer that the #MeToo movement gathered momentum, and I shared the scantest details of what had happened to me with him, explaining that exploitative adults often wear a friendly face, and that victims' own complicated feelings and longing for attachment sometimes make it virtually impossible to see abuse for what it is.

In talking to Theo, I managed to skim the surface, to leave the seething heart of the messy business shut up in that box, but something about the way Jude sees it, his clarity and his budding masculinity, I think, lead me to look again at that strange time. I want to make sense of it, and to think about it from my incredibly fortunate perspective – having come through what destroyed so many of my friends' lives. The 'Family' tree is littered with overdoses, self-harm, suicide, mental breakdowns and even murder. Some (River Phoenix) have been etched into mainstream memory, but many more are long forgotten. The lost children.

I start with my teenage diary, which somehow survived all those years, marking key moments from Costa Rica, India, Greece, Mexico, and London. The communes, the 'missions', the friendships and the relationships. Through it all, enduring faith: in Jesus, in the Prophet (cult leader David Berg), and in the inevitability of the coming end times, which I fully believed would arrive in 1993. I read printouts of the letters I sent after leaving, seeing the truth, for the first time, about what life in the Family was. I read with pain the replies that had been sent to me, the traitor who spoke out about my experiences. These were letters from people that despite everything that had happened, I had loved. I read the court documents describing evidence recovered from cult houses that had documented paedophilia, which the cult recommended as an act of worship.

As I began to pick through the past, the desire to write about it grew, but with it, the wish to remain private, for the sake of my sons. Because at the heart of what was most disturbing about the activities of the Family was the complete disregard for the children within it, in particular for their future. We were there to be used; the world would be over before we were grown up anyway. With the perspective of time, I was curious to think from an adult standpoint about the grown-ups who had been around me – about how they, in particular my own loving mother, could have been so comprehensively brainwashed into putting their own children at such incredible risk.

Post #MeToo, I feel that this part of the problem has been swept under the carpet. Because although I'm happy that women are being listened to and male predators have nowhere to hide, there's a hidden story lurking beneath the surface. It's the story of all the women who are complicit, either turning a blind eye to the behaviour of abusers, or themselves abusing others. The message I would like to get across is that all of us, men *and* women, are capable of terrible things. Destructiveness, and potential disregard for other human beings, is something that lurks within us all.

More than anything, though, I want to tell the extraordinary story of my family, to relive the adventures and the technicolour travels of my early life in order to help me understand what happened and why. And perhaps the spirit of that defiant girl is still in there somewhere, because I am filled with some of my old fight, too – I wish to look into the eyes of 'evil', with its many faces. I want my readers to see it too, to front up to it, so we can send it on its way.

Faith Morgan, Surrey, January 2020

CHAPTER 1: A Carpet of People – Costa Rica, 1970s

In my earliest memory, there is music. The song sounds far away:

'We live in the fifth dimension . . . A very nice place to be . . . We live in the fifth dimension . . . Oh won't you come and live with me.'

There is a strip of bright daylight visible between the curtains that cover the bedroom window, and I can hear an American couple arguing on the landing outside the room. I am crying. I want my mummy to come, to get me out of my cot.

'Shall we pick her up?' the woman asks.

'No. No we shouldn't. We'll spoil her.'

I keep crying and they keep arguing, their voices get louder. The woman sounds worried. After what feels like a very long time, the door opens, and an American woman is striding towards me. She is wearing a long blue dress which reaches to the ground. Her hair is wavy, light brown, and waist-length. She leans into the cot, her hair is all around me now, falling forward. As she lifts me up, I see the man behind her. He has long hair too, he is wearing jeans and a T-shirt, with bare feet. I stop crying, but in the memory, the feeling which is strongest is: *This is not my mummy*.

*

I was the first child in my family to be born outside of the 'system'. 'System' and 'systemite' were words that we used for the outside world and the people in it. I was the third daughter, the middle child in a family of six, and I was the baby only fleetingly, quickly gaining another sister, Beverly, when I was fourteen months old. She was followed by Michael, then Petra, so that by the time I was four, I had three younger siblings.

We were an anomaly in the Family. Although we were disciples, and my parents paid 10 per cent of their income to the group, ours was a privileged status that we were permitted only because of Daddy's unusual position. Daddy (Arturo) was well connected in Costa Rica. His father had been a senior figure in the judiciary, and although Grandfather was semi-retired, he was now the Dean of the School of Law in a prestigious university and sat on the boards of a number of businesses and institutions. He moved in diplomatic circles. Daddy worked in his office and had introduced senior 'shepherds' in the Family to influential figures in the government along with a couple of prominent academics. As a result, the shepherds were happy to turn a blind eye to the peculiarities of our unorthodox family set-up: home ownership (our house was held in trust by our grandfather, so Daddy could not give it over to the group); Daddy's 'systemite' job; children born in a private hospital at my grandfather's expense; daughters who were sent to a 'systemite' kindergarten, and the eldest to a 'systemite' private school, and an English-speaking wife – our glamorous mother Elizabeth, who sometimes read us Enid Blyton and C. S. Lewis's Narnia books at bedtime despite the fact that, in the Family, only Bible and Family-produced stories were permitted.

Every day, Daddy would set out to work in his three-piece suit and ostrich-leather shoes. He was handsome and tall, by Costa Rican standards, and his natural charm made him captivating, particularly to strangers and acquaintances. When there were no guests at home, he grumbled about working for his father, whom he did not get along with, openly wishing him dead around the dinner table (something that upset Mummy a great deal).

Daddy was, he enjoyed telling us, the black sheep of his family. His two older brothers were a successful barrister and a businessman. In contrast, as a young man, Arturo had flitted from one job to the next, facilitated by his father, before deciding to become a preacher after a dramatic conversion experience. 'The Holy Spirit came to me in the form of a gold cord. It floated towards me and hit me straight in the heart!' he told us. 'I changed, right then,' he said, clicking his fingers dramatically. 'I stopped drinking and smoking and decided to give my life to the Lord.' We listened to this story, rapt. 'It happened one afternoon whilst your mother and I visited some old American missionary friends of your grandparents. Handel's *Messiah* was playing in the background.' The transformation in him was radical. This one-time playboy and directionless black sheep was reborn as an impassioned seer and seeker, with a conviction that it was his mission to spread the word of his new God around the world.

'When I saw the change in your father, I was shocked!' Mummy said. 'I had been brought up an atheist, my father used to sneer at religion! Then one day, after a few months of watching your dad's transformation, I said to God: "If you are there, then I want the same as my husband." I felt the presence of God very strongly and I heard the voice of the Lord say to me: "Elizabeth, you do not need your epilepsy pills anymore. You are healed." So I flushed them away and I haven't had an epileptic fit since!'

Daddy got distracted from his religious training at a Baptist ministry in Scotland when he met Faith (I was named after her), the daughter of the founder of the Family, David Berg. Faith convinced him to turn his back on systemite religion (the 'Old Church') and join the 'new wine' of the Children of God, later known as 'the Family'. It was a chance meeting that inspired his move back home with Mummy and my older sisters, Shiloh and Dinah. Once he had become convinced to leave the conventional church for the Family, his zeal was increased. The move back to Costa Rica suited the leadership within the Family, who considered the country a key mission field, ripe for witnessing.

But rather than freedom, Arturo found himself in a bind. Before long, Mummy was pregnant with me. Another three pregnancies followed in quick succession as contraception was regarded a systemite heresy dreamt up by selfish people who had been inspired by the Devil himself.

Despite claiming to be desperate to travel and do missionary work, Arturo was stuck in a position where he was required to work to earn a living and maintain the relationship with his father, which served the Family's interests. He longed for his inheritance, and for independence, reminding us all the time he wanted to travel to China to spread the word. Despite this, he did appear to enjoy the status that his connection to the systemite world, and his family contacts within it, gave him. Also, his job meant he had an excuse to get out of the house, and when he was home to avoid being helpful in any practical way, retreating to his study to 'work'. The house was chaos. Even with the help of visiting maids (another of the 'special' privileges our status and Grandfather's wealth afforded us), Mummy had her work cut out with all the washing, cooking, childcare and gardening there was to do.

Shiloh was the eldest of us kids. She was extremely bright, got top grades at school, and was an invaluable mother's help at home. She was Grandfather's favourite too, a talented poet with a strong sense of right and wrong. From the time I was about three, it was Shiloh (then eleven or so) who bathed, dressed and fed me and my younger siblings.

Shiloh suffered from painful joints, which sometimes made it hard for her to play with us. When I was very little, she was diagnosed with lupus, an autoimmune condition. She had to stay out of the sun, as exposure could cause her to develop terrible blisters. Her illness made her tired, and meant she often had to go to hospital for check-ups and treatment. Our bathroom cabinet was filled with her medication, and I watched in the morning as she swallowed an assortment of pills.

Dinah, who was four years younger than Shiloh, and four years older than me, sometimes helped Shiloh marshal the younger children into nappies, socks and shoes. She went about this with considerably less skill (and care) than Shiloh. As a result, I often had uncomfortable feet as my rucked-up socks were stuffed absent-mindedly into my shoes by Dinah. The socks pressed uncomfortably on my toes all morning, until I found an opportunity to tear off my shoes and socks and discard them. When this was discovered, usually by a sibling, Mummy shouted: 'Put your shoes back on immediately!' We were not allowed to go barefoot and Mummy was particular about us all having properly fitted leather shoes.

On the days we went out 'witnessing', singing in orphanages, old people's homes and schools, Mummy dressed us up. We practised Family songs with Shiloh and Dinah, who both led with the guitar and sang. I joined in with the singing from the age of about four, learning guitar when I was five. I loved our witnessing outings, even though I sometimes felt self-conscious. At Christmas time, Mummy dressed us up as angels, with home-made wings, white dresses and gold satin ribbons. Carolling was an English tradition, completely unknown in Costa Rica, and when we knocked on doors in our neighbourhood and began to sing, our neighbours would often cry.

We were spotted on one of these trips by an agent, Mr Barolo. He was a warm man with a huge smile and explained to Mummy that he could help arrange appearances for us: he had contacts in TV and knew one producer at a popular daily show who he thought would love us. True to his word, the producer was charmed by the vision of four little girls (Beverley can't have been much more than five), and we were given a regular slot. The show was filmed in front of a live studio audience, and Mummy always sat near the front, nodding encouragingly, gesticulating at us to project our voices, to smile.

I enjoyed singing for people and harmonising with my sisters, although I was slightly embarrassed that we were singing about Jesus, telling the people at home and in the audience that Jesus loved them, that they just needed to open their hearts. I could see the pride in Mummy's eyes as she signalled from the audience that we should *smile*, drawing her fingers upwards in front of her mouth to remind us not to frown just because we were concentrating. I liked to please Mummy, and my heart swelled with joy and purpose as we sang. A driver took us to the studio, which was always exciting. Also, the trips meant Mummy and Shiloh got a break from the gruelling domestic pressure of life at home. It was an escape.

Mummy's workload was even heavier when we had visitors staying. She baked bread, made cakes and cooked piles of rice and vats of stew. We were an unusually 'nuclear' family by the Family's standard, but the house was always open and often, at mealtimes, Mummy would welcome extra visitors: members of the Family who dropped in after a day out witnessing. Sometimes young members, in couples or alone, would come to stay for a few weeks or months. Occasionally, whole families would come to stay.

The dinner table was Daddy's pulpit, and he relished every opportunity to preach to visitors, irrespective of their level of interest and spiritual leaning. I found his fervour embarrassing, even as a little girl, but I knew I was wrong to feel that way. The Family taught us that if we didn't preach the gospel at every opportunity, we would be robbing people of their chance to have their souls saved and so would have to give account to God for failing them: their blood would be on our hands. This terrified me and left me feeling terribly guilty.

Daddy's warnings about the inevitable coming 'end times' and his anticipation of Jesus's imminent 'rapturing' of the true believers were welcomed by impressionable new converts, but his rants about systemite life and its limitations were the cause of awkward tension when our dinner guests were outsiders. Sometimes Mummy's sister, Aunty Bridget, who worked and lived in France, would come to visit us. When Dad started up with her, her eyebrow would raise quizzically. She looked amused. There would be a dramatic pause at the end, the cue for an expression of interest, some sign of encouragement or, failing that, indication of provocation. After a while, Bridget would simply say 'Mmmm', then change the subject.

On one occasion I remember, Daddy kept on and on: 'You systemites are flatliners, that's the truth of it, Bridget. Your whole world is two-dimensional. And you may think I am way out there with my ideas, and that is all part of it, you see, that is all part of the systemite thinking ... they will brand us with the mark of the beast and persecute us, they will drive us out. We will be persecuted, and we will rebel ... The illuminati are everywhere, and they paint us as the crazy ones, because we are the real threat.' Aunt Bridget left a second dignified pause, then looked up at me, across the table.

'Could you pass me the salt, Faith, darling?'

Her cut-glass English accent was so polite, and she seemed so unmoved by Daddy's warning. I loved Aunty Bridget, with her fancy French clothes and her perfect winged eyeliner. Everything about her was so *worldly*. But the way she ignored Daddy's speech was confusing. Somehow, I knew that to pass the salt would be . . . a defiance, of sorts, on my own part. I was terrified by the idea of the end times. Even the rapturing sounded unpleasant, although Daddy's eyes sparkled whenever he talked about it.

My gaze darted back to Daddy, who was still staring at Aunty Bridget. Mummy put a hand on his sleeve: 'Arturo, Arturo . . .' she said, using the tone she usually kept for us children. Smiling at her sister, she said: 'Children! Why don't you sing Aunty Bridget that new song you have practised after dinner?' It worked. Daddy loved to hear us sing and never missed an opportunity to ask us to perform for visitors. 'Oh, yes children! Sing for Aunty Bridget!' he echoed in his thick South American accent.

At the end of mealtimes, Daddy would wander off and leave the cleaning up to us. Often, I wondered if he had gone to his study in the basement, to take out his 'book of souls' – the little leather-bound notepad he kept with him whenever he went out witnessing. Inside, he noted down the names of all the strangers he had persuaded to share in a prayer with him, to invite Jesus into their hearts. He was proud of his tally, crowing about it often. 'One hundred and seventy-five souls, children! Imagine them all lined up!' he said. It seemed meaningless to me and I was not impressed when he showed me the pages, with the names, printed in his exaggerated, almost illegibly fancy, cursive writing. There were a lot of them. All the souls he had helped to win.

Perhaps I remember Bridget's reaction so vividly because I recognised it was unusual. The force of Daddy's personality meant that most visitors were either entranced by his charisma or were preached into submission. Most were left with the impression that Arturo's diatribes were no invitation to debate; they were a spectacle to be witnessed and enjoyed. Much of the time, Daddy's speeches were rehashes of David Berg's thoughts, as shared in the 'Mo' letters. Berg was the self-appointed 'Prophet' who had founded the Family. He wrote the 'Mo' letters, which were his followers' main source of spiritual instruction. Berg hated Israel and Jews ('Jesus killers'). He admired Gaddafi, Fidel Castro and Arafat. Berg believed the United States and the West in general were *The Great Whore of Babylon*, described in the book of revelations. Daddy loved to regurgitate Berg's views: 'The precious words of the End Time Prophet, as revealed to him by the Lord himself,' he said.

The ideal crowd for Daddy would be full of entranced listeners, murmuring agreement; relaxed, confident and certain in the truth of their belief. All convivial believers with occasional agreeable suggestions from young admirers. Afterwards, the assembled company, buoyed by talk of the coming reckoning and feeling elated to be amongst the 'elites', would reach for their guitars and tambourines. Shiloh, Dinah and I would stand in the sitting room, gathered underneath the large framed Venus De Milo poster that hung there, and sing our hearts out, blasting Family songs at the top of our lungs, a band of miniature Von Trapps.

The adults would clap us and sometimes they'd join in with the songs, or teach us new ones. Family troubadours sometimes came. One of them, a handsome American musician called Matty, came to stay for a month or so when I was three. He taught Dinah to play properly; she spent hours practising the chord shapes in front of a mirror and proudly showed Matty her progress when he was back from a day out witnessing. Matty brought a load of new songs into the house. Dinah loved the attention and she loved to play. She was a tomboy, and her secret passion was listening to forbidden systemite songs on the radio whenever she could. Playing music herself brought her closer to the outside world, which she imagined was filled with pop and rock stars. She practised diligently.

The evening singalongs were a highlight for us all, at first. There was a party atmosphere, and a real sense of celebration and hope amongst the adults, which was contagious. The morning after, we children would pick our way through the hallway, to find a carpet of people sprawled on our living room floor, sometimes spilling into the hallways and kitchen. I remember long hair, stray maracas and tambourines, sleeping bags, and the potent aroma of strange, stale bodies everywhere. Sleepy voices, speaking in a mixture of languages: English, Spanish, Portuguese, sometimes French, would offer us good mornings and God blesses. The visitors were young, in their late teens and twenties. Mummy and Daddy were unusual in the Family, in their thirties already and with so many children. The young visitors seemed enchanted by us, perhaps partly because we lived still as an intact family unit. We were a curiosity in the Family as well as in the systemite worlds we inhabited.

I understood that my friends at the little school I went to, which was Catholic and systemite in the extreme, did not live like this. The weekend get-togethers, I was certain, were unusual. Mummy and Daddy warned us not to talk too much about our home life at school, and they warned us to be on our guard during the school masses and services. They railed against the systemite Catholic idolatry, the shrines that Mummy had warned me were pagan Devil-worshipping symbols. I particularly feared the statues of Jesus with his gory sacred heart. I became convinced this bloody mass contained the soul of the Antichrist, quite literally. I shook when we trooped into the church, keeping one eye on the redness of Jesus's exposed heart, obscene, like something from a butcher's window. I worried that Jesus, the real Jesus inside my heart, would disapprove of me being there, that he would know.

I don't remember sharing my fears with anyone. I kept them to myself. Shiloh would sometimes comment about how 'creepy' the churches were. She attended a Catholic school, too, and she found the rituals and prayers very boring and tedious. Shiloh taught me to read and she sometimes read Bible stories to us all. She said goodnight prayers with us too: 'Jesus, give the children a good night's sleep, help them to have good dreams, in Jesus's name, Amen.'

I loved Shiloh dearly. She was kind to us little ones and had lots of time for me. If I was being a good girl, she would let me sit on her immaculately made bed for a little while. In my eyes, at fifteen, Shiloh was virtually a grown-up. I hated to see her disciplined. Once, I remember, she had an argument with Dinah over a perfume sample. I heard it all from the landing, where I was playing with my dolls:

'You're such a bitch, Shiloh, I just want one little spray. You're so prissy, with your precious room and your scent that *nobody can touch* . . . Don't you know we are all meant to *share?*'

'*Get out,* you little shit!'

Scuffle. Door slam. Mum heard all this from the utility room downstairs, because they were shouting. Her voice was calm, really calm: always the worst sign. She made her way upstairs, with two beakers in which she had dissolved a large spoon of clothes-washing powder. She summoned Dinah back into Shiloh's room.

'Girls, this is appalling behaviour! A terrible example to the little ones. I will not have that language in this house. It is disgusting. You will both swill these around in your mouths for ten seconds. One more bad word from either of you and I'll get the *chilillo.*'

I was at the door, watching, and Shiloh looked grave. It made me very worried. I said a prayer: 'Not the *chilillo*, not the *chilillo*, please Jesus.' I knew that the pain from the thin, stripped bamboo was so intense that you felt the hurt deep in the centre of your belly.

After they had swilled the washing liquid around their mouths, retching and swilling with plain water to try to get rid of the taste afterwards, Dinah stomped downstairs to play outside. I sidled up to Shiloh her to give her a hug.

'Are you OK? Does your mouth hurt?'

'Oh no . . . wasn't very nice but . . . look.' She smiled wide to show me her teeth, running a finger across them for effect. 'Squeaky clean now! Gleaming . . .'

I knew she was protecting me by making it funny, but I was glad about that.

CHAPTER 2: Break for Freedom – London, 1991

The morning after I made the call to Mum telling her I wanted to come home, I was at the breakfast table with Ruth, an American disciple in her late twenties, and her children, Zachariah, eight, and his younger brother Akio, six, whose father had been a wealthy Japanese 'fish' (the Family word for a friendly, usually male, non-believer who was happy to give money or lodging to Family members in exchange for sex with one or more of the 'sisters') whom neither of the children had met. Zachariah's father was an Israeli disciple Ruth had met when she was twenty. She had lost contact with him, too, ending up in the 'mission field' in India, and finding her way to the north London home after the exodus of the Family from India. Ruth's children were a handful, and her coping strategy combined a general policy of disinterest with vicious and unpredictable discipline. They were not much fun to be around, poor boys. I could see that they were bored stiff, intelligent and full of beans. They weren't allowed outside in the garden because the shepherds said the neighbours would start wondering why they weren't in school.

June, a woman of indeterminate age who just seemed 'old' to me, sat at the head of the table. She was in charge of provisioning supplies for all of the Family homes in the area and spent much of her time upstairs in the 'telephone room' coordinating donations of food and clothes from local businesses. The line she spun them was that the donations would go to homeless children in orphanages. I overheard her patter when I was cleaning the house and knew it to be duplicitous. Provisioning always made me feel very uncomfortable. Sometimes disciples would tell outright lies to get people to make donations: 'We distribute this food/clothing/equipment to orphanages and old people's homes,' they'd say. The only distribution I saw was to the other communes. Along with me, Ruth, her children and June, another couple lived in the house with us, although that morning, they weren't there, having set out early on a witnessing trip. I'd helped to make their packed lunches. They had gone to the West End with a supply of posters and videos, and we knew they wouldn't be back until dinner time. June went upstairs to start her provisioning calls whilst Ruth and I finished breakfast with the children.

Zachariah and Akio were arguing about who got the blue striped bowl. As usual, Ruth ignored them. Turning instead to me, she said: 'Faith, have you noticed how we get sent to this horrible house? Did you know that the home shepherds and their children went to Uncle Charles's penthouse apartment in Knightsbridge?' Uncle

Charles was a very wealthy 'fish'. 'It seems to me that we single mothers are always at the bottom of the pile.'

I was stunned. She is murmuring, (a word used in the Family for complaining) I thought. This was a cardinal sin and one for which, if I were to report her, she would pay dearly. But I felt sorry for her, and I knew she was right. There were many single mothers in the Family with children of all the colours of the rainbow because they mostly had different fathers from all the 'flirty fishing' and sharing. The Family did not believe in contraception of any sort, and I could see women were the ones who paid the price.

'I am going through very big trials, Faith,' she said. 'I feel further from Jesus here in England than I ever have . . . It is so grey . . . I feel sad . . . I need a change . . . I need to find a mate, a father for the children.'

I nodded and mumbled a sympathetic sound. But I didn't fancy her chances. At least she only has two kids, I thought. Zachariah had blue eyes and almost white hair and Akio was half Japanese. Many young mothers had many more than two children, like Aunty Meekness in India . . . She had seven.

After a tussle, the coveted bowl fell onto the floor, clanging against the table leg, and bouncing on the linoleum. Miraculously, it didn't break.

'Go straight to your room, boys, or I'll make you stand in the corner to memorise scripture for half an hour,' Ruth said. They scampered up quickly.

Although I regarded Ruth's mothering with disdain, I shared her views on England. Prospects for the future as a disciple, especially a single mother in one of the London homes (whether a small one such as the one we found ourselves in, or a large one like the ones we had both moved from), felt uninspiring. It was scary, too. The systemites were mounting a persecution campaign against the Family in the media and there were rumours of a court case involving two children being made a wards of court.

Ruth looked rattled. It wasn't surprising; the last few weeks had been odd. I had been bundled (along with Ruth and her boys) into a van one night, from the larger Family home we had been in for months. It had happened suddenly, after a night of burning Mo letters in the home on the instructions of the shepherds, who were convinced we were about to get raided. Ruth, three preteen girls and I had been tasked with destroying the Mo letters locked in the 'Word Trunk', ripping out pictures or passages that the systemites might use as proof against our beliefs. We threw them on a bonfire in the garden. 'The world does not understand the radical teachings of the Prophet,' Uncle Andrew admonished us as we ripped out pages from the books, filled with Berg's sexualised teachings and pictures of naked children. I tried not to look at them.

As we shredded the books and threw the pages into our makeshift incinerator – an old washing machine drum

– Uncle Andrew preached at us. 'What does The Word say?' he asked. 'The Word says in Revelation, chapter three, verse sixteen: *So then because thou art lukewarm, and neither cold nor hot, I will spew thee out of my mouth.* We are not ashamed of being "hot"!' he said, his voice rising as he warmed to his theme. 'And if that makes us extremists, so be it. That is why the world hates us.' We knew these Mo letters were the hottest of all, and that was why they must be destroyed.

We teens – in the Family this meant anyone between the ages of twelve and twenty – were not allowed to go anywhere on our own or even together at that time. And now that I was shut in this home with Ruth and a few others, we weren't even allowed to escape to the scrubby patch of grass which housed some rusty swings at the end of our street. This didn't stop the children from asking on a daily basis. They had seen the swings once or twice, when we had driven past them on the way to one of the larger homes for occasional devotional meetings. We were under virtual house arrest. Strangest of all, nobody would tell us where it was that we were. I had no idea whether I was close to the north London home, or deep in the suburbs on the other side of the city. We had been taken in the night, in a hurry. I didn't think to look properly at landmarks as we rattled our way around the streets, because it didn't occur to me that we wouldn't be told where we were once we had arrived.

I didn't have a proper room in the safe house, just a rolled up mat on the floor of a bedroom, surrounded by a huge mountain of clothing and boxes of whatever June had managed to collect from businesses with surplus stock. Hi-vis tabards jostled with large tins of formula powder that were past their best-before date. There were cardboard boxes filled with crackers and large tubs of the kind of pink soap you sometimes saw in public toilet dispensers. The mattress I had was thin, and I was expected to lean it against the wall and roll up my sleeping bag every morning. Everything else I owned lived in my canvas 'flee' bag, which the shepherds told us to keep packed at all times in case we had to move on in a hurry. More and more, I had the feeling that I was getting close to the edge of something. I had given up on trying to believe by now: I no longer willed myself to feel a connection to the Prophet when June or Jonah read out the morning's Mo letter.

I began to wonder if Jesus really was going to come back when I was twenty. Secretly, I didn't believe it could be true. If Jesus didn't come back, what would become of me? Would I become a single mother with tons of kids from different brothers and 'fish'? Would I have to carry on organising music groups with the kids, in whatever home I was in, to busk in Leicester Square at Christmas? I remembered our stands in Victoria and Marylebone stations, covered in tapes, video cassettes and posters. We played guitar and sang for hours, the children dancing their practised routines with guitar cases on the ground, left open for donations. The money rolled in but we were never given any of it.

I thought more and more of the afternoon when I had burnt the Mo letters, watching as the black and white photo story of a three-year-old boy being abused by his own mother was thrown into the flames. I watched the fire destroy pamphlets entitled 'God's Whores' and 'Lashes of Love'. Pictures of naked women with enormous melons of breasts were everywhere, and photos of the gnome-like Berg, with his wrinkled forehead and wispy white beard, surrounded by an assembly of beautiful women, all of them less than half his age.

Since the burning, I had become more contemptuous of the adults around me and now, in the safe house, found myself staring out of the window more and more. I wondered what thoughts occupied the minds of the systemite men and women I saw wandering past the window, and I particularly wondered about what life was like for systemite teens. They looked so free, so worldly. Even the girls in school uniform. I was frightened about backsliding, about the shepherds' warnings about what happened to those who turned their back on the Prophet.

In the past year or so, there had been an increase in the sharing of 'traumatic testimonies' – gathered witness statements from those who had left the Family. We were warned that some of these backsliders had found themselves homeless, begging for drugs and alcohol, turning to prostitution, or saddened by a life that felt dead and meaningless without the Family. One brother described flipping burgers for a pittance, with no hope of a better life. Another, who had made a great material success of her life after leaving, spoke of the hollow emptiness of her existence, and told how she missed the protection, security and sense of belonging that came with life in the Family. She shared her feelings of emptiness and futility – living in the world just to make money – and described how grateful she was that the Lord and her precious Family had taken her back. Grandpa, (the title we children, or 'Second Generation' were told to use to refer to the Prophet) in his mercy and generosity, had received her, the prodigal daughter. In Mo letters, Grandpa used examples like this to make his point: to live a meaningful life and to maintain your faith and your connection with Jesus, you must stay within His Family.

Even though the rebellious part of me questioned this, I was terrified that by becoming a backslider, I would be breaking from Jesus forever, and the fear of the unknown was almost paralysing. I had no real idea about what the outside world was like, but everything I had heard made it sound sinister and dangerous. I had been trained to be an end time disciple, and the end time was supposedly only two years away. What if Grandpa was right; what then?

We finished our cereal: provisioned cornflakes. 'Provisioning' was another method of 'witnessing'. It consisted of contacting retailers or wholesalers and telling them that we were missionaries. Would they donate any surplus products to help us as we go about our mission to show the love of God to the world? June came back down to find me a few minutes later. I was washing up. 'Honey, the area shepherds are coming to talk to you in the next couple of days.' I was gripped by terror and said nothing. Oh no, I thought. Mum has not managed to convince them to allow me to stay with them. I was worried this might happen, and I'd been careful in the way I had explained it to Mum on the phone. We were never allowed to use the telephone without a grilling by the Home Shepherd first, after which we might be granted permission. The consequences of being caught didn't bear thinking about, but I had plucked up the courage and snuck upstairs one day when June was out and called home. Mum answered. I told her I wanted to 'wait out this wave of persecution' with her and the rest of my family. I was desperate to go and live with them as I knew all my siblings were there. I had felt left out, but now we could be together for the first time in years. My parents at this time had DFO (Disciple and Friend Only) status, what was known as 'half in, half out'; this meant that they wouldn't receive all the Mo letters, only the ones fit for 'babes', even though they still had to give 10 per cent of their income to the Family. Once the persecution was over,

I told Mum, I would come back to a full-time Disciple Only (DO) home, the top membership status.

For two days I agonised. I couldn't eat and had difficulty sleeping. I was worried that I would get sent to a teen home instead. And I knew what happened in teen homes to rebellious dissenters. I could be put on silence restriction. Or perhaps they might do a public spanking and exorcism. Maybe I'd be put on hard labour or be made to do a bread and water fast. What had Mum said to them? I wished I could talk to her. Perhaps I was being deceitful, and perhaps the Lord knew my heart and was going to see to it that I was corrected, to save me from the system. I might be put through a 'breaking'. This meant silence restriction and isolation, prayer and fasting, exorcisms and, in some cases, physical punishment. I might lose my mind. I might never see my family again. Worse than that was the worry that the Lord was disappointed in me.

The shepherds, Uncle Zeph and Aunty Maria, arrived two days later. June showed them in. I could hear them having a meeting in the telephone room with June and her husband and then with Jonas and Mary. Uncle Zeph's loud voice travelled down the stairs. He was an overbearing and authoritarian shepherd and he scared me to death. They were in there for three hours and the entire time I was terrified. My head conjured a carousel of visions of unwanted futures that filled me with dread. Then June called for me.

'Hi, Faith,' said Aunty Maria with a smile. My guts churned. She hugged and kissed me. 'God bless you, honey! We love you. Praise the Lord. Let's start with a prayer.'

We sat down together in the telephone room. The three of us held hands, closed our eyes and bowed our heads. 'Thank you, Jesus, thank you Lord,' Uncle Zeph took over. 'Jesus, we want to thank you for Faith. She's such a blessing! We pray that you show her your love and your will, your plan for her life, to serve you and bring your light into the world, to win souls for you. I pray that she is yielded to your will and that she is sensitive to your holy spirit, in Jesus's name.'

Uh-oh, this is not going to go well for me, I thought. I knew full well what those kinds of prayers meant. 'We've been in contact with your family, Faith,' said Maria, her sickly-sweet smile suddenly disappearing. Aunty Maria had an air of dogmatic self-righteousness. She wore her long flat hair parted in the middle, framing her horse-like bespectacled face. I nodded. My heart was beating like crazy and my stomach was in knots. Perhaps Mum had not covered for me well enough; perhaps she'd caved in. Mum is so easily persuaded, I thought. I felt disappointed; she had sounded willing on the phone.

'We feel as if you need a new challenge. We thought you might join a pioneering home in Siberia. We have a group of dedicated pioneers. You'd be leaving in three

27

weeks' time. We think you'd be a great addition.' My heart sank. Siberia.

'Or, we could send you to Brazil!' said Aunty Maria. 'There are some homes doing amazing things with music out there and we know how musical you are. We don't even need to get your parents to sign over a power of attorney – you don't need your parents' permission, Faith. You are almost eighteen years old and you can leave without needing their consent.' I had heard about power of attorney before. Parents had been coerced into signing over their kids to their shepherds so they could send them wherever, whenever. A new challenge? I didn't believe a word they were saying. It would be the same drudgery, just in another country and further away from my family. I thought: I need to get out, I need to get out!

'Can I pray about it? I'd like to ask the Lord where I should go,' I said.

'OK, we will give you a couple of days to pray about it, honey. How exciting!' said Maria enthusiastically. When they left, my heart sank to my boots: I'm backsliding, I thought. A voice in my head admonished me: 'You are being given the opportunity to go to new mission fields and you would rather stay with your parents. You are a backslider,' it said. I lay on my mattress that night para-lysed with fear and dread. My head was filled with the fear of the Lord, shame about backsliding and dread at the prospects ahead of me.

'Aunty June,' I said as she was downstairs making a cup of tea. 'May I borrow the phone to call my parents about my meeting with Uncle Zeph and Aunty Maria, please?'

'Yes, sweetie,' she smiled.

I dashed upstairs to the phone, my heart beating fast. Mum answered.

'Please, Mum, it's me! They want to send me to Siberia! Or Brazil. Please, I want to come home!'

'OK . . .' said Mum weakly. 'Let me speak to Zeph and Maria again and tell them your decision.'

'Mum, please be careful! You can't say it was my idea or I'll be in big trouble!'

'OK, darling, let me see what I can come up with.'

The next day, June came downstairs looking grave. 'Faith, get your flee bag ready, you will be collected in one hour and taken to the train station. Here's the train fare. Your parents will pick you up at the other end.' I could barely believe my ears. I was so excited!

It was mid-January, less than three months away from my eighteenth birthday. The ground was thick with snow, the streets icy. I climbed out of the van by the taxi queue at Victoria station. The driver, a disciple in his fifties, was someone I had never seen before. He had been silent on the journey. When we pulled up, he said: 'Here we are. Good-bye.'

This was odd and uncharacteristically cold. We were used to hugs and kisses in the Family, it was a ritual. I had promised the area shepherds that I'd come back to the Family, so why was this brother being so hostile? I skidded my way on the slippery pavement clutching my flee bag. I knew I was going to Crystal Palace.

When my siblings told me the story later, they said that they had all exploded when Mum got off the phone to me and announced that the shepherds wanted to send me to Siberia or Brazil. Even Dad was cross about it. When Mum called the shepherds back to discuss it, everyone crowded around her: Dad, Dinah, Bev, Mike, Petra and Maria. Mum dialled. The conversation went on and on, it sounded as though Zeph was convincing Mum and getting her to acquiesce. Suddenly, to my siblings' utter surprise, my dad snatched the phone out of my mum's hand and yelled:

'Zeph! *You send my daughter now, or I call the police!*'

Then he slammed down the phone. My siblings cheered and jumped up and down for joy. They knew he had called the shepherds' bluff. Sure enough, the next day, I was bundled into the van. I only connected the dots afterwards – that was why they were so hostile. The Family was suffering persecution and the last thing they wanted was my dad calling the police on them.

Ordinarily, in Family homes, Christmas was the busiest time of the year for us. We spent the run-up to Christmas working our arses off, busking in Leicester Square, Covent Garden and train stations with our posse of singers and dancers. We'd set up a stand with our tapes, posters and video cassettes to sell. People would leave tips in the guitar case and buy merchandise from us. Our hands froze and we played the guitar with fingerless gloves. I watched through windows enviously as other teenagers got to sit in coffee shops sipping hot chocolate and eating mince pies. Why can't we just be normal? I thought.

This year, I hoped, I could be. Finally, here I was, on my way home. I called home from the payphone on the concourse at Victoria, reversing the charges. 'Oh Faith, that is wonderful. We will come to meet you at Crystal Palace!'

As the train pulled in, I saw my whole family on the platform waiting for me: Dinah, with two-year-old Robert in his buggy and baby Tito, Mum and Dad, Beverly, Petra and Michael and little Maria, who had grown so big, she was eight now. I was looking forward to getting to know her properly. I was so happy to see them. There were big hugs all round. Michael picked up my suitcase, and Maria held my hand as we walked up the big snowy hill to home. They were full of questions.

'Where was the house you were living in, Faith?' Beverly asked.

'I don't know. I wasn't allowed out and we weren't told.'

'Why didn't you come to see us when Tito was born?' This was Maria.

'I wasn't allowed to, Maria,' I said sadly.

'Do you have to go back?' Petra asked.

The question hung there. The sound of eight pairs of feet on snow, which was still falling.

'I don't know, Petra,' I answered truthfully.

I had a long bath when we got to the house, and Dinah lent me one of her jumpers. She was upstairs putting the children to bed, and I kissed their sweet smooth foreheads. 'Ni-night Tatty Faith . . .' said Robert.

I made my way back downstairs and sat down next to Beverly in the living room. She was watching TV with Petra and Michael. 'Wow,' I said. 'You're allowed to watch TV?' They grinned. 'Yeah,' said Bev smugly. I got up and sat cross-legged on the rug in front of the fire and stared into it. It was a gas coal-effect fire so there were blue flames dancing about as well as the orange ones, licking the lumps of fake coal. I mulled over Petra's question to me earlier as we trudged up the hill in the snow from the train station, 'Do you have to go back?' I'm never going back, I thought to myself. It was then that I realised how utterly comfortably that thought sat within me, and how easily my fears of leaving the Family had disappeared, like in a little puff of smoke.

The weeks that followed were spent catching up with my family. Everyone recounted their experiences and adventures. Dinah had stayed in Mexico, Beverly and

Michael at the teen home in Wantage. I shared my stories about London and the caravan trip around Europe, Hungary and Romania.

'Wanna come to the pub, Faith?' said Dinah.

'What?! OK, sure!'

As soon as we'd closed the front door, she produced a cigarette, lit it and blew rings of smoke in my face. I was shocked. 'Want one?' she said with a twinkle in her eye. Without thinking twice, I stuck out my hand. It was disgusting. I coughed and spluttered.

'We are systemites now!' Dinah laughed, and we cackled as we walked down the hill to the pub through the snow. We had enough money for one drink each and bought a pint of lager, taking it to a corner table. We made it last, and I felt a real thrill, surrounded by systemites in a pub – what David Berg had called 'the Devil's playground'. the barmaid was friendly and already knew Dinah. Dinah told me how happy she was that Dad had finally stood up for something.

'We could all tell that Mum was wavering,' she said. 'The shepherds were on the phone to her, putting the pressure on, saying you should join the mission to Siberia. She was starting to soften towards them. Then Dad came out of nowhere, he snatched the phone out of her hand and shouted that they had to send you back or he would call the police. Can you imagine that?'

I laughed. Dad had always been unpredictable.

So that was how it happened. It hurt, that Mum had been wavering about letting me go to Siberia or Brazil. Because it seemed to me that if I had gone, that could well have been it.

When we got back to the house, Mum had made a huge cheesy lasagne with salad and green beans. We all sat around the table and Dad said: 'Let's sing "Thank You Jesus!"' and proceeded to tunelessly sing 'Thank you Jesus for this food and for our home so fair, help us Lord to do some good and keep us in thy care, and bless our loved ones e-e-everywhere . . . In Jesus's name, we pray!' We cringed and laughed at him.

'Hey Bev,' I said, 'remember in Costa Rica that time we put Josie's fleas in Uncle Simon's hair when he was reading a Bible story to the boys?' We laughed and looked at each other knowingly. On one of the many day-long fellowships at our home everyone had said their good-byes at the end of the day except Uncle Simon, who stayed on. Dad had taken himself off to 'witness' for the weekend and it was just Mum and us kids in the house, but Uncle Simon, he stayed put. 'Mummy?' we had asked. 'When is Uncle Simon leaving? Why is he still here?'

'None of your business, girls.' And then we knew that Uncle Simon would be 'sharing' with Mummy that night. It was disgusting but also frightening for us.

'Bev, it was your naughty idea, ha-ha-ha-ha!' I remembered Josie spread out on the wooden floor snoring away. Her pink belly was alive with plump black fleas. We carefully picked them out and dropped them onto Uncle Simon's scalp as he sat chatting to Mum. We sniggered at our sweet revenge. 'Lucky we didn't get caught, ha-ha-ha-ha!'

'Careful!' Mike said. 'Ooh! Watch out or Uncle Andrew will make you chalk up a double demerit on the demerit chart for being "foolish"!'

'Or Aunty Rula might make you clean the toilet with a toothbrush!' piped Bev. More gales of laughter. Dad was engrossed in his plate of food; he finished and left the table. Mum sat with us and listened as we reminisced. My brother Mike's face went dark.

'Why did we get so many spankings all the time?' he said. 'They were always looking for excuses to beat us. I used to try to be so good all the time, to cover up for Petra. I don't know what was worse, the beating or hearing my sister getting beaten. Uncle Shay and Uncle Francesco were sadists! They were sadists! Why did they have to humiliate us by forcing us to pull down our pants first?' Mum began to look upset.

'Bastards,' we all chimed. 'And it wasn't just us, guys,' said Dinah. 'Everyone else was getting beatings or being put on silence restriction too.'

'Yeah, we took some huge risks though, Dinah. Didn't we? What a buzz!' I said. 'Remember when we teens were allowed to borrow the Walkmans? How we'd have scripture on one side of the cassette and contraband systemite and old-time Family music that was banned for being "too cool" on the other? We'd flip the reverse switch if an adult asked to listen in . . .'

We were laughing again, but could see that Mum was upset.

The next few weeks were giddy. We all had chores but because none of us were in school, we had a lot of free time too. I relished the new freedoms I had and found some favourite places. I went for long walks in Dulwich Woods with my siblings. I spent hours in the local library, having previously been banned from reading systemite literature. I devoured books, taking out the maximum seven every week on my ticket. One of the ones I found was about cults. I flicked through it, reading about the Hare Krishnas, the Moonies and the Scientologists; their practices sounded so alarming, their beliefs so dubious. Then I stumbled upon it: a whole section on the Children of God. When I got home, I showed Mum. 'Look Mum, we're in this book!'

She looked at it, running her fingers over the picture of David Berg, a bus full of grinning young hippies clutching guitars and tambourines. 'Oh yes, darling. I've heard about this sort of thing before. The mainstream church has always accused the Family of being a cult . . . I wouldn't pay too much attention to it. Now, where have all the tea towels gone?'

It was a brush-off and I recognised it. I took the book upstairs. I'd read it properly later.

CHAPTER 3: Spare the Rod, Spoil the Child – Costa Rica, 1980

Shortly before my fifth birthday, there were two arrivals.

Shiloh began her campaign for a puppy immediately when we heard our neighbours' German Shepherd was having a litter. She made a long list of the pros and worked on Mummy daily. It would be good for the little ones and would mean we had a guard dog to keep us safe when Daddy went off on his overnight 'witnessing' sorties. These often coincided with sunny weekends, and he would head to the beach, leaving Mummy with us at home, reappearing on Sunday afternoons. Shiloh also pointed out that with a guard dog, the house would be safe when we were out performing with Mummy and Mr Barolo. German Shepherds made excellent guard dogs, she explained, because they were menacing and wolf-like to look at, but gentle, loving and obedient in their nature.

Mummy, a great dog-lover, was not too hard to convince and as soon as the puppies were born, we all trooped round to visit them and picked out Josie.

She was black with caramel-coloured eyebrows. We played with her constantly and she defended the house with a fierce bark and a sixth sense for danger. When strangers approached the gate, she would appear out of nowhere, barking until she could sense they were welcome.

Long-suffering 'Jo' allowed us to pull her ears, pinch her nose, stick our fingers in her mouth, pull her tail and dress her up in old clothes. She quickly became the heart of our family. We threw stones and sticks for her to catch and rode on her back. Sometimes somebody would take her for a walk, but mostly, she would escape from the garden and take herself off for a wander in the afternoon, always coming back. Because we didn't have her spayed, she got pregnant on these walks. She had a litter of puppies every year (fathered by a range of stray neighbourhood mongrels), which provided us with endless pleasure. Mummy would make milky oatmeal or semolina for the puppies to help relieve the pressure on Jo's nipples, and Jo would only permit Mummy to be close to her in the first week after the puppies were born. She would snarl at the rest of us, which was upsetting.

The second new arrival, at around the same time that Josie came, was a 'brother', a Family member in his twenties, Nathanael, who appeared at our lunch table one day. Mum introduced him: 'This is Nathanael. He's coming to live with us! He'll be helping us around the house and to look after you kids.'

'*Hola chiquitos!*' he said. He was from Honduras. A relatively new disciple who spoke no English. We thought that was a bonus because we could talk about him behind his back. However, unfortunately for us, we found out later that he could understand quite a lot.

We glanced at each other from across the table, worried and unhappy. Why did this guy have to come and live with us? I didn't like his unsmiling eyes. He had dark frizzy hair which he wore in a big seventies Afro, pale skin and thick lips. He seemed a bit too familiar with Mummy as he joked and chatted with her over lunch. It was my turn to help Dinah with the washing-up after, and we wondered together if this new visitor would be strict or a pushover, like the last young disciple Mummy left in charge of us for an afternoon. Josiah was tall with dark hair. He was good natured and smiley and a bit goofy. We had a field day, running rings around him in the back garden, and he took it in his stride until we realised that Petra, the youngest, was no longer anywhere in sight. Worried, he ushered us all back inside and there we found our little sister who can only have been around two, squatting in the middle of the dinner table, ladling black beans that had been left over from lunch into the water jug: slop, slop.

She had eaten a few fistfuls as she went, smearing the gravy down her chin and plastering it through her fluffy hair. She then shook the bean-and-water mixture up and down, like a large rattle, sloshing it about excitedly, speeding up and making excited 'Gah! Gah!' noises and blowing kisses when she realised she had an audience. 'Yuya!' she said, raising her chubby bean-covered arms above her head. This was her version of 'Hallelujah!', an imitation of adults, observed at collective prayer meetings, which were a frequent occurrence at our house and other Family houses we visited for 'fellowship'. Petra was filthy, and there were beans everywhere: tablecloth, rug, walls.

It didn't take long before I found out what kind of helper Nathanael was going to be. Whilst Mummy and he were chatting away, I asked if I could leave the table.

'Mummy, may I leave the table please?'

'Yes, darling, take your plate.'

I took my plate to the sink and slunk off down the stairs to the basement, knowing no one would notice. One of the rooms in the basement was smaller than the rest. It was damp and gloomy in there and I switched on the bare bulb. Speckles, our semi-feral cat, who had had kittens the week before, was asleep with them in the corner, surrounded by a smelly nest of old newspapers and rags. I was desperate to see the kittens, but we had all been strictly forbidden. I sat cross-legged next to

Speckles, picked up her kittens and gently placed them in my lap. Oh! They were so cute. I turned one over. I was fascinated by its soft pink tummy crawling with fleas.

Suddenly the door opened. I looked up and saw that Nathanael was there.

'*Que estas haciendo aqui?*' (What are you doing here?) His voice was angry.

I said nothing.

'Come here!' he said. Meekly, I took the kittens off my lap and put them back into Speckles' nest. I walked over to him. 'Hands out!' he said. I obeyed. Smack! Smack! Smack! Smack. 'Your mother told me that if I found you here, I was to smack you, for being disobedient,' he said in Spanish.

The tears rolled down my cheeks. I felt betrayed by my beloved Mummy for sending this man to smack me, and yet, I knew I deserved it. I had broken the rules and there were no excuses.

I didn't like to break Mummy's rules because she was the centre of our world. She was very loving and affectionate. She would shower us with praise when we were good, and never shooed us away the many frequent times we would rush up to her, kiss her face all over and wrap our arms around her legs, waist or neck. When she wasn't busy, she was fun, too. Sometimes in the evening when we were in our pyjamas and ready for bed, she would pick up the guitar and start to sing little songs. 'The little bunnies are hopping up and down, hopping up and down!' The four of us little ones would make little bunny ears with our hands and start hopping about; Shiloh and Dinah would watch us and clap. 'The little snakes are slithering away! Slithering away!' We would slither away, furiously trying to outdo each other.

Mummy was incredibly strict but always scrupulously fair and showed no partiality. She went out of her way to tell us she loved us all the exact same amount. 'Who do you love more, Mummy?' we would ask her as we fought over who would sit on her lap during story time. 'I love you all exactly the same, kids. My love never diminishes the more of you there are. It only ever multiplies!'

We were used to receiving smacks on our legs or hands for even minor offences. These included: not doing what we were told, snatching a toy from someone, borrowing something without permission or being stubborn. Other transgressions included walking around barefoot and bad manners at the table, a huge bugbear of hers. She would sit at the head of the table with a wooden spoon next to her as a reminder: no elbows on the table, eat with your mouth closed, use your knife and fork properly and most importantly, no bickering, arguing or fighting over food. It seemed to me that her punishments were always justly meted out: Mum was utterly consistent in her discipline. For more serious crimes, such as backchat, using bad words, hitting or lying, we would have our mouths washed out with soap or be spanked on our bare bottoms. Hard. Pants down, over her knee. Her weapons of choice were, in order of preference: the handle of a plastic fly swatter, the *chilillo* and a hairbrush.

Daddy, on the other hand, would just lose his temper and start shouting. He wouldn't often hit us but when he did, he was arbitrary and inconsistent. Most of the time he just ignored us, preferring to go out witnessing than to spend any time with us.

Physical punishment of children was considered biblical and essential by the Family: any adult, so the belief went, was permitted to spank a child if they were being 'out of the Spirit' – disrespectful, insolent, angry or disobedient.

Mummy wasn't happy with the idea that other adults could discipline her children. Once, an American family came to stay and the father, Ezekiel, spanked Bev and me for giggling when we kept getting wrong the passages in the Bible verses we were memorising:

Ye adulterers and adulteresses, know ye not that the friendship of the world is enmity with God? whosoever therefore will be a friend of the world is the enemy of God. (James 4:4)

We stood to attention in front of a seated Ezekiel trying to get the verse right. Increasingly frustrated, he grabbed my hand, pulled me to him, pulled my knickers down and gave me six hard swats. I was shocked and humiliated and I cried. Then he did the same thing with Bev. I felt indignant because I thought he was being unfair, and I immediately ran to tell Dinah. She told Mummy, and Shiloh overheard Mummy and Daddy talking to the couple later, explaining that they had to ask permission in future before laying a hand on us. 'Mummy didn't sound happy,' she said.

Nathanael, on the other hand, was given a free pass to discipline us as he saw fit. He had full permission to spank us whenever he liked. He was brutal and he liked to use his thick black belt. He beat us often, and severely. He smacked my hands for spreading crackers with cream cheese in a way that displeased him (not enough coverage); spanked me for leaving my dolls out in the living room. He spanked us for 'being foolish', for chattering and giggling as we did our chores when we had been told to be silent. All six of us were united in hatred of our common enemy. I remember one beating when Bev and I were spanked, hard, one after the other, with his black belt. Shiloh was standing behind Nathanael as he belted us, and I caught her eye. She was pulling faces behind his back, her best angry imbecile face, flicking the bird with all her might. It gave me so much comfort, the fact that

45

she hated him as much as I did, and that she was on my side. If he had turned around and caught sight of her, she would have been in big trouble, although Nathanael never dared touch Shiloh.

He gave her a wide berth and the only person who was allowed to discipline her was Mummy. Her punishments were rarely physical because she was a teenager, and because of her illness. Dinah, who was nine, would sometimes take great pleasure in telling on us to Nathanael. Perhaps it was to deflect the heat from herself, because she got the worst of the beatings.

When the belting was over, Nathanael would shout: 'Shut up! Stop crying! Enough crying! If you don't shut up after I finish counting to three you will receive another six beltings! One . . . two . . . three!'

It took all of our strength to stop our little bodies from convulsing as we tried to keep the sobs inside. Then he would pray:

'Repeat after me: Jesus (Jesus), help me to be a good girl (help me to be a good girl), help me to be obedient and do as I'm told, in Jesus's name, amen (help me to be obedient and do as I'm told, in Jesus's name, amen).'

Our greatest fear was that we might have displeased Jesus. Mummy reminded me, often: 'When you do something naughty, Faith, even though I may not find out, Jesus will know because He's always watching you, He's always with you. When you tell a lie or are disobedient, you make him very sad. He will always forgive you if you confess and say you're sorry but it makes him very sad.' I didn't want to make Jesus sad.

One Saturday morning, Bev and I were summoned to Nathanael's downstairs room for a misdemeanour – throwing scraps to Josie straight from the table during breakfast. Nathanael said: 'Come over here, *chiquitas* . . . You know you're forbidden from throwing food at the dog from the table. Why did you do that? Why? You are being disobedient! Right? Why are you being disobedient?' We shrugged. His face was bright red and he began to remove his belt. 'Come closer!' We edged closer to him and it suddenly occurred to me that a belting was too hard a punishment for such a small thing.

'Jesus, help me,' I prayed in my head. 'I know I was being disobedient, please forgive me! Please save us from this spanking!' As I said that prayer, the strangest and totally unprecedented thing happened: his face drained of colour, and he put his belt back on, and said: 'Get away then. Don't do it again.' We scuttled off and I said to Bev: 'That was because I prayed, Bev. Jesus saved us from that spanking.' Neither of us ever forgot it.

It had been Mummy who asked me, when I was five, whether I wanted to let Jesus into my heart, whether I could let him love me, and love him back. I said yes, and from that moment, I had a sense of connection that I have never lost. His mercy, shown to me when I really needed it, cemented my faith, and I began to believe that the Jesus I had inside myself was different from the Jesus we heard about from Nathanael and visiting Family members. I always had the feeling that the Jesus we were made to read about in the Mo letters, the doctrinal leaflets that appeared in our house, distributed by the local area shepherds, was different to my Jesus. The Mo letters showed the Prophet, David Berg. He had a long white beard and was often shown surrounded by young women. The letters were sometimes accompanied by Marvel-style cartoon strips featuring conversions, miracles and warnings about the end times, and Mummy would read them out to us at breakfast.

The idea of the end times was worrying in a vague sense, but the immediate threat was Nathanael, as more often than not, my prayers to be spared his beatings went unanswered. One day, when five of us were being quarantined with measles in our one room (Dinah and I were in a room with Bev), Nathanael found reason to beat us. We were feverish and covered in spots but we were bickering, too, fighting over whether the curtains should be opened or closed, and squabbling about who was the sickest. Nathanael appeared at the door, red-faced and breathing heavily:

'Nobody else can get a moment's peace with your incessant arguing . . .' he said.

He held Dinah's hands above her head, the way you would hold a chicken if you were plucking it, and he slapped her face with his free hand, twice, hard.

'You will be next, Faith, if I hear another squeal from either of you. You understand?'

Afterwards, Dinah cried into her pillow for a long time. I listened as I lay there, feeling utterly miserable and wracked with guilt. Shiloh came up with some lunch a while later and was furious, but we knew there was nothing she could do about it; only Mummy had any power over him. One time I dreamt that I was watering flowers in the garden and when I woke up, I realised I had wet the bed. I was horrified and terror-stricken. As soon as I heard that Mummy was awake I rushed up to her. 'Mummy, I had an accident! I did a wee-wee in my bed, please don't tell Nathanael, please Mummy!' I started to cry. Mummy hugged me and said, 'Oh, darling! Never mind! It was just a little accident. Come on. Let's clean this up and I promise I won't tell him.'

Nathanael had a friend, Emilio, who sometimes came to visit. Emilio was also in the Family. He lived in another home across town. He was fun and funny, playing with us and greeting us with big hugs, so we looked forward to his visits. He would appear at the door saying *'Hola Niñas!'* and we would run to him, launching ourselves into his arms.

One day, at dinner, we were sitting around the table, and Shiloh asked when he was going to come by again. The rest of us piled in: 'We love Emilio! He's so fun! He's so funny . . . When can he come again, Nathanael?'

'Soon, I'm sure he'll be back soon,' he said. Then he turned to my mum and said, in a gossipy tone which we all heard: 'Although you know, Rachel (Mummy's 'bible' name), he told me . . . if he has one weakness, it is for little girls, that is his biggest temptation, he said.' His tone was tentative.

'That's disgusting, really disgusting,' Mummy said with a frown.

But she still allowed Nathanael to invite him over.

CHAPTER 4: The Suburbs – London, 1991

January was cold and wet and the snow returned in February, heavier this time, so we were stuck inside a lot. Dinah, Bev and I were there 24/7 with Mum and Dinah's two boys. We all mucked in with chores and sometimes we minded Dinah's boys, but although we adored them, Mum made it clear that they were her responsibility. I felt sorry for my sister. It must be terrible to be a single mother, I thought. I knew I was lucky that I had the freedom to go to the library whenever I fancied. Dinah had to ask Mum if she could go anywhere, even the new church she had started visiting, because of the boys. I had always dreaded becoming pregnant young and thanked my lucky stars that it hadn't happened to me.

In early spring, Dinah moved to north London to her own flat. Michael gave her all the money he had earned the previous summer from his weekend gardening job and helped her move. Robin, a man from her new church in north London, gave her a lift in his car. Michael and Robin stuffed her bags in the boot of the car and the two little boys were strapped in. Dinah grabbed her guitar and jumped in too, waving at us through the back window. The new home she found for herself and her boys was close to her new church, and that was the reason she gave us for moving, but I think she must have been fed up with all the fights that would break out amongst us. There were a lot because we were all so traumatised, five teenagers trying to adjust to normal life after a disturbing start. The house in Crystal Palace was crowded and noisy, and she wanted her own space. I was concerned about her new involvement with the church. It was a fundamentalist evangelical church and she would complain that the leaders there were judgmental about her being gay. I said, 'Dinah, you are a sucker for punishment. Why in the hell would you go from a cult to another religion? You need to get away from those people as soon as possible and spend your time learning to love and accept yourself as you are, not as others think you should be.' I was angry with her, furious she was putting herself through this hellish purgatory yet again.

Watching my sister and the struggles of single parenthood underscored my fear of getting trapped. I resolved that I was going to educate myself on the subject. I thought about what would happen if I ever got pregnant by accident. Would I ever have an abortion? We were taught in the cult that contraception was wrong and that abortion was murder. It was a view that had always seemed incredibly unfair to me. I decided that my position would be to fully respect and support a woman's right to have an abortion, but that I didn't want to ever be in a position where I would be faced with that choice, if I could help it.

I devoured novels with the appetite of somebody starved of stories for too long. I consumed non-fiction, ravenous for information, for context and for other people's history. I read *Foucault's Pendulum* by Umberto Eco and *Papillon* by Henri Charrière. I read about the Knights Templar, the Freemasons and the Crusades, about the Renaissance, ancient history and space exploration. I picked out books about other cultures and religions, including Hinduism and Buddhism. I read the Koran and the Book of Mormon as well as the Gnostic Gospels and the Apocrypha, the gospels that did not make it into the Bible. I realised that the Bible was a collection of books chosen by a group of men, the Council of Nicaea, over three hundred years after Christ's death. I wondered what gave these men the right to determine what books to put in the Bible and define the word of God. In my searching, I came across Thomas Aquinas. He believed Aristotle's idea that women were 'misbegotten males'. He thought that women should be subordinated to men, that this was part of the created order. He argued that this was for women's own good. Yeah right, I thought. Fat lot of good it's done me.

I remembered the writings of St Paul that we were made to memorise, Ephesians 5:22–23

Wives, submit yourselves unto your own husbands, as unto the Lord. For the husband is the head of the wife, even as Christ is the head of the church: and he is the saviour of the body.

And 1 Corinthians 14:34–35

Let your women keep silence in the churches: for it is not permitted unto them to speak; but they are commanded to be under obedience as also saith the law.

And if they will learn anything, let them ask their husbands at home: for it is a shame for women to speak in the church.

My blood boiled. Although both boys and girls were treated badly in the cult, girls definitely had it worse, and it was because writings like these gave these men permission to treat us like objects to be used and abused physically and spiritually as they saw fit. It wasn't just Grandpa and his mad rantings; there were centuries of precedent enshrined in doctrine. We had to submit to them 'as unto the Lord'. I decided that I hated the idea of this 'Lord'. That I hated religion, full stop. I decided then that it was a load of bullshit and that God didn't exist. God was the figment of the imagination of misogynistic men who used him as a way of dominating and controlling women for their own pleasure. I was literally 'Losing My Religion', as the REM song playing on the radio constantly that year reminded me. And I felt completely justified and free from the fear of displeasing God and the wrath that it might bring upon me, because, guess what? He didn't exist.

The more I read, the more I realised how black and white the world we were brought up in had been. There was no space for anything in between. I was realising that the truth lay in those spaces we had been denied.

It was also clear that the 'real' world, for all its grey areas, could be incredibly cruel, too. Michael and Petra had just started, in years nine and ten respectively, at the big comp a thirty-minute walk away up a steep hill. Michael said it was a different flavour of hell to the teen home. Having had no formal schooling, both of them struggled with the work, but it was outside the classroom that the real danger lay.

My siblings stuck out like sore thumbs, being neither black nor white and skinny with wiry Latino hair. Petra was pretty, and a particular group of white girls took against her and made her life hell. Michael was bullied, pretty relentlessly he told me, by the black and the white gangs. But Petra's tormentors would wait until after school to do their worst. Often, she came home shaking, pumped up with adrenaline having managed to escape or having been beaten up on her way. She was bright, astute and quick witted, and the bullies seemed particularly outraged that she dared to speak up for herself. Michael was more academically minded and relished the challenge of a formal education. In the teen home, he had found ways of studying, even though it was prohibited. He developed a passion for maps, spending hours studying them, and had honed an encyclopaedic knowledge of stamps. Now, thanks to the support of a retired ex-schoolmaster that Mum had met one day at the library, who agreed to give him extra lessons in the afternoon after school for free, he quickly started to do well academically. By the summer term, he had found a way to make himself valuable to the bullies: he offered to do their homework for them. This worked well and they left him alone.

For Petra it was harder. She found schoolwork unbelievably boring and found it harder to focus. She also had the misfortune of landing in a year with a particular group of girls who were led by a terrifying alpha, Donna, who seemed to have a psychopathic relish of cruelty and humiliation. Often, they would chase her home from school. One day in spring, she arrived home at a sprint, pursued by Donna and three others, like a pack of rabid dogs on the chase. She crashed through the back door, swinging her arm through a textured glass pane. It shattered, almost severing three of her fingers. She cried out and ran into the laundry room, where Bev was looking for her jeans. I heard her scream and I flew downstairs as Dad emerged from the sitting room. Dad started shrieking hysterically when he saw what had happened. Poor Petra stood there in shock, the colour draining from her face as she looked down at her three almost-severed fingers dangling down. When I saw what had happened, a deadly calm came over me and my mind became very focused. I told her to sit down on the bench and told Dad to calm the fuck down and call an ambulance, now. I asked Bev to pass me a long sock from the basket in front of her, and asked Petra to raise her arm high, tying a tourniquet tight on her forearm. I wrapped a tea towel around her hand to control the blood, and asked Bev to make a strong and sweet cup of tea. Somewhere in the back of my mind I remember Mummy saying that sweet, warm tea was good to give to someone who was in shock. I sat with her and supported her arm to keep it upright whilst we waited for the ambulance. Mum was out at the supermarket.

The ambulance arrived. 'What happened here then?' the paramedics said. 'Let's have a look at the damage, shall we? What is your name?' Petra replied and explained that she had slammed the door and her hand just followed through. No mention of the bullies and there was no way I was going to say anything about that. 'Have you had anything to eat or drink in the last few hours?' they asked.

'My sister gave me some sweet tea just now; I drank a bit of that.'

'Pity!' they said. 'You are going to need surgery to save those fingers and you must have a completely empty tummy before you're given anaesthetic. That means you are going to have to wait longer!'

I felt very silly and guilty about that.

Mum was shopping, so I told them I would go with her to hospital. 'Dad has to stay here,' I said dismissively. There was no way I was going to send my sister to the hospital with my neurotic father. Petra was very brave and kept calm the entire journey. I was very proud of her. We arrived at the hospital and ten minutes later, Mum showed up in a taxi, looking worried. 'There you are!' she said. 'What happened to you, you silly sausage!' Mummy always put on a brave face. It was a relief to see her. 'Thank you, Faith. You might as well take that taxi back home. I think we're going to be here for quite a while . . .' She gave me a tenner for the cab.

Bev, Michael and I talked it over before bed that night. We all agreed there was no point talking to Mum and Dad about the bullying. They would probably do nothing, or if they did, it was likely to make things worse.

Michael said he would try to make sure they walked home together from now on.

Mum called a few hours later to say Petra was in surgery. It would take ten hours as the operation she needed was extremely complex microsurgery. The surgeon had explained that although they would be able to save her fingers, she might lose some feeling in them as the nerves had been severed. After the operation, Mum and Dad decided to let her recover before returning to school. The time off gave Petra a welcome break from Donna, and during this time, she set about reading up on self-defence, and cultivating a new 'goth' look that was designed to push people away.

By the time she was back at school, she had had a growth spurt, and with her new look, something shifted. The bullies didn't threaten her as much. Donna switched to mocking, jeering at her crazy hair. But she didn't chase Petra home any more. Petra had no friends in school, but as she moved into the latter part of year ten and then year eleven, she slotted into one of Bev's and my friendship groups from years twelve and thirteen. I liked Petra; she was fun, outgoing and a bit wild. In later years we smoked weed together and laughed for hours.

Michael was much more conservative. Mummy had started to attend a local evangelical church and he would often go along with her. I thought Mum was bonkers, going to church. It was my view that she had traded one cult for another. She started to talk about how sex before marriage was wrong. I openly scoffed at her: 'Oh for fuck's sake, Mum,' I snorted: 'Really? Puh-leesss!'

Whilst Bev, Petra and I would go out partying, Michael would plonk himself at the dining room table with a huge maths-problem book. We would come home half cut and merry and Michael would greet us with: 'Eureka! I solved the problem! I solved the problem!' We would fall about laughing.

'Michael, you're such a freaking nerd!'

'Yes, I know!' he would say, beaming with pride. I loved Mike and felt very proud of him. He would often start explaining something about physics or chemistry and I would feel as though I could totally understand it all. Pity I would forget after five minutes! I would often see him and Petra playing chess together. Mike was nerdy about chess and would spend hours memorising the different moves.

For Bev and me, our siblings' experience of being thrown into the bear pit of a south London comprehensive with no formal education and zero street smarts looked like something to be avoided at all costs. We were in no hurry to join them, although we craved education and realised that, one day, we would have to leave home and fend for ourselves. 'Perhaps Jesus isn't gonna come and "rapture" us after all, eh?' we would tease each other. I lived for the evenings and weekends, when Bev and I would hang out with the group of friends from Pistols wine bar. They were in their early twenties and had proper jobs.

Our little group was mainly boys, but there was another girl, Vicky, whom I liked. After the pub, we started going back to the boys' bedsits, to smoke spliffs. My friends thought it was hilarious that I had never smoked weed before. I remember the first time a big reefer was passed to me: 'Go on, Faith!' I took a few puffs and coughed. They laughed. 'Nothing is happening!' I said after a few minutes. But then my mates started giggling and so did I. I laughed my head off for what seemed like hours. It was a huge relief.

At first, I struggled to understand British humour and British culture. Mum had talked about it but I had never experienced it so I never quite knew if my friends' teasing was because they were being mean or not. I soon worked out that 'having the mick' taken out of me was actually their way of making me part of the gang and including me. Everyone was fair game for mick-taking and banter. At first, I watched and kept quiet. After a while, my confidence grew and I gave as good as I got. I finally felt I was beginning to find my feet. My new friends were stunned at my complete ignorance of pop culture. They talked about Led Zeppelin and I told them I'd never heard of them. 'What planet have you been on, Faith?' they asked, falling about laughing. Andy passed the spliff and Steve picked out the CD and put on *Stairway to Heaven*. I was transfixed and transported to another world. A world of beauty and wonder and warmth. I was utterly amazed that such beauty actually existed.

I started listening to Radio 1 at home and noted the names of the songs I liked. Prince, David Bowie, Madonna . . . I listened to Tramp, The Who and Pink Floyd. I loved sitting in Andy's bedsit, surrounded by my new friends. I sat there, hazy from the hash, enjoying the laughter and the banter and the freedom of it. Sometimes, in a stoned haze, I would go quiet and ponder on the books I had been reading. I longed to be able to talk to my new friends about the existential questions swirling around in my head. I wanted to discuss history, philosophy and art. I would spend ages marvelling at the wonder of art and music. The way I saw it, any art was the physical manifestation of the imagination, an idea that was birthed in a person's brain, or a group of people's brains, and it blew me away that I got to share in that experience. I wondered what kind of evil caused people not just to stifle, but to attempt to suffocate that essential aspect of human experience, one that was at the heart of all that was meaningful and beautiful. That's what was going on in the cult, I saw that now – what was *still* going on in the cult. No wonder we were all so utterly miserable and messed up. I knew that my thoughts on this would land on stony ground with Andy and the rest of my friends. They wanted to talk about cars. When Vicky was around, though, I could talk to her about anything. A year older than me, Vicky was worldly wise and fashionable. She carried a big bag around with her all the time with her make-up, spare bits of clothing and books. Vicky was intelligent, curious, ambitious, generous and optimistic. She was very artistic and loved to paint. I enjoyed chatting with her and learning from her.

One Friday night, after chucking-out time at the pub, my mates said they were all going to pile back to Andy's. I went home to grab some things and told Mum, who opened the door in her nightie, that I wasn't staying, I was going out again.

She looked at me dismissively and said: 'Don't be ridiculous. It's past eleven o'clock. Get to bed.'

I suddenly felt enraged and empowered. For the first time ever, I defied her: 'I am over eighteen, I can come and go as I please and there is nothing you can do about it.' I glared at her. She looked shocked and hurt but said nothing. She walked to her bedroom and I carried on packing. Dad came out five minutes later: 'Look what you've done, Faith!' he said dramatically. 'You have made your mother cry!'

'I don't care!' I said as I slammed the door shut behind me and jumped into the waiting car.

I began to trust my new friends and open up to them. One spliffed-up afternoon, whilst listening to music, when I had missed yet another universal cultural reference and they asked me again how I could be so ignorant, I decided I would tell them the truth.

'I may as well have been on another planet, guys. I've been in a religious cult my whole life. We weren't allowed to listen to ordinary music, read books, watch TV and we didn't go to school.'

There was wide-eyed stunned silence and although I was nervous, saying it, I needn't have worried. My friends were fascinated, and curious and bombarded me with questions.

'What kind of cult?'

'Oh, you know, one of those hippy cults that came out of California in the sixties . . .'

'Where did you live? Did you live in communes?'

'Yes, we lived in communes in India, Mexico . . . we travelled . . .' I said vaguely and hoped that the questions would stop. I was worried they might ask the name of the cult. What if they found out it was a sex cult, and worst of all, full of paedophiles and abusers? That would be too embarrassing for words.

'What sorts of things did they believe?' they asked.

'Well, they were sorta Christian . . .'

How on earth was I going to explain that they believed the Holy Spirit was a big-boobed woman who would have 'sex in the spirit' with 'The Prophet'? Or that Jesus was our 'husband' and that both men and women should imagine that they were having sex with him? I felt it was just too outlandish, too crazy and frankly blasphemous for this group of suburban youngsters to get their heads around.

'They believed a load of bollocks, guys, and there were stupid rules we had to follow, ha-ha!' I laughed it off.

The subject was changed and from then on, they went out of their way to explain things to me, giving me a backstory so I didn't have to ask, but not before taking the piss: 'You better explain that to cult baby over there!' someone would pipe up. Or someone would ask me a question and if I didn't know the answer, I would say, 'How the hell should I know? I been in a cult all my life!' and we'd all fall about laughing. They were kind, not patronising, and I was grateful for it.

After months of late nights, Mum had had enough. She sat Bev and me down and told us she was going to enrol us at college. 'It's time to study, girls, you need to get some qualifications.' We were terrified, and I remember the feeling of dread that settled on me the day of the interview.

Mum, Bev and I met three tutors from the college together. We arrived at the college, which looked enormous to me, and asked a group of students the way to the admissions office. The building had a strange smell, like watered-down disinfectant, rubber flooring and chip fat. A grey-haired man in glasses and one of the women, an admissions tutor, led the questions. They seemed welcoming, which set us at our ease, asking us to tell them about our background.

'Where have you been to school?'

There was a silence.

'We've been travelling . . .' Mum said.

I looked at my knees.

'Whereabouts?'

'Europe . . . India . . . Mexico . . .'

'So international school?'

'They were, I suppose you'd say . . . home-schooled . . .'

At this, Bev and I locked eyes.

The tutors looked puzzled and continued to ask questions.

Bev and I began to blush furiously and then, mercifully, the questions stopped. The tutors seemed to understand.

'Well, do you like books? Reading?'

'Oh I love books . . .' I said. Bev agreed.

'Perhaps you should both start with GCSE English . . . That's a good one to have . . . And there's a secretarial skills course . . . IT.'

They suggested maths too. I looked at Bev and I could tell that, like me, she was internally freaking out. I mumbled, 'Maybe next year we'll give maths a go . . .' There was no way I was going to tell them we hadn't done maths since Bev was nine and I was ten. The idea of GCSE maths filled us with despair and regret. That day, it was right in front of our now-adult faces, nineteen and almost eighteen, that no one had bothered to teach us maths and all we had were the very basics: adding up, subtracting, multiplying and dividing. Oh, and we knew what 10 per cent meant, because that is how much 'tithe' each home or any person receiving any money should give to the cult.

By the end of the interview, Bev and I had signed up to do CPVE, a secretarial and business skills course, which meant we would learn to type, and operate word processing and bookkeeping software. We would also do Spanish GCSE and English and two other subjects. I chose IT and design and technology and Bev chose IT and home economics. The tutors were so encouraging that I felt much less daunted by the end of it.

Just before college started, Dad announced to me that he was going to take me on a special trip with some new business associates of his. 'Would you like to keep me company, Faithy?' he asked.

'OK,' I said. 'Why not?' It would be fun to have a little holiday before college, I thought.

CHAPTER 5: Dark Day – Costa Rica, 1982

When I picture Shiloh now, I see her pulling goofy faces and telling us little ones funny stories, testing my reading with homemade flashcards, and playing games with us whilst we had our bath. But by the spring of 1982, the symptoms of her lupus had become severe and her spirit was fading. Mummy accompanied her on her frequent trips to the hospital, which meant the rest of us were left with Nathanael whilst Daddy was out at work or witnessing – this was most of the time. We dreaded these times, and during the rainy season, May to November, when Shiloh's illness got particularly bad and we were stuck inside the house with an ill-tempered Nathanael, it rained incessantly. The boys would cry for Mummy, and we all felt jealous of Shiloh's special status, and all the attention and Mummy-time she got, even though we understood that our sister was very sick.

When Dinah, Bev and I weren't at school (by now we were walking ourselves, never missing a day as it was a welcome break from Nathanael), we would do our best to amuse our siblings, building dens and playing endless games of snap and chess. We would sometimes dress Josie up in cast-offs we had dug out of the 'forsake all' pile in the living room – clothes left by members of the Family who had passed through. We even tried strapping her paws into Mummy's old high-heeled sandals and fell about giggling as we threw scraps of bread for her, watching Josie lollop after them gamely in her drag. We counted the hours on the worst days and spent a lot of time looking out of the window to see if we could spot a taxi (we didn't have a car). It was Dinah who missed the company of our eldest sister most, and increasingly got the worst of Nathanael's attentions.

In between her hospital visits, Shiloh spent more and more time resting, shut away in the room she shared with Dinah. When she did go out, covered in long sleeves and floor-length skirts with a huge hat or umbrella to protect her face, she only had the energy to sit and watch as we played. On the rare occasions we ventured out as a family, people would point and laugh at Shiloh in the street, because to cover up so much at that time of year was unheard of in the tropics. I felt their ridicule deeply and wanted to defend her, but I was also embarrassed: she was another reason why our family was not normal. In her room, Shiloh kept the curtains drawn, and although I loved my big sister, I dreaded going up to visit her because it felt so heavy and sad, sitting with her in her old pink nightie in the half-light.

One afternoon, Mummy explained to us that Shiloh had had enough of systemite medicine. Shiloh had written to Grandpa, David Berg, asking his advice on how best she could pray to get better. He wrote back publicly, advising her to read the Mo letter called 'Pilgrimage', a shortened version of the letter he wrote to her privately. He suggested that her illness may have been a punishment from God, a reaction to her over-consumption of systemite literature. He also suggested that systemite medicine could not cure her. Shiloh was devastated by this as she knew that Grandpa had written so much about natural medicine; she believed that she was being disobedient. Besides, she was already feeling fed up with the cortisone that made her swell up and feel rotten, and the aspirin she was taking for her sore joints, which gave her dreadful tummy aches and made it difficult for her to eat.

Shiloh decided to stop taking her medication, against the advice of her doctors. Her tummy hurt a lot of the time and she had lost a lot of weight. Her skin had taken on a greyish hue. Not only had she lost her appetite, but when she did eat, it would cause her pain. More than anything, she was sick of all the pills and creams. She resolved instead to focus on prayer and follow the advice of Dad's American friend Smith Howells, a 'naturopath' healer who had come to visit a few times and had offered to treat her. All of this was her choice, Mummy explained.

Smith was a brash American whom Daddy had met on one of his witnessing trips. He was very tall and fat with a wart on his nose, like a large toad, Bev and I agreed. Smith was opinionated and railed against mainstream medicine and 'big pharma', both of which he believed to be exacerbating, rather than treating, Shiloh's illness. Smith ordered Shiloh to sip a glass of distilled water on the hour, every hour, and a glass of distilled water with lemon on the half hour. Smith also told us all that we needed to rub Vicks into her feet at four-hourly inter-vals. Shiloh explained to me that Smith said the lupus was a sign the pH balance in her body was out of kilter. The lemon would help to make her system more alka-line, and the Vicks should 'eliminate the toxins' from her body. Often, Shiloh called out for me to come up to rub the Vicks into her feet. I was her second favourite nurse, after Mummy, she said, and she made sure I understood that by helping her I was sparing Mummy another job to do.

Shiloh told me funny stories to entertain me whilst I rubbed, about what she liked to do when she was little.

'My favourite make-believe was to baptise the ants in the garden,' she told me. 'When we first moved here, I missed the other children I had got to know in the village in Scotland, so the ants became my friends. I would put on my most holy face and would fill up a bowl with water, scoop them gently into my palm, sprinkle them with my holy water, and say: "With this water I have blessed you. I baptise you in the name of the Father, the Son and the Holy Ghost.'"

When I was done rubbing in the Vicks she'd say, 'Thank you, darling Faith. Hop along now, you go and play.' I felt bad leaving her in her dingy room, but it was always a relief to be dismissed so I could go back out into the sunshine and play with Josie and my siblings. I prayed afterwards for Jesus's forgiveness, as I knew it wasn't loving, my reluctance to go to Shiloh's room.

Daddy was away in Europe on Family business, introducing senior figures in the Family to important people, so he told us later. Meanwhile, Mummy, helped only by Nathanael, did everything at home. During this time, the only break she got was when we went to visit her friend Paul, a fellow Brit, who was a disciple too, and a single father with four daughters. The two eldest were the same age as Bev and me. He made Mummy laugh and massaged her shoulders whilst we all sat around talking. We teased him for looking like an egghead and having a huge nose. He was nice to us, but we were suspicious of him. Sometimes, the four of us little ones would stay the night with Mummy. It was not long afterwards that, to our delight, Mummy became pregnant again, when

Petra, the youngest, was five years old. Aurelia and Chloe, Paul's two eldest daughters insisted that the baby in Mummy's tummy was their sister, not ours. 'She's our Mummy now too!' they said. They told us that the new baby would be born with blond hair, and then we'd see.

The thought of this drove Bev and me mad with jealousy. And when Mummy laughed along with them, it made it worse. Bev and I told the girls that they were wrong, but privately, we feared that they might be proven right. She was our Mummy, not theirs. After one of our sleepovers, I was upset to wander past Paul's bedroom door and see Mummy in his bed, with naked shoulders visible, sleepily waving at me: 'Hello, darling! Good morning!' We had wondered the night before where Mummy would be sleeping and Bev said: 'I think Mummy will be sleeping in Paul's bed.' It was too disgusting to think about.

At night, Shiloh's sleep was increasingly affected by her condition. Her limbs would twitch when she was dreaming, forcing her awake. She began to have nightmares. One night, she woke up the whole house screaming like a crazy person after she had woken from a bad dream.

The screams that night were piercing. I still remember the sound: it sliced through my belly, and I was very frightened that there was a fire, or that somebody had died. It must have been well after midnight, and Bev

73

and I scrambled out of our beds (the two littlest both slept through the commotion). Mummy got to Shiloh and Dinah's room first, followed by Daddy and then by Nathanael, who had apparently sprinted up the stairs from his basement room. Bev and I pushed our way in, past Nathanael and Daddy, and clung to Mummy's legs. Shiloh was inconsolable, sobbing that in her dream, a huge gorilla had been standing over the bed. Dinah was hovering in the background, her eyes wide and her face deathly pale. Dad started praying in tongues loudly saying:

'Arabarashanda barashondo! I rebuke the Devil in Jesus's name!' This made us all even more frightened. After the prayers, we were shooed back to our bedrooms.

It wasn't long after this, a week or two perhaps, that I overheard a commotion. Mummy and Daddy were in their room, and were calling different people into it, including Nathanael and Dinah. There was an air of charged excitement, and a feeling that an event of some sort was imminent. I heard raised voices. Bev dared me to see if I could find out what was going on, so I crept up to the bedroom and stuck my ear to the door. Shiloh was standing in the hallway.

'What's happening?' I said.

'Nathanael is going to be leaving!' Shiloh whispered. 'Tell the others.' She smiled her old smile, and I felt full to bursting. I ran down into the living room, where Bev, Mike and Petra were standing still, trying to listen in. 'Nathanael is leaving! He's going! He's not going to live here anymore! Shiloh told me!'

The four of us jumped up and down. It seemed like a miracle! We all hugged and Bev and I looked at each other, incredulous. Shiloh came to join us as we heard the upstairs door open and Nathanael's footsteps in the corridor. We formed a big huddle, stifling giggles. It felt good.

Mummy came in a few minutes later and asked us to sit down. 'Nathanael will be leaving us. He is going to live elsewhere.' Later that day, I knocked on Shiloh's door. She was sitting at her desk, writing in her diary. 'Yes, Faithy darling. What do you want?' I walked up to her. 'Why did Mummy ask Nathanael to leave? He didn't stop to say goodbye.' Shiloh blushed and looked down at her diary.

'Well, for a long time he had been touching Dinah . . .'

'Oh,' I said knowingly, looking down at my shoes. I understood what had happened that night, then. The 'gorilla' in Shiloh's dream had been Nathanael, standing by Dinah's bed. 'Run along now, Faith. We can all be cheerful now! No more horrible spankings from Nathanael anymore! Right?'

'Right!' I smiled and ran out of the room.

Once Nathanael had packed and left, Mummy went to the hardware store and bought some sheets of plywood. She cut it into three triangles, and made a pyramid for Shiloh, which she set up in the basement next to Daddy's office. Mummy worked hard at the pyramid, late into the evening. I wandered down to find her, sleeves rolled up holding nails between her pursed lips, her now swollen belly pushed up against the plywood as she drilled holes along the sides of each panel. Sometimes she would let me hold the screws or pass her a screwdriver. She was good at DIY. Once finished, she filled it with cushions and blankets, and a lamp that had been Nathanael's. Shiloh liked her pyramid and would often decamp there for an afternoon. She said the pyramid had healing powers and it would help her get better from her lupus.

One afternoon, a good few months after Nathanael had moved out, Smith Howells came over, wanting to check up on his patient. Shiloh's health by now had deteriorated considerably and she was in bed almost permanently, slipping in and out of consciousness. Smith and Mummy helped her out of bed and together they took her into the light of the garden. Shiloh looked so weak, she could barely hold her own weight, but Smith stepped back, looked her over and started waving his arms up and down frantically with a huge hysterical smile on his face. He proclaimed: 'She is healed! It is

wonderful! You are well again, Shiloh! Do you hear me?
You are healed, Shiloh!'

Shiloh looked at him blankly. I could see that she
wasn't taking in anything he said – she was barely conscious. I was worried that she had been taken out into
the sunlight just in her pink nightie without an umbrella,
but the strange episode meant that Bev and I began to
hope that Shiloh would soon be her old self again. Dinah
had none of our optimism: 'That man is creepy,' she said.
After a minute or two Mummy said it was time for Shiloh
to go back to bed to rest, so Smith helped Mummy to
tuck her in and then he left.

That evening, while I was playing with the other
children in the garden, I heard sobbing coming from
Daddy's basement office, which had a door that opened
onto a small paved area with steps that led up to where
we were on the grass. It sounded like Mummy was crying. This was unheard of; I had only seen her cry once
before, when her father had died a few years earlier. I
angled my head to look into the office and saw that
Mummy was sitting on Daddy's lap: very strange. Her
arms were around his neck, and she was sniffing and
sighing, saying, 'Oh Arturo . . .' This was his systemite
name; we were used to her calling him Jed, or Jedediah,
which was his 'bible' name.

He was stroking her back, shushing her. I had the feeling that I had intruded on something deeply private, far

more so even than when I had glimpsed Mummy in Uncle Paul's bed. I ushered the other children away and decided not to mention it to anyone.

Two months later, in early July, Bev and I returned from school one afternoon to find a police car and an ambulance parked up outside the house. My heart beat fast.

'Is it the persecution, Bev? Have the systemites come for Mummy and Daddy?'

We ran inside and were shocked to see Mummy silent, sitting on the sofa with her hands behind her back, looking up at a strange man in uniform who was saying something to her authoritatively. Had they hand-cuffed her? They were going to arrest her, I felt sure. The systemite policeman and the ambulance man who was there too didn't smile at us. Perhaps they would take us all away? Were they going to take her somewhere else, apart from us? I scanned the room to see if there were Mo letters anywhere. We had been trained to understand that under no circumstances should we let the systemites see the Family's literature. It was 'strong meat' — too strong for them — and was meant for disciples' eyes only. I saw that Mummy's blue-grey eyes were wide with shock and I felt a bolt of fear shoot through my body.

Before I could say anything, Elias, an American disciple who had come to stay for a few weeks with his wife and small kids, appeared in the doorway and took us by our arms, saying: 'Come here, girls.' He marshalled us into one of the bedrooms, and behind us I heard the policeman say to Mummy that he would be sending some paperwork over and that it must be attended to immediately.

Elias sat us down on the bed. Keeping hold of our hands, he said: 'Girls, Shiloh died this morning. Your mummy needs to talk to the police and the medical people . . . Stay here girls, you must stay here.'

I sprang up, twisting my wrist to release his grip and pushed past him, flinging the door open to find Mummy. Bev followed me and we ran to her and buried our faces in her swollen belly, great heaving sobs wracking our eight- and nine-year-old bodies. Eventually the police and ambulance people left. Dinah, who was now thirteen, simply walked out of the house without a word. Mummy said we should let her have some space – Dinah needed to go out, to see some friends. Daddy shut himself in his office and wailed, for hours. I felt so empty. A light had gone out. After a while, when we had stopped crying, Mummy got up and started preparing dinner.

Bev and I sat very close to each other at the dining room table and watched Mummy chop the vegetables. I was so grateful Bev was there and made a promise to myself that I would never let anything bad happen to her. That night, she crawled into my bed and we slept cuddled up.

Daddy's family took over to arrange the funeral for us. Mummy was grateful, because Daddy was absorbed in his own grief she had us to look after and the baby was only two weeks away from arriving. Shiloh had been Grandfather's favourite, and although he had died, our grandmother, Antonia Isabel, was fond of her too. She explained to Mummy and Daddy that the Family would pay for everything and organise it all. Shiloh's death was also particularly difficult for Daddy's brother Ernesto. He had lost his own daughter to leukaemia only three years earlier, and Shiloh's death affected him profoundly. He was a wealthy lawyer with a strong personality, and he despised my father. I overheard him calling him a 'good-for-nothing' one time when we had visited him and my Aunty Consuelo. We found out later that he had had to pull a lot of strings to halt a criminal investigation into Shiloh's death, which the coroner suggested had been inevitable once Shiloh was allowed to stop her medication. She was a few weeks off her eighteenth birthday when she died, at the beginning of July.

The funeral was about as far from our usual Family gatherings as you could get. Everybody was dressed in very smart black clothes. My aunts and distant cousins, whom I barely knew, wore their finest jewels. All around, the smell of expensive perfume and hairspray hung in the air. The mood was sombre, and strangers kept coming up to us to give us their condolences. I wondered if Shiloh had known who all these people were.

Daddy was crying. I held his hand as we approached the coffin, which was at the front of the chapel. I had expected my sister to be there, still but beautiful, but the coffin was closed and I wondered why. I wanted to say goodbye. Later Mummy explained that Shiloh's body was very swollen and that she and Daddy felt it was important we didn't remember her like that.

The chapel was full of white lilies. The service was long and boring, and very strange. Being scared of Catholic churches, and believing them to be full of demons, it seemed so odd that Shiloh was being buried there. And by a systemite priest.

Afterwards, we walked the short distance to the mausoleum, where Grandfather, and our cousin who had died, had been laid to rest. It was all white, with an angel at its front.

We stood in the graveyard, and lots of people came up to Mummy to tell her how sorry they were. I only recognised a few of them and there was nobody from the Family there. Everyone seemed to know Mummy well and greeted her with affection and familiarity. It made me realise that my parents had been a much closer part of my extended family prior to joining the Family and that they had separated themselves from them, as was the norm for disciples. We were taught our systemite families were a worldly influence and that we should stay away from them but still witness to them when we had a chance. If they were not receptive to the gospel then we should 'not cast our pearls before swine'. This was a familiar line from a passage from the King James Bible that was quoted to us often when we asked about meeting up with systemite friends from school.

Maribel, our new maid, fitted into our house immediately. She was young with long, straight glossy black hair. She took Nathanael's old room and made it her own. She put a pretty plant on her bedside table and some cute little glass and pottery ornaments on the shelf. Her en-suite bathroom had lovely smelling soaps and sprays in the cupboard. She was kind but strict and expected us to do our chores without complaining. She would invite Bev and me into her perfectly neat room and tell us stories about her village. Her family were very poor and she had been born in a native reservation area. Her Spanish was littered with native words we didn't recognise. Sometimes, we would perch on her tightly made bed, or the little upholstered chair in the corner, and she would help us memorise scripture in Spanish. When she spoke to us, and particularly when she spoke to Mummy and Daddy, she made an effort to enunciate her words in Spanish.

Maribel was an excellent cook. She made us typical foods that she learned how to cook back home. She fixed up rice and beans and delicious fried yucca. Sometimes, for a special sweet treat, she would fry very ripe plantains and serve them with *nata* (soured cream). She looked up to Mummy. I could tell because she spoke to her very respectfully and would speak of her admiringly. She never laid a hand on us but would sometimes reprimand us when we were naughty: 'Faith and Beverly! Have you stripped your bed yet? I asked you two hours ago!' 'Sorry, Mari,' we would chime. She sometimes combed and platted our long hair: '*Niñas*, when you brush your hair you must start from the bottom and work your way up carefully so as to not break the strands, like this,' she would demonstrate.

After the funeral, Mummy busied herself preparing for the baby. Mummy was not one to show grief or fear and although she prided herself on her stiff upper lip, we knew not to talk about Shiloh instinctively. We all feared she might crumble if she gave herself over to grief. So when a gloomy mood descended, we let her distract us by thinking about things we would do when the new baby came. Shiloh's old mattress was taken out of the house and disposed of. I watched as some men carried it out and put it in a truck and I felt hollow and sad. Her books and diaries and personal belongings were stored away in a box. I was given her precious gold earrings. I wore the little round hoops day and night. Bev was given an intricately crafted gold butterfly brooch.

Mummy ordered a new Moses basket and a changing table. We got the muslins, nappies and Babygros out of storage, and Bev and I folded them into perfect squares, ready in the drawer in Mummy and Daddy's room. We gently ran the soft baby brush on our cheeks, and lined up the baby bath, shampoo and lotion. There was a feeling of expectation in the air, and everything smelled lovely and new. We watched as Mummy prepared her overnight bag.

One morning on 18ᵗʰ July 1982, I woke up and Mummy wasn't there. I knew this because I went into her room early and the bed was neatly made. Her slippers and overnight bag weren't there. I went down the hall and Mari was in the kitchen, making porridge.

'Where's Mummy?' I said.

'*Se fue al hospital con tu papá. A tener al bebé!*' she said with a big smile. 'She's gone to the hospital with your dad to have the baby!'

Daddy had gone with her in the taxi, but he came back because it was going to take a long time for baby to come, Mari told us. He would be taking us to the hospital to visit as soon as we received a phone call from the hospital to say Mummy was ready to receive us. We were to wait for a call to hear more. The morning went painfully slowly. Sometimes, Bev and I would pick up the phone, just to check it was working OK. It was. We discussed what we were going to do to help Mummy and to welcome our new Pascale. Mari helped us to make a banner, which we stuck on the front door for when Mummy came back from the hospital.

Finally, the phone rang. We jumped and ran excitedly to the hallway. Daddy, who had been pacing around all morning, answered it. We were gathered around him, straining to hear.

'It's Mummy . . .' he said excitedly. 'It's a girl!'

Was it a blond baby, I wondered? Would Mummy be going to live with Uncle Paul and his daughters? Bev and I looked at each other anxiously. We were desperate to see for ourselves and waited impatiently as Daddy milled about getting ready. What's taking him so long? I thought. He's had all morning to get ready.

'Hurry up, Daddy! We want to see the baby!'

'Patience, children, patience!' he said looking into the mirror carefully combing his hair and beard.

We arrived at the clinic and there was my beautiful mummy with a radiant smile sitting up in the bed in a lovely sunny room. The cot was next to her and the five of us children rushed up, arms outstretched to hug her. Bev and I peered into the cot. 'She has dark hair,' we whispered to each other, relieved. We took turns to sit on the chair and hold the baby. I marvelled at her perfect little face and tiny hands. I felt flooded with love at first sight.

Mummy brought Maria home from the hospital two weeks after Shiloh had died, and only a week after her funeral.

CHAPTER 6: College – London, 1992

The trip Dad had asked me to go on was to Hungary. It meant I'd get to return to some of the places I had seen when I was in the 'missile' team (the Family word for a missionary expedition), except that this time instead of sharing an ancient camper van with five people, I'd be staying at the five-star Grand Hotel Corvinus. I loved hotels. When I was little, and later in my early teens in India and in London, when we performed in various singing groups, we would often tour hotels to entertain the guests and would sometimes be given a room to get ready in. Sometimes, the grown-ups would 'provision' a room nearby to where we were singing so we had somewhere to get dressed and do some final practising, or occasionally, sleep for the night.

Dad had met these associates at the embassy where he liked to hang out. In his fantasy world he considered himself a diplomat. In fact, as a young man he was offered a diplomatic position which he turned down because it was in the back of beyond, not 007 enough. Dad loved the finer things in life: clothes, art, classical music and wine. He never had any money to spend on these things yet he somehow managed to acquire them. When his father was alive, he was the source of Dad's tailored suits and handmade shoes. After he died, he became resourceful about hustling and (I suspected) scamming freebies from a range of contacts in return for shady favours and introductions.

Moving to England had provided him with new opportunities to exploit his charm. He had persuaded the three Hungarian businessmen that he was a fixer and could help them set up offshore accounts to avoid tax, promising to introduce them to influential and wealthy VIPs in South America who could offer very cheap loans and invest in their scheme. He was hazy on the details and I wasn't interested in them anyway. He told me that we'd be put up at a swanky hotel in Budapest with a spa. Mum lent me her handbag and earrings for the trip and Dad explained he was going to introduce me as his 'secretary and daughter'. I asked if I needed to do any note-taking or anything like that. 'Oh no, my darling girl,' he said. 'You just keep quiet and look pretty.'

When we arrived at the airport in Hungary, a car came to collect us with two burly men dressed in suits and dark glasses. I wasn't sure if I should be worried or amused. They looked like heavies from a movie. They greeted us and led us to a waiting Mercedes with blacked-out windows, opened the back doors and we got in. The driver sat down and the other guy hung out of the door, looking around as we drove off. He didn't sit down and close the door until we were on our way. Just like in a heist movie, I thought. 'What the hell is going on?' I whispered to Dad on the back seat. He smiled impishly at me and winked. Uh-oh, I eye-rolled internally, wondering what he was up to this time. We checked in; my suite was huge and there was champagne in the mini bar. Dad went out the first night and I had a long bath, put on my hotel robe and poured myself a glass of champagne. I called Vicky on the hotel phone, sitting on the bed with the champagne. We chatted for three hours.

Dad and I did some sightseeing the next day, and all the while the same routine with the 'security detail' in the car. They would look around, let us in the back of the car, the driver would jump in, the other guy would half hang out looking around as we drove off. I would look at my dad, and he would smile and wink. By now, I was starting to get nervous, wondering who the hell these people were and what it was that Dad was doing here. Later on, when we had lunch alone at the hotel restaurant, Dad started teasing and laughing, hunched over his soup.

'Oh Faithy!' he teased. 'What fun with the bodyguards, eh?' His giggles turned into roaring laughter. I stared at him, shocked. 'Can you believe it, darling, it's the royal treatment we are getting here!' Tears poured down his face. Later that evening, we all had dinner together in the hotel restaurant. I had never seen so much cutlery. We were served around seven courses on big plates with huge silver cloches that the waiters would take off with great fanfare at the same time. The Hungarians ordered caviar, chateaubriand and fine wines. The food was delicious.

I listened to the conversation, which I found boring: my dad waffling away about his diplomatic connections, his fancy family in Costa Rica. Blah, blah, woof, woof, I thought, as I carried on slugging away at the wine, getting quite tipsy towards the end of the main course. When the coffee was served, three women appeared at the table. They were young and extremely glamorous, with high heels and very tight dresses. I noticed, when one of them smiled, that she had bad teeth. The women were giggling and talking to each other in Hungarian and I noticed that their English was poor. I sensed something was up. 'We're going to the nightclub,' Dad said to me.

'Great, I want to come! I'll go upstairs to freshen up,' I said.

'No, no. You can't come. It's for men only.' He waved me away as everyone got up from the table.

Ugh, I thought, prostitutes. I headed up to my room, ran a bath and watched a movie.

I made a few phone calls too. I had numbers written down in a little address book for my new friends as well as one or two ex-Family friends who had also managed to escape. There were precious few of us in those early days and we checked in with each other fairly regularly. We talked about various injustices that had happened to us when we were in the Family and we would rage and vent for hours. Often, we talked about revenge. Other times there was sad news: a suicide or a drug overdose of a mutual friend.

I phoned Andrea. 'Hey girl!' she said when she heard my voice. 'How the heck are you?' I told her about my whereabouts and the bizarre little adventure I found myself in the middle of. 'So here I am, in a five-star hotel, in a fluffy bathrobe sipping champagne and running up a huge telephone bill!' I said cheerfully. We cackled with laughter. 'How are your studies going?' I asked. Andrea was my age and the smartest person I had ever met. Her parents, like mine, had joined the cult in the early seventies. She had endured the most horrendous ordeals in the Family in Argentina and, after escaping in the middle of the night, she suffered unspeakable abuses at the hands of the 'fish' who said he would help her get back to the USA, only to keep her prisoner as his personal sex slave for a year.

She had finally escaped from him and managed to make her way back to the USA. She was now studying to be a corporate lawyer and reading philosophy. She spent the next half-hour enthusiastically recounting the philosophy of logic. 'It's amazing that thousands of years ago, Aristotle was busy trying to teach people to use their reason. To get us to at least attempt to distinguish good reasoning from bad reasoning.' I listened in awe, enthralled by her crystal-clear thinking.

'It's so fucked up how we were taught the exact opposite,' I said. 'How we were made to unquestioningly accept as the "the Lord's Will" whatever David Berg or the home shepherds arbitrarily dished out, however unreasonable, illogical or plain disgusting it may have been.'

Andrea became animated. 'Those bastards are perverse. They deliberately go out of their way to be pathologically controlling.'

'Remember how, if the shepherds found out that teens had fallen in love with each other, they would separate them and forbid them to be together? And the reason? "Forming a selfish, worldly and exclusive little unit",' I said, putting on an exaggerated American accent.

'And yet they tried to force us to share with anyone else, except the very person we might love,' said Andrea, sadly. She told me how that had happened to her. She had fallen in love at sixteen with a young man who had recently joined the Family in Argentina. He was twenty years old and had been sent to live in the same home as her. His name was Juan. When the shepherds found out they had fallen in love they got into big trouble and were not allowed to be alone together.

'You're so brave, Andrea,' I said.

'You too, Faith,' she said. 'Love you!'

'Love you too,' I replied, and we rang off.

The next morning, Dad and I were on a flight out of Budapest back to Gatwick. After take-off, Dad leant across to me and said: 'That was a party, wasn't it, Faith? We had fun!'

'I guess so . . .' I said dubiously.

I was annoyed and embarrassed about the women the night before and I felt disgust and contempt for him. I bet Mum wouldn't be surprised if I were to tell her, I thought to myself sadly, looking out of the window at the Danube snaking underneath us.

'You know what, though . . .' he said, a wicked twinkle in his eye and foolish grin spreading across his bearded face. I could tell he was dying to tell me something. 'There's no money, and no investors!' He looked at me, pleased as punch.

'What on earth do you mean, Dad? You mean you pretended you could get them millions of dollars of cheap loans and connect them with investors, and all the while you were lying to them?'

'You got it in one, my girl! Ha-ha-ha-ha! Oh, Faithy, did you see how they fell for it?' He shook with laughter.

I was horrified. I had thought they seemed shady, and I knew my Dad was up to something, but this was so brazen. It was like something out of the *Dirty Rotten Scoundrels* movie, I thought. I lost any scraps of remaining trust I had for Dad at that point and resolved to forget about maintaining a relationship with him. He had no sense of right and wrong: this was proof.

Back home in Crystal Palace, my evening adventures continued. I moved on from the pub, and along with Vicky, started to hang out at Yates wine bar and Alley Cats, a club with live music. Bev would usually come with me. I loved the blues bands that played in Alley Cats and Vicky, Bev and I would get blind drunk with our mates down there, downing pints of ale that came with a free whisky chaser. I enjoyed these nights, but often found that, once I was drunk, I would go from super happy and fun to overwhelmed with sadness, locking myself in the toilets to cry. I didn't understand why this was and I hated myself for it. I was meant to be out with my friends, having fun. I was finally free. Vicky always came to find me, and she'd hug me until I stopped sobbing, telling me it was all right. 'It's all right, darling, it's all right!' she would say. 'Come, let's sort out your make-up, you silly moose, you can't go out there looking like a panda, can you?'

I would smile weakly and let her fix my make-up. 'I'm such an idiot, Fluff,' (my pet name for her). 'Why do I have to start crying when I'm having so much fun? I hate myself for that.'

'Don't be silly darling,' she said, dabbing at my cheeks.

It was through our family discussions around the dinner table that I began to process what had gone on. My siblings and I began to recall more and more of our memories and we shared stories that we had experienced or had witnessed. Michael and Bev told us about gruelling exercise regimes they were forced to complete to the point of collapse. They were beaten when their muscles gave up. We all remembered friends forced to wander around the homes with boards around their necks saying, 'Don't speak to me, I'm on silence restriction.' We recalled endless beatings and had witnessed and suffered sexual abuse by the adults around us and, sometimes, other children. Our discussions would start off light-hearted: 'Remember Uncle Josh earnestly laying hands on a banana, praying in tongues before eating it? Ha-ha-ha-ha-ha!' 'Remember Nathanael standing in the bathroom with a towel around his waist and calling us kids over so he could whip it off and dance around naked in front of us? Ugh!' We would screw up our faces in disgust. Then the stories would grow more serious.

Mum sat and listened. She said very little, but sometimes she looked close to tears. After one of these confessional sessions, she said: 'Children, I am so sorry about what we put you through, I am really, truly sorry.

I want to tell you that we are leaving the Family forever. I have decided to stop giving my 10 per cent tithe so we are now out.' We all cheered. I was elated and at the same time I realised what a big deal this was for my mum. She had given her life to the group and now she was admitting that she was wrong all along, that she had been duped and had followed blindly, choosing to deal with her doubts and concerns by 'wrapping them up into a little bundle of faith', so that she could syphon off all of the practices she saw going on around her that she found distasteful, compartmentalising the worry to maintain her faith and loyalty to the organisation. I realised it must have taken a huge amount of courage to make the decision she had made.

It was around this time that I started to have bad dreams at night. One in particular returned at least three times a week, for months. In it, I was lying in my bed at home and there was a frenzied banging on the front door. Mum would open the door and two male home shepherds would walk in.

'We are coming to take Faith back, where is she?'

'Well . . .' Mum would mumble weakly.

'She's been totally out of the Spirit, disobedient and backsliding. The Lord wants her to turn back to him and his family,' the shepherds' voices said.

I'd hear footsteps on the stairs of the house. I would jump out of my bed and cower by the side of it, shaking with fear, my arms over my head as I heard the two cult shepherds pushing past my mum and into my basement room. They were faceless but terrifying, and I knew they had come to take me back. I'd wake up, covered in sweat, panting, my heart racing. My first feeling was anger and fury at myself. 'Why are you allowing yourself to be intimidated and abused again, Faith. Why? You're such a spineless idiot!' It felt so real, and the malingering paranoia and feeling of being cornered like a wild animal stayed with me through the following day.

One day, after another sleepless night, I decided enough was enough. It was before bedtime and I was scared to turn the lights off and go to sleep. What if I have that dream again? I can't stand it, I thought. I looked at my bed and across the room at myself in the mirror. I walked over to the mirror and looked closely at my face. I spoke to myself out loud:

'Look me in the eyes, Faith. Look me in the eyes!' I said as I stared myself down. 'Listen. If you have that dream again you are going to get up off the bed, you are going to rush upstairs past Mum, you are going to confront those motherfuckers and you are going to scream at them with all your might to fuck off out of your life forever. You are going to remember me saying this to you when you have that dream tonight, Faith, because you are not afraid of them anymore. OK?'

'OK,' I said to myself.

Sure enough, that night, the dream came back. But this time, I took control and I did exactly as I had instructed myself to do. I woke up feeling elated, empowered and in control. I never had the dream again.

Starting college was challenging, but I found I enjoyed it. Mercifully, it was nothing like Michael and Petra's school, although I was just as much of a misfit as them amongst my new peers. But that didn't really bother or surprise me. I realised by now that I would never quite fit in anywhere, no matter what I said or did: I had an American accent although I had never lived there, I was half Costa Rican, and I had been living on the outside of society for my entire life. The other students were a year or two younger than me and were set in friendship groups from the feeder schools they had come from. I didn't mind; I had Bev and we stuck together like glue. We had some classes together and for the ones we didn't, we would always plan to meet up at break and lunch-time. To my complete surprise I realised that Bev and I were no dumbos. We did very well at college and got As and Bs. I found it easy and we were both keen to learn. It was such a novelty that our teachers wanted to hear our opinions and actively encouraged us to think critically. What a revelation! Both Bev and I took to it like ducks to water and whenever there were any discussions about life topics, we would jump in enthusiastically, opining and debating with the teachers. Sometimes the other students looked at us, baffled and amused, but we didn't care.

Although I did well at college, I didn't enjoy the secretarial course much at all. I found it boring, and besides, I didn't want to be someone's secretary. But I loved English and IT. I whizzed through Spanish and was allowed to jump on to the Spanish A-level course and finish it in one year. It was surprisingly challenging but I was chuffed to come out with an A.

One day, Bev noticed an ad on the college notice board: Cleaners wanted, part-time 3:30–5:00 £50 p.w. The job was paid fortnightly. 'Let's check it out, it's here at the college!' The head cleaner, who was recruiting for the new cleaners, was surprised when a couple of students bowled up, but we got the job. After our last lesson we walked to the caretaker's area where there was a little room where the cleaners gathered. It was foggy with fag smoke. All the other cleaners were over thirty and what Mum would have called 'fag-ash Lils'; they were nice enough to us but bemused by two foreign girls with American accents wanting to clean their own college after lessons. But Bev and I were too skint to be proud. And besides, we were used to cleaning toilets and floors.

Mum was always reminding us how tight things were, especially now she had stopped receiving money for me from the social because I was nineteen. Bev and I were given the art rooms and the sports hall to clean. We were relieved because those were in a building on the other side of the playing fields and by the time lessons were over, no one was around. We would often bicker. I was always running out of cigarettes and tried to ponce off Bev. We would also debate whether we would spend our 50p bus money on a cheese and onion pasty or take the bus home. The cheese and onion pasty always won unless it was raining! We gave mum half of our wages every fortnight.

Bev and I had made friends with a new group who were into the grunge scene. They listened to Butthole Surfers, Chickenhawk, Alice in Chains and Mudhoney. We would go round to either Simon or Rob's house where we would gather to drink beer, smoke weed and play computer games. Sometimes, we would sit in silence listening to music with the TV on and sound off, passing spliffs around and getting drunk. It was boring, but I had nothing better to do. By now I was a fully paid-up grunger. I lived in bottle-green overdyed 'mom' jeans, Dr. Martens boots, lumberjack shirts I bought from the charity shop and a holey fisherman's jumper. My broken glasses were stuck together with Blu Tack. I was glad that grunge was all the rage. We were so brassic that I wouldn't have been able to afford new clothes anyway.

Although the bad dreams had stopped, I began to think more about the people I knew who were still in the cult.

I started wondering if anyone was going to do anything about it. My friends were stuck in there. I felt a strong sense of 'us and them' (us being the second generation, those of us unfortunate enough to have been born and raised in the group). Would I be willing to stick my neck out and speak up? Hell yes! I thought. Why should those bastards get away with it? I felt shocked and saddened knowing what I did now and having heard my brother and sisters' testimonies about life in the teen home here in the UK. Somebody had to speak up.

Because my family was well connected within the organisation and known amongst the ex-member network, a handful of young people who had recently left would show up on our doorstep. Mum would take them in, help them get settled and sorted. I think it was her way of righting some of the wrongs she had turned a blind eye to for years.

Some of the kids who came to stay were quite seriously disturbed. One young man, a white-blond American who had lived in a teen home for three years, had been subjected to countless beatings and 'retraining' at the victor camp. The victor camp was a department within the teen home that was reserved for those teens who had what they termed 'serious spiritual problems' and as such were subjected to a concentrated form of reprogramming including beatings, head shaving, silence restriction, forced fasting, forced memorisation, hard labour and isolation. He came to stay in the spring of 1992. As soon as he arrived, babbling incoherently, it became clear he was having a nervous breakdown. Bev and I gave him a pretty wide berth, but I felt sorry for him. Somehow, Mum managed to contact his grandparents in America who paid for a flight back. He wasn't with us for long and I remember her driving him to the airport and feeling grateful that at least we had Mum and that we hadn't been abandoned or kicked out, like some of our friends had, after rebelling and deciding to leave.

Dad was a different story. We knew we could never count on him to do anything for us, unless it suited him. The only thing I felt he had ever done for me was to facilitate my escape from the group by threatening to call the police unless the shepherds let me leave. During this period, he kept coming and going from the family home in south London. When he was around (he would disappear for months at a time, who knew where), he made it clear he didn't approve of the disdain we felt towards the cult. Whenever a new dinner-table discussion sparked up about our experiences in the communes and teen homes, he grunted and went upstairs. He refused to acknowledge anything was wrong and would leave the table to avoid hearing about what we had experienced. For months, he continued to read the Mo letters in front of our faces. Mum seemed increasingly distant from him, irritated by his reappearances, especially when he demanded to stay in Mum's room. She had had enough of him by now. 'I think I'm going to divorce him,' she announced one day at the table. 'About time, Mum!' we all chimed in.

Another of the escaped teens who came to stay, Justin, had left an Austrian teen home and had got in touch with us through a friend. He was a year younger than me and utterly lost. He had nothing, just his passport and a few clothes. He was huge – well over six foot – with the body of a weightlifter. He explained to me that he had found a way to build himself up in the cult, turning his body into a deterrent for the sadistic shepherds until they no longer dared to beat him. Justin had trained himself to be hypervigilant. Everybody was afraid of him, but he and I got on like a house on fire. He was traumatised, I could see that, but he was kind and resilient too. After a couple of weeks at our house, he found out that there was a place in town where local labourers would go to get picked up for work. The foremen would come by and choose a team every morning. He did well with them, he was a hard worker, and he quickly earned enough to pay rent on his own bedsit. I remember I stayed with him a few times at his bedsit, as friends. He always let me have the bed and he stayed on the bare floor, explaining he had trained himself to sleep that way; it was part of his (self-taught) martial arts regime. One night when I was staying there, there was a noise outside and he leapt up, looming over me, his eyes wild. He was half asleep and I had to shake him awake.

'It's me, Faith! For fuck's sake, Justin, stop being such an idiot, it's only me!'

He would come out of his panicked state and look at me sheepishly, like a six-year-old, his huge bulk looming over me in the dark.

'Sorry Faith . . . sorry!' I worried he might reach for the baseball bat he kept under the chest of drawers.

Poor, broken Justin. His experience, and all the other stories I heard from my siblings and friends who had either left or, mostly, who were still in the Family, acted as lighter fuel for my growing anger. I became more and more convinced that it was my duty to call these people to account. To stand up and speak out against these sick abusers who had broken my family, traumatised and abused me and my siblings. I would add my voice to those who were beginning to campaign in earnest.

At this time, an English couple who had been to visit the Holloway home when I lived there got in touch with us. Their daughter had joined the cult and they believed their grandchildren were now trapped in it. Mr and Mrs Saberton were determined to build a legal case to try to win custody of them, and they asked our family if we would give affidavits to help them prove it was a dangerous setting for children. We all agreed to help. At the same time, my mum began to receive approaches from organisations and the media who wanted to look into what they rightly could discern was a terrible evil happening under the noses of the authorities. I told her to pass those enquiries on to me. I was going to call it out.

CHAPTER 7: The Get-togethers – Costa Rica, 1982–86

Having a baby in the house was a welcome distraction. I loved my little sister. I was crazy about her cosy smell and soft, peachy skin. Beverly and I sang to her, which she loved. She would coo in her baby way and try to join in with us. It was my job to bath her, and to change her nappy in the morning. When she woke at night, I volunteered to have her sleep in my bed after Mummy had fed her. I loved the feeling of her scrunched up on my chest and would lie awake listening to her little baby breaths. I liked helping Mummy, too, who was tired. Her afternoon nap was sacrosanct, and I was in charge of looking after Maria whilst Mummy slept. Dinah would shut herself in her room for whole afternoons, so as the eldest by default, I took charge of the little ones and helped Maribel with the endless washing and folding.

Sometimes, when I was playing in the garden with my siblings and Jo, or preparing a snack for Maria, I would hear Mummy complaining about the house and the neighbourhood. We lived just off a main road, which was getting busier.

'It is too noisy, and it's dangerous, Jed, one of these days somebody will get run over.' Her other bugbears were the endless repairs – leaking pipes, cupboards with broken hinges, windows that needed repainting and creaking floorboards. Dad was no help whatsoever with any of these and Mummy mended most of them herself. But there were bigger jobs that needed doing: the roof, and the damp in the basement.

One day, when Mum voiced these familiar complaints, we heard Daddy say: 'OK, Macha,' (this was his nickname for her, it meant 'blondie') 'you are right. It is time for a change, we have outgrown this house, and now we have my inheritance, we don't have to stick around. We can have some brothers and sisters from the Family look after the house and we can rent a bigger property further down the valley into the countryside. Why don't we rent a property near Ernesto's holiday home?'

Mummy was enthusiastic and excited by the move to a new home and her mood was infectious. 'The weather will be a little warmer, kids! We will move to the countryside near Uncle Ernesto's holiday villa and he said you are welcome to go swimming whenever you like! We will choose a house on a little country road with a much bigger garden than this one.'

We all loved the sound of this. We all had fond memories of the rare times Daddy and Mummy took us to the villa to see Uncle Ernesto and Aunty Consuelo and our cousins. Uncle Ernesto was a loud, larger-than-life character; he always greeted us kids enthusiastically, shouting *'Hola chiquitos!'*, wrapping us in a big hug then chasing us to the swimming pool, making us jump in the deep end.

He and Consuelo had five children, three who were a number of years older than us and two who were much younger. We thought our cousins were quite stuck up. They went to private schools and had all the latest clothes and gadgets. They even had quad bikes! We took the edge off our envy by reminding ourselves that we were special, because we spoke perfect English and were talented musicians. They always made us feel welcome, though, and the idea of being able to swing by their home and their pool was exciting.

Mummy got along well with Ernesto and Consuelo. When we went to visit, Daddy would often head off for the day, leaving Mummy and us children there. Daddy's older brother would often criticise him, and sometimes, I'd hear Mummy, Consuelo and Uncle Ernesto complaining together about him. Uncle Ernesto regarded Daddy as a waster.

'He's good for nothing . . . so useless . . .'

Mummy would agree with them and say frustratedly: 'Let's not go on about it, Ernesto. There is absolutely nothing I can do about it.'

The only one of us who did not want to leave the house in town was Dinah. This was because she was in love with the daughter of some high-up leaders in the Family who had been staying nearby. They belonged to a World Service Unit, based in the Caribbean, which had been temporarily closed down as the group was making a shift in the merchandise it was producing. They had closed down their radio show *Musica con Vida*. The Spanish version was produced in the Caribbean and the English version, *Music with Meaning*, was based in Greece. These two units were responsible for the creative output of the group. They produced the merchandise that the 'workers' would peddle: videos, posters and literature. The units were very 'selah' (secret) and Grandpa and his closest advisors and entourage lived in one of them, although we never knew whereabouts in the world.

Grandpa was paranoid about security and his whereabouts being kept secret. He told his disciples that the systemites were on the lookout for him because 'They that live godly in Christ Jesus shall suffer persecution' (2 Timothy 3:12). We, too, as his 'children' should be vigilant because 'The servant is not greater than his lord. If they have persecuted me, they will also persecute you' (John 15:20).

I would overhear Daddy and Peter, the head of the Caribbean crew and an old friend of Daddy's, talk about how Grandpa was 'the Prophet who spoke Truth into the world'. Peter said, 'The systemites hate him because their deeds are evil and they can't stand the light of the truth, and they will stop at nothing to extinguish the light.'

'Praise the Lord!' exclaimed my dad, excitedly. 'What a privilege to suffer persecution for the sake of the revolution for Jesus!'

The conversations would carry on after dinner. Talk about persecution, the end times and the Antichrist. The system and the great whore of Babylon. The illuminati and the old church. 'Well, thank you, Jesus,' Mummy would agree, 'we are the new church!'

A special kind of disdain was held for the 'old church', which was compared to the scribes and Pharisees in the New Testament: 'Woe to you, scribes and Pharisees, hypocrites! For you are like whitewashed tombs, which outwardly appear beautiful, but within are full of dead people's bones and all uncleanness' (Matthew 23:27). I knew all these Bible verses by heart as we were made to commit them to memory, and yet this kind of talk would fill me with abject terror. I wondered whether this meant the systemites I knew – the teachers at school, Grandma, Aunty Bridget or my friend who lived on the opposite side of the street, Patricia – would persecute us if they found out that we belonged to the new church. Patricia's family were staunch apostolic Catholics. 'That means she's from the old church,' Daddy warned me. But they seemed so nice.

We knew about the importance of keeping Family literature 'selah', especially *The Book of Davidito*, a copy of which every Family home (commune) possessed. In it, photo-storyboards documented the 'love-up' time David Berg's wife and an assortment of nannies shared with her young son Davidito, who looked to be about five in the pictures. I found this book in a top cupboard in our bedroom. We had bunk beds so I could easily reach the top cupboard and there I made a discovery of that book. It had a brown cover with gold font at the front: *The Book of Davidito*. The pictures were graphic but the grown-ups' faces were disguised with cartoon drawings. As well as that book there were other ones with drawings of vaginas and penises and people having sex. It was a confusing and frightening discovery. I was curious but I was also aware that something wasn't right about it. The pictures frightened me.

Peter was part of a 'thrupple'. In other words, his wife, Kerenina, had a second younger 'husband', Seeker, who was in his twenties. Seeker was from Ecuador, a talented musician and choreographer. Dinah's sweetheart, Sarah, was Peter and Karenina's eldest child. She was very pretty with long wavy caramel hair, green eyes and full lips. Dinah, who was then fifteen, and Sarah, who was thirteen, were inseparable. They sat for hours mooching in Dinah's room, writing songs and playing their guitars. We all noticed that Dinah seemed happy. Her moods disappeared overnight. She even let me borrow her guitar!

Beverly and I had just made some new church friends too, Sarah's siblings, Regina and Abigail, who were around our age. The fact that their parents were part of a 'thrupple' didn't seem unusual to us; there were a number of these threesomes in our group. Some had two wives and some had two husbands. Also arriving with Sarah's parents were Joshua and Tirzah. They had a couple of kids too. The two families came as a pack. There were five children, ranging from seven to thirteen. The older girls became playmates for Beverly and me. We would often go to their house to practise Family songs together. Seeker taught us dance routines and new arrangements for our newly formed witnessing group, which he called 'Little Rays of Love'. We appeared on some local TV shows and toured around orphanages and old people's homes, the same ones we had visited before. I really enjoyed the performances by now and the trips out were a break from the monotony of our usual routine.

Mummy and Daddy invited the whole lot of the Caribbean crew to the house. Daddy was excited that Peter was in town. The two of them had met back in the early seventies when Mummy was pregnant with me, and Daddy was on a witnessing trip. Daddy had got to know Peter when he was a nineteen-year-old dropout. Originally from Los Angeles, Peter had left his family after flunking his first year of college, setting out to travel through Central and South America. By the time we met him, Peter had become a shepherd and had 'spiritual oversight' over my dad. In other words, in the Family, he had higher status. This change in status didn't appear to interfere with their ability to get on, although at times Daddy would complain that Peter had 'rebuked' him for something or other.

The first night they came over, Daddy and Peter told us stories from that time – they set out to preach the gospel, with very little money, charming their way from Mexico City through Central America. A crazy gringo hippy drifter and a reformed Costa Rican playboy, with a boot stuffed full of Bibles and boxes of 'hot' Mo letters. They were held up by bandits and police, and once smuggled a fugitive over the Guatemalan border. He was wanted for fraud back in the US, but Dad and Peter took a liking to him after they had witnessed to him and he had received Jesus into his heart. He agreed to join the Family, and Dad and Peter decided to let him hide in the boot of the rusty blue Plymouth Valiant they had picked up outside Cancun. Daddy and Peter got excited when they talked, whether it was about the gospel, the funny and exciting adventures they had on their mission trips, the fallout from the Falklands conflict and the forthcoming election, which marked a return to democracy for Argentina after Peronism, the 'Dirty War' and disappearances. They would settle on a topic then get sidetracked trying to remember the name of a bar where they had witnessed to young traveller hippies who were 'ripe and ready for harvest' or stopped to read out the latest Mo letter from the Prophet and comment on Grandpa's bold new exposition of his radical interpretation of a piece of scripture, 'strong meat' that we should all take our time to digest and never share with systemites.

The Mo letters featured more and more in our family life, and sometimes Mummy and Daddy would read aloud from them in the morning. One time, a new Mo letter arrived about Grandpa's visions and dreams of heaven. He would go into the spirit world and there he would encounter people he knew who had passed into that world. He described meeting his mother and Phoebe, one of the sisters in the 'Music with Meaning' World Service Unit in Greece who had died from an ectopic pregnancy. He wrote about how happy everyone was to see him and how all the women, including his mother, lined up to have 'precious love-up time' with him. He would describe the 'lovemaking' sessions. In one of those letters, our sister Shiloh featured as one of the young women who had queued up to pleasure him. When Mummy read out the description, I felt sick to my stomach. My siblings and I protested, outraged. It was a disgusting thought. Mummy was tight-lipped, but I could tell she felt as I did. Daddy looked flattered that the Prophet had been with Shiloh in heaven.

'That's gross, Mummy. He's an old man,' I said, ignoring Daddy's reaction. 'Shiloh would never do that.'

I began to wonder why Grandpa's letters were so full of sex. The whole idea of 'flirty fishing', of female disciples going out into the world as 'God's whores' to have 'love-up' time for any old man who might be ripe for witnessing, was disgusting to me. I saved these bigger complaints for when I could catch Mummy on her own, because I knew Daddy would disapprove of me questioning anything the Prophet said. Once or twice, though, Daddy overheard us talking about it. 'Stop your murmuring and bellyaching, you must not criticise the Prophet!' he told us. Mummy's reaction was meek. 'Your father is right, Faith. It is wrong to criticise him.'

Mummy would shush us more and more when we questioned the Family's beliefs around sex. She told us about the importance of 'sharing' and in particular the importance of winning souls for Jesus, no matter what the cost or sacrifice. That meant that all of us, particularly us girls, should be willing to share our bodies with 'needy, lonely men', so that they too could experience the love of God and go to heaven. Often these 'grateful men', systemite outsiders seduced by what Grandpa would call his 'hookers for Jesus', would give donations, or become 'supporters', 'big fish' or 'kings', pledging money and properties and vehicles to the Family. I wondered if that was what Mummy was doing when on the odd occasion she would go out in the evening. Beverly and I would watch from the door as she sat at her dressing table putting on her make-up. We would glance at each other knowingly, our hearts sinking when we saw her all dressed up. Her shiny gold hair, her pretty dress and heels and the worst part – her rarely worn expensive perfume, which hung in the air after she'd gone.

I made no secret of my dislike of 'flirty fishing'. On the rare times I got Mummy alone, I told her I thought it was disgusting. Mummy explained that now was a good time for me to read the volumes of Mo letters that Grandpa had written on the subject so that I could 'understand the doctrine, the theology behind it,' she said.

'Will I have to do flirty fishing, Mummy? Yuck!' I would ask.

'Faithy darling, one day, you will be more than willing to share and sacrifice your body with others in the Family as well as with "fish" outside the Family as a way of demonstrating your love for Jesus and to save souls.

You're old enough to understand now, Faith,' she said, handing me the pile of books. There was an ink drawing of a woman with enormous breasts on the cover. I had seen those books before when I discovered them along with *The Book of Davidito* in the top cupboard of our bedroom.

'It explains how generous Grandpa is, letting his little fishes go out into the world to give themselves to needy men, to win souls for Jesus.'

'Mummy,' I asked, 'was Shiloh a virgin when she died?'

Mummy looked at me, shocked.

'No, darling. She gave her virginity to a boy from school who was her boyfriend, when she was sixteen, a year before she died. She confessed to me that she wanted her first time to be special and she was worried that she would have to "share" with a "brother" from the Family soon.'

Six months after the Caribbean crew arrived and at the peak of Dinah and Sarah's romance, a Mo letter was published. Shown in stark black ink in comic-book style, it told of an incident that occurred one day in the commune where Grandpa lived. Word had reached Berg about a young female member of his staff called Keda who refused to share with one of the brothers in his home. Berg was furious. He ranted and raved in this Mo letter that such reluctance was selfish.

'She withheld herself when she should have sup-
plied the sex you required willingly,' he wrote, advising
that true believers should '[d]o it in love, sacrificially,
just to make their brothers happy. Maybe it's because
she's lesbian and only wants to share with the other
girls,' he said. 'I have allowed the women to share and
get together with each other but I'm going to forbid it
from now on because it leads to selfishness!' he raged.
'She's a Rebellious Woman! And the Word says "For
rebellion is as the sin of witchcraft, and stubbornness
is as iniquity and idolatry. Because thou hast rejected
the word of the LORD" (1 Samuel 14:23).'

Grandpa warned that such behaviour was demonic,
yielding to the Devil himself. It was straight from the
pit of hell. This was a complete U-turn from a Mo
letter he had written a few years previously berat-
ing another young woman for not wanting to 'share'
with this same 'sister', Keda. This arbitrary about-turn
of Grandpa's spelled the end of Dinah and Sarah's
relationship. What the grown-ups, or at least the Caribbean crew, had regarded as sweet and lovely, 'cute
teen love' that was tolerated and even encouraged, was
now regarded as 'demonic, rebellious and the sin of
witchcraft, straight from the pit of hell'. My parents,
who were never keen on my sister's relationship and
had a problem with homosexuality, seized the opportunity to separate them.

One night, Dinah snuck into our room and said: 'Faithy, I think I'm going to escape. I'm going to run away.'

'Why?' I said, wide-eyed and terrified.

'Because Mum and Dad are going to exorcise me for liking girls, and they are sending me to Mexico to separate me from Sarah. I'm going now, bye.'

As she turned to leave the room, we heard Dad's voice. 'Dinah! Come here . . .' She meekly entered my parents' room and I snuck out to stick my ear to the door. 'I REBUKE THE DEVIL IN JESUS'S NAME!' Dad's voice boomed. Then I could hear Mummy and Dad both praying in tongues. 'Shondo! Arabarashandabarah!!!' Dad yelled. I felt confused and angry.

Why had Grandpa changed his mind? I thought he was the Prophet! The very mouthpiece of God! Instinctively, I knew there was nothing wrong with Dinah. I liked Sarah, and they were happy together. Why were they saying she had demons? I felt very indignant on her behalf. A day or two after that episode, Dinah was sent off to Mexico to a teen home there. My parents were of the view that she should get as far away from Sarah as possible.

Sarah herself was sent away to the 'babe's ranch', a cult Bible-study centre in the mountains owned by a wealthy 'fish' (a systemite widow who had been flirty-fished and allowed her home to be used for Family business). Life carried on as normal for the rest of us and Beverly and

I carried on hanging out with Sarah's younger siblings, Regina and Abigail, and the rest of the Caribbean crew. Regina told us that sharing and 'love-up' time was the most natural thing in the world for them. She explained that her sister liked boys and girls. Sometimes, the kids shared 'love-up' time with other children or even grown-ups during the big regional church get-togethers or in the communes where they lived, sometimes even with their own parents, they said. Beverly and I were horrified.

I wonder if I will be made to share with Daddy? I thought. 'There is no way . . . no way I could!' I told myself. But inside, I was worried and scared.

On the occasions when Mummy would go out and leave us with Daddy, I would lie in bed paralysed with fear that Dad would come into our room for 'love-up' time. Tirzah's daughter Abigail told us that her mother had helped her to prepare by showing her how to stretch her insides, covering her fingers in Vaseline. She had encouraged her to practise, helping her to have intercourse with a nine-year-old boy once when she was eight. One afternoon, she offered to show us how, but she was spotted smuggling the Vaseline out of the bathroom by her mother, and had it confiscated. Regina and Abigail were also used to performing naked 'veil dances', a Family custom and a regular feature of the get-togethers, also known as Fellowships, where naked women and children shrouded in voile would swing their hips in time to Family music whilst they removed the sheer layers. Videos of these dances were shared within the Family and many were dedicated to Berg himself. The first time we saw one of these videos was at the Caribbean crew's home. We didn't have a TV at home, much less an expensive video recorder. Mummy was a strong proponent of the Family doctrine that said systemite music and TV was demonic and a worldly and polluting influence on our minds and spirits.

The only music that was allowed in our house was either Family music or Daddy's classical music. He was a huge fan and had a big collection of records. When he was around, he would put the record player on and the sounds of Beethoven, Bach, Rachmaninov, Tchaikovsky and other composers would fill the living room. I remember those times fondly because I loved the music; it had a calming effect on Daddy's nerves. Daddy was quite a neurotic person, fidgeting and stressed out except when the music was playing.

The first time I was asked to join in, I was eleven. I was at the house where the Caribbean crew were staying. Mummy and Daddy weren't there. The grown-ups had invited other Family members from nearby communes for lunches of salad, brown rice and beans and creamed tuna with fruits and homemade banana bread. The adults were in high spirits, and Tirzah proposed a dance show.

'We'd love to see you all dance, children.'

'Can we sing instead?' I asked.

'You can sing as well!' she said.

'I don't want to dance,' I said, but Regina, Abigail and the other children enthusiastically scrambled upstairs to get undressed and put on their floaty diaphanous veils. They brushed their long hair and put in pretty clips with flowers on them. They loved the positive attention and praise the grown-ups lavished on them on these occasions. It made a change from being told off constantly.

Tirzah came to sit beside me. She took my hand in hers. She had armpit hair showing out of her strappy dress top and she smelt of cocoa butter: sickly.

'You have a beautiful body, honey . . .' she said. 'You shouldn't be ashamed to share it.'

I wished my mummy was there. Beverly, who had come with me for the playdate, stayed stuck to my side. There was no way she was joining in either and Tirzah didn't try to persuade her.

When Peter dropped us back home that evening, Beverly and I told Mummy that the children did naked dances for the grown-ups but that we didn't want to, so we said no. She looked taken aback and then kissed our heads and said, 'You don't have to do naked dances if you don't want to, girls.' A week later, I broke my leg. No more 'Little Rays of Love' performances for me, and no more school, either. The accident happened when I cycled over a branch on my friend Patricia's bike. She lived across the busy road we lived on. I coveted Patricia's bike, a Chopper, and sometimes she let me borrow it. I loved the feeling of speeding around a corner, and bunny-hopping up and down kerbs in the patio of her back garden. The wheel caught a branch that I had spied earlier but had been too lazy to get off my bike to pick up and chuck out of the way. I rode over it at the wrong angle and I flipped over, the bike landing awkwardly on my leg. There was a loud crack; I saw stars and the pain winded me and made me feel sick. I watched in agony as my leg swelled and turned purple, but I didn't cry. Patricia's older brother saw what happened and ran across the road to call Mummy.

When she arrived, Mummy was shocked. She went pale and looked very worried. Composing herself, she got down on the floor next to me. 'What happened to you? You silly banana,' she cooed as she held me tight. I was very upset at myself for causing Mummy more pain. After all, it hadn't been that long since Shiloh had died and I didn't want to be the cause of more tears for her. I cried then. Patricia was busy calling the ambulance. When the paramedics arrived, my leg had blown up to twice its size. I held in my screams as they eased a big plastic boot on to my leg all the way up my thigh. They then attached a pump to it and blew it up to cushion my leg. The young paramedics were kind and compassionate. 'What's your name, *chiquita?*' they tried to distract me.

'My name is Faith,' I blurted.

'You are such a brave little girl! So brave!' they said to me as they put me on a stretcher and eased me into the ambulance. Mummy got in next to me and held my hand reassuringly. 'Would it be fun if we put the super loud sirens on?' they said. 'C'mon, let's put the sirens on and zoom past all the other cars!' they agreed. I smiled and nodded.

They are trying to cheer me up, I thought. And I felt very grateful for that. It was very painful but I didn't cry. Mummy explained I wouldn't go to school whilst it was broken. 'Well, well! There'll be no school for you for a long while!' she said.

We didn't get home until midnight. We had to wait for hours in the hospital until someone saw me and I wasn't given any pain relief. I was exhausted. When I was finally seen, the jaded doctor looked at my X-rays and turned to Mummy, saying in Spanish '*Señora*, this is a very bad break. She has broken her leg at the growing point. She will need to wear a cast all the way up to her thigh and will not be allowed to put any pressure on it whatsoever as this could stop her leg from growing.' I was moved on to a table. 'Now, *chiquita,*' the doctor said. 'Are you going to be a very brave little girl?' he asked as he scissored off my plastic boot.

'Yes,' I said.

'I'm going to count to three and when I get to three, I'm going to tug on your leg to set your bone back in place. OK?'

'OK,' I said.

'Now, close your eyes and hear me count . . . one, *two!*' Crack! My entire body was overwhelmed with pain and I saw black.

'Well done, Faithy, well done, my darling!' I could hear Mummy say in English in the distance. I was crying quietly. I was never one to make a scene or a fuss. I was taken for another X-ray and then my leg was put into a cast. I watched, fascinated, as the junior doctor went to work on my leg, putting a thick sock on first, then dipping the bandages into warm plaster and wrapping my leg up in layers all the way up to my thigh.

Life with a broken leg was deathly dull. Beverly was my designated nurse as we shared a room together. Mummy brought Maria's potty into the bedroom and told Beverly to help me wee if I needed to in the night. I couldn't move on my own. I was stuck. Poor Beverly. I would wake her up in the middle of the night for the first week.

'Bev!' I would whisper loudly. 'BEVERLY!'

'What?' she would growl.

'I need the potty; please, Bev . . . help me . . .' She would peel her exhausted ten-year-old self out of bed, pick up the potty and ease it under my bum and then take it away when I was finished. I was so humiliated and desperately upset. For the first two weeks I stayed in bed. I watched Beverly enviously as she got up to get ready for school. I was bored, staring at four walls all day until my siblings came back from school.

One day, Mummy's 'fish', a Serbian called Liubo who sometimes came to visit, brought me ten beautiful yellow apples. Liubo would tell us stories about his gold-mining expeditions in the Yukon in Alaska. He said the wolves out there were actually very friendly and would eat apples out of his hand. We had grown used to Liubo. He had a very big nose, a balding crown with lots of curly hair on the sides. We nicknamed him 'Bubbles' and sniggered at his funny accent behind his back. He was nicer than Mummy's other 'fish', Gert, who was German and very tall. Gert made no secret of his obsession with our mummy, and we hated him. He started visiting not long after Shiloh had died. We thought he was going to take our mummy away from us because Mum and Dad were fighting so much all the time. Daddy made it worse. Sometimes when the phone would ring, he would call out:

'Macha! Get the phone! It must be your boyfriend!' he would tease and laugh.

'Stop it, Jed,' Mummy would say, embarrassed.

Lying in my bedroom waiting for my leg to recover, my thoughts turned to the future. I longed to grow up, to be a big girl. Dinah and Sarah had already got their periods, and they seemed so mature. I longed to be like them, or so I thought. I began to wish for its arrival. I felt very self-conscious that I still hadn't hit puberty. I hated my puppy fat and goofy teeth. I wanted to be a big girl, because I looked up to Dinah and Sarah, and I had idolised Shiloh. I wanted to be beautiful and grown up like them, even though I knew that, for disciples, coming of age meant there were all sorts of expectations and pressures. In the Family, you were considered an adult at twelve. I had heard hushed stories about fourteen- and fifteen-year-old mummies in Family homes. I didn't want to be one of them. I also knew that some families sent their teens away to live in independent teen homes, like the one Dinah had been sent to temporarily, or with a mixture of other families in one of the bigger communes. I didn't like the sound of that either. In the Family, over-reliance on traditional family bonds was believed to get in the way of serving the Lord. We all belonged to each other in the Family. We were 'one wife, wedded to the Lord', as Grandpa liked to remind us.

Finally, my wish came true. Three months before my twelfth birthday, my period came. But instead of feeling happy when I saw my knickers were covered in blood, I was devastated and instantly filled with regret.

Mummy gave me sanitary pads and congratulated me. It didn't feel like a cause for celebration. I made her promise not to tell anyone. The first night, I asked Beverly if I could sleep in her bed with her, like we did when Shiloh died. I felt better with her next to me, and for the whole week, would crawl into her bed when it was lights-out. Beverly asked me what was up. 'I got my period. It is horrible. I'm frightened.' Beverly hugged me and we slept, curled up together.

Soon after my period came, and when the cast on my leg had finally come off, Daddy approached me to inform me that I was to go to the babe's ranch, in the mountains. Dinah's Sarah was already there, so I would have somebody familiar to show me around. 'It will be fun!' Mummy chipped in. I would be staying there for a couple of months, and it would be a great way to practise being more independent, and to deepen my Bible study. (I wondered why I wasn't being sent back to my old school, but didn't think to ask.) I was nervous about the trip, but three months without school had been so boring and I liked the idea of an adventure.

I was driven there in a pickup truck with a posse of euphoric and excited new disciples who sang songs and quoted Bible verses. This was all so new to them and they were very keen to receive 'training' so that they too could be equipped with the love of God and knowledge of the Word, the Mo letters and the Bible so as to 'go into all the world and preach the gospel to every creature' (Mark 16:15).

When I saw the house emerging from the trees, I was relieved. It was a beautiful chalet-style building with huge windows and a balcony. The house was high up in the mountains called Monte Verde. A brunette woman with a big German Shepherd dog, barking ferociously, came out to meet us. She welcomed us enthusiastically. She was Peter's 'fish', I realised. I had heard the grown-ups talking about her in hushed tones. Her husband had recently committed suicide and she was very lonely and needed the love of God. She was also very wealthy; it was her house. I told her I knew Sarah and she said we'd be in a room together, with some other women. She asked me my age and told me she had a son and a daughter of her own, who were younger than me. She explained that they were at school. She was very sweet and kind. The next day, I watched, fascinated, as she sucked her thumb during Bible study time, just like a child.

I was shown to a big dorm and put my bag down on a high bunk. Sarah came in as I was unpacking. 'Hi Faith!' she said and gave me a hug.

'Put your stuff here.' She opened a drawer and I plonked my meagre belongings in. 'C'mon, I'll show you the bathroom.' She picked up a little bag in the bathroom, opened it and produced a hairbrush, a lip gloss and black eyeliner. 'Would you like some?'

'Yes!' I nodded enthusiastically. She put the cherry-smelling lip gloss on my lips and showed me how to put on eyeliner.

'Let me do your hair,' she said, combing it into a high pigtail. 'There!' she said. 'You look cute.'

I felt so special. I was in awe of Sarah and I thought she was the most beautiful girl I had ever seen. I could see that all the male new disciples thought the same and she loved all the attention. That made me feel uncomfortable and I remembered how it made Dinah crazy-jealous. I would overhear her rants sometimes. 'Why are you flirting with that creep?' she would shout.

For the first few nights, I struggled to sleep and I missed home bitterly. Sarah reached an arm up, and tapped on the side of my bunk, and we held hands for a while. I was shivering. Compared to the climate I was used to at home, it was incredibly cold at night up in the mountains. A few days in, I found a cupboard full of extra blankets and took a few; it hadn't occurred to me to ask if there were any.

There were lots of new disciples at the ranch; people were very enthusiastic. Apart from Sarah and me, everyone else was a grown-up. The day started with devotions – communal prayer, where Mo letters were read and Family songs were sung. Then, after breakfast, teams of grown-ups would go out witnessing in the day, driving into the surrounding countryside to villages where they sold merchandise and preached to the systemites who lived there. Sarah and I would stay home and help with the chores around the house. These included sorting endless piles of laundry, food preparation, sweeping and mopping floors, and cleaning toilets. After a few months, I was told it was time to go home. I was to go back to the city with a group of disciples who had graduated from 'babe' status to 'disciple'. This meant that they could now be trusted to receive the 'stronger meat' of the hotter Mo letters. When I arrived home, Mummy was preparing for our house move. 'Pack up, children! We're finally off!'

CHAPTER 8: Justice – London and Argentina, 1992–94

I had spent a lot of time worrying about my friends and all the children still living in the Family. I had heard that there were some court cases and police investigations in various locations around the world but I knew that only a small handful of second-generation children had left the cult. Of those, hardly anyone had been willing to speak up.

Mr and Mrs Saberton – the grandparents who had contacted us about the court case they were building – seemed nice, and I wanted to help them. They were desperately worried about their grandchildren growing up in the cult and were determined to expose what was going on in the communes. Mum mentioned they had found out about us when another sympathetic ex-member told them about our family and said we might be willing to help. Their daughter had joined the Family ten years earlier and had given birth to three grandchildren in it. Their contact with her and with their grandchildren had dwindled to nothing, although they had been friendly toward the organisation at first. I remembered Mrs Saberton coming to visit the Holloway home once when her daughter and grandchildren were staying there.

It was the custom in the Family that whenever we had visitors (a very rare occurrence), we would tidy up the house and put away any literature lying around. Children would be hidden away, apart from the ones who would be appearing in carefully orchestrated musical performances. Usually, one or two of us would play the guitar with three or four other boys and girls who would do a little dance routine. We would sing our hearts out, harmonising with great beaming smiles on our faces. 'We need you to be a good example of the Lord's love, so sing with all your hearts,' the adults reminded us. When Mrs Saberton had come to visit, we were wheeled out, and she looked happy enough with our performance. However, she explained to me now that she had quickly become suspicious and increasingly worried, especially after Uncle Mark and Aunty Sabine, a married couple she remembered from her visit, had disappeared from the Holloway home in the middle of the night taking their camper van with them, reappearing in the *Daily Mail* the following Sunday in a spread filled with the lurid details of life in the Family.

The Sabertons told Mum about the case they were building. 'I'm going to help them by telling them what I can and they are looking for other witnesses, especially children. I told them I'd ask you,' she said.

'OK, sure, I'll do it, Mum,' I said.

'And me too,' said Bev. Mum didn't ask the younger ones because said she felt they had enough on with school (it was Michael's GCSE year).

The first time we met, I could see that the Sabertons were good people. I went to meet them at their house in Mayfair, central London. They asked me lots of questions. I asked them what they'd need from me.

'We would need you to write an affidavit that we will submit to the court, and in time, you may be asked to testify in the High Court. Would you be willing to do that?'

'Yes,' I said. I felt a big responsibility to speak up. 'You are right to not want your grandchildren to grow up in the group. It's a horrible place for children and it's not safe,' I told them.

It was important to be specific, they said, so a week later I went to their barrister's office. The barrister was a large and attractive lady in her late forties with a Spanish accent. She had short dark hair, a big smile painted red, and smoked a pipe. She took out her tape recorder and asked me about all the places and names I could remember: Costa Rica, Spain, Greece, India, Mexico, London. However, most of the names I knew were people's cult names; I had no idea what most of them had been called in the systemite world as we were told we should keep our legal names 'selah' from one another as much as possible.

After these conversations, which were more like interviews, I would come away aware of the gaps in my memory. Sometimes it worried me – what had I forgotten, and why had I forgotten it? Later, around the dinner table, my siblings would often help me fill in the blanks. It always amazed me that, despite the fact that we had spent so much time apart, when it came to the limited time we had been together, in various combinations, my brothers and sisters always recalled details I had lost, and vice versa. 'Do you remember that time in India when all the boys were lined up and belted in turn for playing "Bible battles"?' Bev asked. I remembered that day. Some of the boys were quite hardened to the beltings and beatings, but my brother Michael was horribly affected.

I spent afternoons with Mr and Mrs Saberton. Mrs S explained there would be no jury, just a judge. The Sabertons' barrister Rafaela said that the barrister acting for the cult was likely to try to make me look like an unreliable witness. I should be ready for some tough questions and this might make me feel hurt, angry and misunderstood. I was ready for it.

The Sabertons, with Rafaela, had assembled documentary evidence compiling a selection of cult films showing women and girls dancing naked with diaphanous veils and flowers in their hair. They had evidence from international investigations along with piles of Mo letters and *The Book of Davidito* – I wondered how they had managed to get one of those. The homes had been charged to either destroy or keep it under lock and key along with the 'flirty fishing' material and those letters where the Prophet had said that girls should be careful about 'going all the way' once they had got their periods to avoid pregnancy but that they could 'share' as much as they liked before that. The case sought to demonstrate that the Children of God cult was not a fit environment in which to raise children, the ultimate goal being that Mr and Mrs Saberton would make their grandchildren permanent wards of court. They didn't want to take the children away from their parents but they wanted the court to have a part to play in their lives, ensuring that they received an education in school, that they received medical attention and that their living conditions were adequate, that they were not going to be whisked away to another continent or live in cramped conditions, having to share a bedroom with their entire family or other children.

I was happy to play a part in taking on the organisation itself. We were out to prove that the cult was too dangerous an environment in which to bring up children. If we were to win, I knew it would set a precedent and open up all manner of persecution for the cult. Unsurprisingly, they wanted to avoid this at all costs so they went on the attack to try to discredit all the witnesses. I believed that our attack on the cult leadership, and our work in exposing what went on in the communes (one of a number of similar campaigns around the world at the same time) could do serious damage to their reputation and their ability to recruit and function. They were no longer under the radar thanks to this case and others like it.

I became more and more angry, the more I thought about the beatings and abuse my siblings and I had experienced and our lack of education, and the more I saw of the evidence Mr and Mrs S had uncovered. Rereading the Mo letters, including the Davidito book, and all the 'flirty fishing' leaflets with new perspective, I was shocked that this had been the organisation in which I had grown up. An organisation where institutionalised paedophilia and incest were rebranded as 'love-up' time, and where the man whom we were encouraged to call 'Grandpa' believed in smashing the bonds of family in the name of God's love. Mrs Saberton had been very upset by how openly David Berg talked about destroying families. She picked up a Mo letter from the pile on the coffee table. 'Look at this one, Faith, this is horrendous!' She read it out:

'God is in the business of breaking up little selfish private worldly families to make of their yielded broken pieces a larger unit – one family, one wife.'

'Yes,' I nodded. 'I know that one, Mrs Saberton . . . that's what we were all trained to believe.'

I could see the absolute shock on her face. Every time I saw regular people appalled by what they heard about the Family, it was as if I realised again, for the first time, just how topsy-turvy the world of my childhood had been. I couldn't laugh it off with outsiders like I could with my siblings. If I tried to make a joke or a flippant remark with Rafaela, it would hang in the air unanswered, excruciating. What the wider world considered good and healthy, the group considered 'selfish and worldly'. What the cult considered 'selfless, loving and revolutionary', normal society considered appalling and evil. I saw now that Berg's poisoning of followers' minds was nothing but evil. All the while, I was intensely aware of how this court case would be called a 'systemite persecution' by the cult.

Sometimes, this worry would cause me to fret and I felt guilty that my action in supporting it might contribute to renewed control, violence and abuse for the young people who were still trapped in the communes, as the shepherds reacted to the threat in their preferred way, through channelling their bad feeling into punitive rage. I imagined my friends in the houses in London, Bangalore and Mexico City. It was likely they didn't still live in those homes, as families were constantly being moved around the country and indeed, the world. Would they understand what I was doing? Would they realise that I was trying to save them? Would they forgive me for the fear and distress I knew I was causing them? Would they believe me if I were to tell them that I cared about them and that I wanted the abuse to stop? That they were worthy of an education and of receiving medical attention? Justin had told me that every morning at devotions they would read the latest Mo letters ranting on about 'our enemies', naming them all one by one and putting curses on them.

They would say, 'We curse Mr and Mrs Saberton in the name of Jesus!', breaking out in tongues and praising, 'Thank you, Jesus, thank you, Lord, *shondo laberoudo, abarashanda!* We rebuke the Devil in Jesus's name!'

Then the children would be drilled on how to answer to 'our enemy, the authorities' should they be questioned about their beliefs, about schooling, about doctors, about sharing, about spankings, about silence restriction . . . They must be totally terrified, poor kids, I thought. Perhaps in the future they would understand, when they too had a chance to escape.

I helped Mr and Mrs S to gather more witnesses. I persuaded Justin to testify. He hated the cult. He had suffered unspeakable abuse in Macau. His stories of violent beatings and ritual humiliations were heartbreaking to listen to. Female 'childcare workers' in the homes regularly performed oral sex on him as a nine-year-old boy.

A fourteen-year-old girl was hit forty times by a man who was sexually abusing her. She found out she was pregnant by him, and miscarried. Justin described what it was like to live in a 'victor camp' – a home designed for the punishment of 'detention teens' where the children were so disturbed that many were hallucinating and suicidal. In the victor camp, Justin was forced to wake up at 4 a.m. every day and to do eight to ten hours' hard labour, digging trenches and filling them again. Apparently, this was the best way to help rebellious and 'out of the Spirit' teens to 'get the victory' over their spiritual problems. I had other friends who had been in victor camps and had described being forced to do calisthenic exercises to the point of collapse (they were beaten if their arms or legs gave out before the allotted number of press-ups or squat-walks had been completed).

I persuaded two of my other friends, Jack and Diego, to talk to Rafaela, too. The more I thought about it, the more convinced I became that what my friends and I were doing by supporting Mr and Mrs Saberton wasn't a choice, it was a duty. I felt this case was more important perhaps than anything else that was going on in my life. Word got out that I was one of a number of ex-members helping the Sabertons with their case, and I felt compelled to write to some of the adults whom I had been fond of within the Family to explain my actions. I was acutely aware of what was likely to have been said about me in the communes. I wrote to Steven and Violet, the shepherds from Bangalore, whom I liked because they were fun and more understanding towards us teens than most adults. Violet wrote back, denouncing me and saying I was lazy, selfish, self-centred and unyielding. It hurt to read her words.

My boyfriend, Rob, acted as a welcome escape from the trauma of recalling my experiences with Mr and Mrs S and Raphaella. Rob was an antidote to overthinking and to seriousness. He was one of the grungy gang, and for some reason he was besotted with me, which was a novelty. He wore leather jackets, cowboy boots, Levi jeans and cut-off T-shirts and had a shock of long curly golden-blond hair down to his shoulders, which he would sometimes put in a ponytail. To my horror, three months into our relationship he turned up one day with a new elaborate tattoo on his chest: my name in big letters surrounded by roses. I was mortified but I didn't show it. We didn't have anything in common whatsoever. He was kind but extremely boring and we had nothing much to talk about. What made up for it was the sex. He was fit and for the first time I got to experience what good sex was like in a relaxed environment. During almost all of my other sexual experiences, I had felt like a voyeur in my own body, going through the motions with no connection to sexual pleasure. I would be left feeling frozen and dissociated. With Rob, I was able to relax and properly experience making love. At first, he seemed to know exactly what I needed, and the sexual chemistry we had between us was good, but once the novelty wore off, the sex dwindled and there was nothing left to talk about.

Rob and I hung around with friends, smoked weed and went to the pub and to gigs. The best was Rage Against the Machine at the Town and Country Club in October 1992. The spirit of rebellion was contagious, infecting everyone in the crowd. 'And now you do what they told ya (now you're under control), and now you do what they told ya (now you're under control)! Fuck you, I won't do what you tell me!' they screamed from the front.

I loved it. And whilst they were raging against police brutality, I was raging against something I thought was off the Richter scale: a tyrannical, sadistic, unrepentant cult. 'Fuck you! Motherfuckers!' I raged along. Rob and I split up not long after that; we drifted apart, but the relationship had been just what I needed at the time.

My second year in college was easier than the first. I found that I enjoyed studying and although I hated the idea of becoming another grey commuter, like my systemite friends' parents, I knew I needed to get some qualifications. There were days when I felt utterly hopeless and nihilistic. What is the point? I thought. Life felt meaningless. On the worst days, I convinced myself it was all just suffering with a few glimpses of happiness here and there. I fell into a horrible, black depression. Even though I had managed to get the recurring dream to go away, the blackness was something else.

Sometimes, I would have to get really stoned and listen to music at night to be able to go to sleep, then I'd wake up feeling horrendous, with no motivation to do anything.

'Get up, Faith!' Mum yelled at me. 'You're going to be late for college!'

I'd peel myself out of bed, jump into my jeans, shake my long dark hair, wash my face, brush my teeth and ten minutes later I'd be at the bus stop, still half asleep. At least I'll be keeping my brain occupied with college work for a few hours, I thought. I started to entertain suicidal thoughts. 'I could just end it all . . . how would I kill myself?' and then I'd follow dark mental tangents, exploring different methods. 'OK then, do it!' I said to myself one day. But as soon as I said it, I realised I wouldn't. What about Mum? She had already had to bury a child. In any case, I was too frightened to go through with it.

New Year's Eve 1993 saw my siblings and me partying hard. For the latter part of my childhood, the year 1993 was talked of in expectant and reverential tones. This was because it was the prophesied 'end times'. David Berg had a revelation foretelling that Jesus would return in

1993. For years, it had been suggested that the leader of the 'end time army' was in fact his stepson, Davidito, the child of his second wife, Mama Maria, who conceived him on a flirty fishing mission with a waiter in the Canary Islands. This was the boy whose graphic sexual abuse was documented in *The Book of Davidito*. He would later go on to murder one of his old nannies, a cult member, and shoot himself in 2005, leaving behind a video to say how he felt it was his duty to avenge us, the second generation of the Children of God.

Berg's conviction was that Jesus was going to come back and rapture us, so we needed to be ready for him. It had been drummed into us and we were made to commit to memory, Matthew 25:1–13:

[1]   Then shall the kingdom of heaven be likened unto ten virgins, which took their lamps, and went forth to meet the bridegroom.

[2]   And five of them were wise, and five were foolish.

[3]   They that were foolish took their lamps, and took no oil with them:

[4]   But the wise took oil in their vessels with their lamps.

[5]   While the bridegroom tarried, they all slumbered and slept.

[6]   And at midnight there was a cry made, Behold, the bridegroom cometh; go ye out to meet him.

[7]   Then all those virgins arose, and trimmed their lamps.

[8]   And the foolish said unto the wise, Give us of your oil; for our lamps are gone out.

[9]   But the wise answered, saying, Not so; lest there be not enough for us and you: but go ye rather to them that sell, and buy for yourselves.

[10] And while they went to buy, the bridegroom came; and they that were ready went in with him to the marriage: and the door was shut.

Mum and Dad believed it; all the adults in the Family believed it. Our lives were geared around this event. Why bother educating the children or planning for the future? To us children, or at least to me, Berg's prophecy meant we had no earthly adult future to look forward to. Because of this, I refused to believe it even when I was still in the cult: it would have meant the end of hope. After leaving, the idea that the world would end in 1993 seemed utterly ridiculous and laughable. Of course, my siblings and I, with our newfound scepticism, joked about it that New Year: 'We may as well get totally plastered because tomorrow morning, we may not be here! Ha-ha-ha-ha-ha!' Bev said.

I laughed. 'Let us eat, drink and be merry, for tomorrow we shall die!' I added dramatically.

January and February 1993 came and went.

The date for the court hearing was months away still. I'd been contacted about a separate case in Argentina; Mrs S told me about it and said they were looking for witnesses – children who had grown up in the cult around the world and were prepared to give testimonies to the Argentine police. I told her to give them my name. An investigative magazine doing a piece about the cult in the Philippines also contacted me and asked if they could fly me out there so they could do an article. They wondered if I would be willing to be interviewed on television. I told them I would.

I went to Argentina and bonded with the other witnesses. We spent hours giving statements to hard-boiled but patient detectives in airless Buenos Aires interview rooms. We were driven to a different city, in the south of the country, and interviewed by different detectives there. The police were building up enough evidence to raid the homes there. There were similar operations going on around the world. A huge raid in Australia the year before had led to sixty-five children being taken into care. This was a fact that startled me, because I worried about what it would be like for those children, for children who were taken away from their parents to be thrown into a care system. Children who had no understanding of the outside world, of how to survive. Would life be better for these children in the system? The answer wasn't always clear. We also heard that homes were raided, children were examined but no evidence of physical abuse was found. It didn't surprise me. For the best part of 1989 through to 1991, all the homes divested themselves of any incriminating writings and punishments were such that no marks were left on the body. Although this was the rule, it wasn't always the case in reality, as Justin and the other teens who had endured the teen homes and victor centres could testify.

The long drive from Buenos Aires to the south took a couple of days. We stopped over on the way, and I got to know the other witnesses. I was delighted that Andrea had also been invited. She was my age and deeply traumatised by her experiences. From the US originally, she had contacted me a year or so before, when she had escaped from the cult in Argentina; we became firm friends and we wrote regularly. There was Peter, whom I knew from my childhood in Costa Rica (Dad's old friend and the father of Sarah, Dinah's sweetheart), and a man called Jeremy who had been the main editor of the Mo letters and had spent the best part of the last twenty years in a World Service Unit, some of it in Berg's own compound. This was a huge surprise. It was encouraging to discover that such a well renowned 'brother' within the group had come to his senses and denounced the Family. Together, we swapped stories of life inside the cult.

One evening, after a long day of separately giving statements, we sat at the restaurant in the hotel to eat.

Andrea barely ate anything the entire time we were in Argentina. Her large blue eyes were filled with sadness: 'I can't understand how they were so cruel . . . so cruel to me.' She looked searchingly at Peter and Ted, a tear rolling down her cheek. I knew she was looking for answers from them, two first-generation adults who had joined of their own free will.

'I'm so sorry, Andrea . . .' said Peter. 'When we joined the Children of God, we thought we were joining a force for good, we wanted to change the world, make it a better place. I was eighteen, a hippy, a dropout wandering the streets of California off my head on acid. Then I met the Children of God. They were so full of fire, full of zeal, we were going to change the world, we were going to start a revolution. A revolution for Jesus.'

Ted nodded in agreement. He was truly wracked with guilt. Now in his early forties, he had realised that for his entire adult life he had been brainwashed and manipulated. He had done things, said things, behaved in a way that he now acknowledged was wrong on so many levels. He had confessed to being put on the sharing schedule with little girls. He said he didn't like it, he only enjoyed sharing with the adult women, and that he deeply regretted never having had the courage to say no. I wondered if I should believe him. Could his case be similar to what happened in Nazi and later East Germany, or in the Soviet Union, where ordinary men and women inflicted unspeakable horrors on their country-men and even their own relatives? I had been reading books about the Russian Revolution and the Second World War and I wondered if I'd also be capable of violating my own conscience to conform to a group. Even so, that day I felt relieved to be in the victim and not the perpetrator camp. I didn't think I could live with myself if I had willingly made the choices Ted and Peter had made.

'Why didn't they take me to the doctor?' Andrea continued. 'They could see I was on the verge of death's door for days. That infection nearly killed me and when they finally took me to the hospital it was too late to save my womb and I was given a hysterectomy. At seventeen! Why?' Her lips trembled and tears fell down her cheeks. 'I will never be able to have a family,' she wept.

I felt desperately sad for my friend; it was so unfair. Yes, I was doing the right thing by adding my voice to the campaign against the Family. I might be saving a life. My sister might still be alive and Andrea might still have her womb if someone had spoken up much earlier on.

Back home, a month after I returned from Argentina, I threw myself into my college work. My exams were that summer and I wanted to do as well as I could. I worked particularly hard at my Spanish A level and GCSE English and IT. My plan for after exams was to get out there and get a job. We had to move house that summer too. Mum would be stressed out every year when her tenancy agreement came up for review. It was always a worry – that we might have to up and leave with a couple of months' notice – and this time round, it happened. It was clear that there would be no space for me in the new house so I would need to get my skates on. I passed my GCSEs and my A level along with the City & Guilds secretarial course: a relief.

The campaigning was starting to take its toll; I was tired and thoughts of all the children left behind and the trauma they might experience as a result of being wrenched out of the Family kept me awake at night.

The dates came through for the court case with Mr and Mrs Saberton. I was to testify on the same day as Justin. When the day came, I was nervous. I walked across the bridge from Waterloo and along The Strand, arriving at the Royal Courts of Justice, with its grand white stone entrance. This was the heart of the 'systemite' machine, I thought, and here I was, ready to denounce the shepherds, and Grandpa himself, on the record, no incriminating detail spared. I went through security and on the other side was Justin.

'Hi, Justin . . .' I looked at him fondly. There he was, all six foot two of him, shock of blond hair, dressed in jeans, T-shirt and his awful goofy glasses, which were too small for his face. I have to convince him to get contact lenses, I thought. He was so brave, leaving the cult on his own with no support system, and now to testify in the High Court in London whilst his entire family remained inside. It was a big risk. He would probably never see them again.

A smile crept over his face. I noticed a naughty glint in his eye.

'Wussup, Justo . . .' I said, looking at him suspiciously.

He leaned in to whisper in my ear: 'I've got an eighth of hash in my sock . . .'

'Shit! You're freaking crazy, Justin, oh my God!'

'Ha-ha-ha-ha!' he laughed with glee, pleased as punch that his revelation had had the desired effect.

'When this shit is over, Faith, let's buy some beers, go to the park and skin up!'

Rafaela walked into the waiting room, and motioned us to follow her; she showed us which courtroom to go in. There was a bench outside the room where whoever wasn't testifying would sit until it was their turn. She showed me where to go. I took the steps up to the witness box, which looked very imposing. It was made of mahogany. I sat down. The barristers were wigged and gowned. 'All rise!' We all rose as the judge entered.

A Bible was placed in front of me. 'I swear by Almighty God that the evidence I shall give shall be the truth, the whole truth and nothing but the truth,' I said.

Rafaela asked her questions; I gave details of places, people and events as well as beliefs and practices.

Then the cult's barrister, a young, pleasant-looking man, cross-examined me. I felt puzzled by his approach. His questioning seemed strange to me. It was as though he was simply repeating the same questions Rapha-ella had been asking, with one exception. After each response I would give, he would say: 'And would you say that it made you angry?'

'Yes,' was my reply.

Both barristers and the judge were so emotionless, so professional. The cult's barrister asked me, in about six different ways, if I was angry with the Family.

'I am angry about what happened to me, angry that I lost the right to an education, angry at the violence I experienced and witnessed, at the sexual behaviour, about the way my family was treated . . . yes, I am angry about that. Wouldn't you be?'

It felt clinical and odd. By now I was used to any-body who I told my story to reacting with sympathy and shock, but I couldn't pick up any emotional cues from the judge or the barrister, even from Raphaella, who seemed to slide into cold professionalism in front of the judge.

I knew the verdict would take time. The court case dragged on for a number of years. We didn't expect to hear anything for months, possibly years, but as far as we were concerned, we had done our bit, along with a number of other first- and second-generation members who, during the course of those years, left the cult too.

Although the verdict took a long time, there was one fairly quick win from the Sabertons' point of view. For the interim, the children had been made wards of court.

Job done, I thought.

CHAPTER 9: Too Much Too Young – Costa Rica, 1985

It was so good to see Dinah again, but there was a new sadness about her. She was tight-lipped on the details, but it was clear that the teen home in Mexico had been an ordeal. From the teen home she had been sent on to a babe's ranch in a different city in Mexico. There, they demoted her to 'babe' status because she was being 'rebellious and unyielding and refusing to be put on the sharing schedule'. She told me she protested and asked how she could be demoted to 'babe' status when she had been in the Family since she was four years old? They refused to listen to her and packed her off. At the babe's ranch, she was treated terribly. She had to endure endless chores, cooking, cleaning, laundry and daily public rebukes during devotions and Bible study times, which was humiliating. She had no word from home and didn't know how long she would be staying in Mexico. Were Dad and Mum ever going to send for her? Was she stuck there permanently? She told me that she started to fantasise about escaping but was too frightened to go through with it. She was in Mexico, a foreign country, and she was only fifteen years old.

One day, Dad appeared out of blue. She was so relieved and happy to see him. She threw her arms around his neck and he said: 'I rescue you now.'

'How did he know I needed rescuing?' Dinah asked me. 'Why did he send me away if he knew I would need rescuing?' I shook my head, baffled.

She asked me how Sarah had been at the babe's ranch I'd been sent to. 'Did she ask after me?' she said.

'Oh yes. She misses you, Dinah, so much.'

Sarah had stayed on at the babe's ranch after I left. We hugged and said goodbye. She had no idea when she'd be allowed to leave or whether she and Dinah would ever get to see one another again. Dinah's way of coping with the loss of her first love was to defy Mummy and Daddy's orders and spend lots of time with systemite teenagers in the neighbourhood. She went out, and sometimes didn't come back until it was breakfast time. She cranked up the systemite music on her radio whenever Mummy and Daddy were out, posting one of us younger kids in the front garden to act as lookouts, to alert her to turn off the music if we could see Mummy or Daddy coming up the lane. We didn't mind because it meant that we too got to listen to cool music once in a rare while. There were lots of screaming arguments, too, especially when she refused to join in with devotions.

Barely a month after Dinah had got back from Mexico, and a week after I had returned home from the babe's ranch, Mummy and Daddy announced that the time to move to the countryside had arrived. They had found a home close to Uncle Ernesto's holiday cottage. It happened quite suddenly, because Daddy had no trouble finding a willing assortment of Family members to caretake our house, for a peppercorn rent. The house we were moving to in the countryside was a twenty-minute walk from our Uncle Ernesto's fancy villa, which was set in a park of rolling hills with a big pool and tennis and squash courts. The little village where we would be living was residential, not as upmarket as the holiday complex but a definite improvement on what we were used to. Ours was a colonial-style bungalow, elegant and white with an open-plan living area. It had a huge outside terrace with garden furniture. We had brought all our furniture with us and Mummy went about the house making it cosy and welcoming. Even Daddy joined in, picking a premium spot for his record player and sound system and putting pictures up on the wall. The Venus de Milo and Van Gogh framed prints came too. Daddy had said he and Mummy had bought them way back in the early sixties when he had been studying in Bible School in England and he'd had them professionally framed. The bungalow had four bedrooms in the main part of the house and a little maid's bedroom and bathroom on the other side of the kitchen.

Maribel had left us a couple of months before the move, whilst I was away. I was sad she had gone when I arrived back. Mummy said that she had decided to move to a new home. I found out the real reason why she left when a couple of young disciples from the group dropped by and stayed for lunch one day. The young woman came downstairs to see Josie's new puppies.

'So,' she said, 'Maribel has left then?' Yes, I nodded. 'Do you know why she left?' 'No,' I said. 'It's because your dad was forcing her to share with him.' I felt disgusted and very sorry for Maribel. She was only nineteen and my dad was in his forties! I was not surprised to hear about it, though. I had walked in on my dad one day when we had another young French woman, Isabella, staying. She was the same age as Maribel. It was around 10 a.m. in the morning and my parents' bedroom door was ajar. I was looking for Mummy but instead I saw my dad on top of Isabella, huffing and puffing and red-faced. When he saw me there, frozen in shock, he yelled, 'Get out! Get out!' I felt sickened and ashamed.

Thankfully, we were allowed to bring Josie with us to the new house. I had been worried that moving to the countryside meant we'd need to leave her behind. Josie loved the new garden, which was big and full of shrubs and shady tree canopies for her to nap underneath.

Once the initial excitement had worn off, after a day or two, I started to feel low. I went off my food completely, which Mum commented on as it was unlike me. I was always teased by my siblings for my appetite, for being the chubby one. But now, it was as if my hunger had disappeared overnight. I grew breasts, which seemed to appear from one day to the next.

When I wasn't moping inside, I was down by the local creek with my younger siblings. Dinah had quickly made friends with beautiful twin girls from a nearby town and hung out with them most days, so Bev and I kept ourselves entertained whilst Mummy was inside with Maria. Daddy was often out, supposedly witnessing and 'winning souls for Jesus'. We spent a lot of time trying to catch guppies in our homemade nets that summer. Sometimes we succeeded and let them go again. The air around the creek was full of mosquitoes, and they feasted on my arms and legs. I swelled up, covered in huge welts which itched ferociously. Everything felt different, strange. I was wired, restless and not like myself. I couldn't sleep at night and began to experience strange out-of-body episodes.

More than once, lying in bed, I would hear the clip-clop of horses' hooves outside my window. I couldn't tell whether the sound was real or not. I tried to get out of bed, but couldn't, and I wondered if I was asleep. I noticed a loud buzzing sound in my ears, like white noise, and felt an overwhelming tiredness come upon me. Then I floated out of my body, wandering around the bedroom. I hallucinated, believing I saw women in Victorian dresses in front of me. They had long skirts and sleeves. I could see they had horses and carriages behind them. I had seen pictures of Victorian ladies like the ones I now saw in the *Encyclopaedia Britannica* that Mummy and Daddy had bought from a travelling salesman. It was one of only a handful of systemite volumes that were kept on the bookshelf.

As I travelled in my lucid dream, I reached my parents' room. I wanted to tell Mummy what was happening. I knew she would want to hear, as in the Family, the spirit world was often talked about and she was very interested in it. But I saw that my parents' bedroom was all boarded up. Planks were nailed across it. I was not allowed in. I turned back to my bedroom and found myself floating above my body, looking down on it. I thought, I have to go back in now, and dropped back in, falling forward, watching as each hand slotted back into its place and then sinking fully into my body, which was still.

The next morning I told Mummy about it.

'How interesting, darling!' she said. 'You've always been a spiritual little girl. I'm the same. I taught myself to astral travel. When you're between awake and asleep, you imagine a cloud above your head and imagine you are jumping over it. You might hear a rushing sound and before you know it, you're wandering around outside your body.'

Some of the kids in the neighbourhood became curious about us newcomers and began to hang around the front of our house on their bikes. We soon became friends with a few of them. Adriano was sixteen and very handsome. He had a cool BMX. The first afternoon, Bev, Mike, Petra and I hung out with them, Adriano offered me a ride on his crossbar whilst he pedalled. I perched on it and we sped along, forest streaming by.

'How old are you, Faith?'

'I'm twelve.'

'You look like you are fifteen. You are very pretty.'

I was embarrassed. I didn't think I was pretty.

'Would you like to be my girlfriend? We can go exploring together . . .'

'OK then.'

Adriano would come to our house along with other neighbourhood kids to play football with my brothers in our huge garden. The girls would come too and Bev and I would chat and play with them. One time, Adriano proposed an adventure. We would pack some picnic food and head out further into the countryside and explore. He had kissed me a few times already. There was a spot he liked in a field a fifteen-minute ride away from our house. I didn't mind the kissing, but it didn't do much for me. He seemed to enjoy it though, moaning his 'Mmmms' as his big wet tongue flicked about. I enjoyed feeling grown up. A big girl, at last. He started to warn me about the other boys in his group, particularly Emil, who he thought had a crush on me. 'Don't worry about it though, Faith, I make it clear that you are *my* girl,' he said. 'If he looks at you another time, and I catch him, he knows what's coming.' I had no idea what he meant. Emil just seemed friendly to me; he was funny and I liked his jokes. But there was a novelty to this language of possession that excited me, so I nodded and smiled.

A week or so after I'd agreed to be his girlfriend, Adriano took me to a stream. We sat down, and I started to spread the food from my little backpack out on the blanket. He leant down into some bushes nearby and said: 'Oh, look what I found!' It was a porno mag. It wasn't the first time I'd seen one. One day I noticed Nathanael's bedroom door was open. I saw him sitting on his bed with my five- and six-year-old siblings either side of him, showing them the porno mag. He was leafing through, pointing here and there. The little ones were enthralled. 'We're reading magazines of naked women, Faith! Look!' he said as he turned the magazine around. I saw him do that on several occasions and I knew he kept his stash on the top shelf of his wardrobe. I was curious, so one day when he was out witnessing, I went to his room and stood on a stool and looked at the magazines on my own. I was eight. I was confused by the weird feelings those magazines stirred up, but I knew instinctively I mustn't tell anyone.

The magazine Adriano had found in the bush looked in suspiciously good condition for a chance discovery. He sat down next to me and started to flick through the pages. He stopped at a picture of a woman in white suspenders with no knickers on, she was on all fours and a man behind her was holding his angry-looking penis, enormous and pink, so that it was almost touching her private parts. I froze.

'You like this?' he said.

I looked away. 'It's OK,' I said dubiously. I felt a little frightened.

'Do you love me?'

'Yes!' I said.

'I don't believe you.'

'But I do, you know I do.'

'Then show me. This is how you prove your love for me. I would like to have sex with you. Let's have sex . . .'

He kissed me, hard.

My heart was beating fast. I felt cold, and lightheaded. I pulled away.

'I'm not ready for that . . . I'm too young, I'm only twelve and I'm not ready for that.'

He jerked away from me, a hand on each of my shoulders, looking at me, irritated.

'Then we'll have to break up. You don't love me. If you loved me, you would have sex with me.'

The ride back was silent. 'Bye then,' he said when I jumped off, just outside the gate to our house.

'Bye,' I said, turning away from him. I felt relieved that I had said no, and that was the end of it.

Two days later, he was back, telling me he missed me, that he had made a mistake. He promised he wouldn't ask me 'that' again. He seemed to be making an effort to be more gentlemanly. He held my hand in front of the other boys, kissed me with renewed tenderness.

I took him to my uncle's holiday home for a swim a few times. The walk to his house took us through an orange grove, past manicured lawns and tennis courts with other residents in whites. 'Your family is wealthy . . .' he said, I could tell he was impressed. His mother stayed at home and his father had a car repair workshop. Money was tight, and along with the other local kids, the families with holiday homes at Las Cabinas, where my uncle's cottage was, were known locally as 'Ricachones'. We are not wealthy, I thought, when I heard the local kids talk about it. My uncle certainly was, but we weren't.

At Las Cabinas, I said hello to a few of the children I recognised from previous visits – friends of my cousins. Adriano didn't like it. 'They were looking at you funny, Faith. No wonder, in those shorts. If a teenage boy asks you a question when you're with me, just keep quiet, I'll put him in his place.'

I didn't like his controlling behaviour, but I started to enjoy the kissing and groping more, and my feelings for Adriano grew. After a few months, the pestering started up afresh, but this time, it had a slightly subtler approach. One day, we were sitting at the same spot where Adriano had found the magazine. He took my face between his hands and said:

'If you loved me, you'd show me.'

'How?'

'By giving yourself to me . . .'

'Please . . .' I said. I felt the panic rising. I was upset.

'We've been together for six months now,' he said

'Give me a month, I'll think about it . . .'

'OK. But if you don't want to in a month, that's it. We're over . . .'

'I understand,' I said.

For a month I worried and fretted. I knew I wasn't ready for sex. I knew I was too young and that it was wrong. I struggled with the dilemma. In the Family I was considered an adult. Even Shiloh took the opportunity to lose her virginity to someone she loved . . . she was sixteen, though. My internal monologue became a fierce debate.

'I'm too young! I don't want to do that! I'm scared . . .'

What if I was forced to 'share' with someone I didn't love, though? I was sure Mummy had had to share with all sorts of brothers and 'fish' she didn't love. What if I regretted being forced to give my virginity to someone I didn't fancy? I didn't want my first time to be like that.

In the end, I gave in. It happened at the back of my parents' garden one evening when Adriano had come over to hang out after dinner. The garden was large, with lots of shady corners. It was twilight, and I could hear a dove cooing in a tree. Adriano had a determined look on his face, he kissed me distractedly, and I felt rigid. 'Relax, Faith!' he said. I was scared. It hurt like hell. My body was rigid, and I waited for him to finish. Before he did, Josie appeared, snuffling around us, and we heard Daddy calling after her, so we scrambled up. I said goodbye to Adriano, not meeting his eye, and ran inside, straight to the toilet. There was a lot of blood, and I felt sad. I felt sad that it had hurt so much, that I hadn't really wanted it, and now I'd had my first time and I knew I could never get it back. I was terrified about getting pregnant, too. I didn't know what a condom was. All I knew is that Mummy had mentioned that if a guy doesn't get sperm inside you, you are unlikely to become pregnant.

The next day, I said to Adriano, 'That's it, I showed you I loved you . . .' and he seemed to accept it. We reverted to kissing and heavy petting, which I enjoyed a lot more. He gave me my first orgasm, and after that I began to see the point of it all, and felt I was glad I had given my first time to Adriano rather than a Family grown-up. At least Adriano was handsome, and young.

He was also crazy jealous. He started a few fights over me, with other boys from the neighbourhood, and his aggression and sense of ownership over me frightened and suffocated me. He became very concerned when I told him Mummy and Daddy were planning on moving back to the house in town: that we wouldn't be staying, because they had plans to go travelling, to take us all to the mission fields in the East, but first, we would stop off in Europe. A new Mo letter had been published to say that those Family members who didn't 'get out of the Americas' (which Grandpa also called 'The Blob' and 'The Whore of Babylon') to preach the gospel in the East, where people did not know about Jesus, would be excommunicated or demoted to 'babe' status.

'Perhaps I should get you pregnant, then you won't have to go anywhere,' Adriano said when I told him we were leaving imminently. The idea filled me with horror and I began to feel trapped. I told him absolutely not, I wasn't even thirteen yet! I could see how controlling he had become, and how quickly. I managed to persuade him this was a terrible idea and that his mother would be furious. That brought him to his senses. He adored his mother and knew she would be disappointed and that he would be in big trouble if that were to happen.

There were tears when we said our goodbyes. Adriano said he would come to the airport to see us off, and I promised to write to him with the details. We packed up our things and a van came to transport us all, with Josie, back home. Mummy and Daddy explained that they had asked the Family members to move out so we could move back in for a few weeks before the flights. Daddy had been delighted and pleased that this new Mo letter had come out. He wanted to travel, to be a real missionary, so the ultimatum suited him. Mummy and Daddy became energised with plans.

We would fly into Spain, they told us, then make our way from Madrid to Gibraltar, where Daddy would convert his remaining inheritance into gold Krugerrands. Spain would be our 'springboard' into other mission fields. My parents explained we would be going to India: there were a number of Family homes (communes) there and the land was ripe for witnessing. We would all finally be given the opportunity to prove ourselves, to show our faith, and to win souls in quantities unimaginable in Costa Rica. The idea of Spain, let alone India, felt impossibly exotic. Daunting and exciting.

Flights were booked and clothes were mended ready for our new adventure. Every day there were fewer and fewer bits of furniture. We waved goodbye to the Venus de Milo, the record player and sound system, the lamp and bookshelves made of precious tropical hardwood, Mummy's sewing machine, Shiloh's old bed frame. There were a few other things to tie up before we left. The worst was to say goodbye to Josie, who was going to be rehomed with another cult family, along with the litter of puppies she had just had. Mummy said:

'Who would like to volunteer to take Jo to Abishai and Jodiah's house?'

I raised my hand. I said I would accompany her in the van with the new people and help settle her into the new home by walking her in and leaving her there. This was harder and more painful than I realised it would be. I sat in shock for the entire half-hour journey and insisted on riding in the back of the van with Josie rather than up front with Jodiah, the shepherd who had come to collect her. When we got to the house, I walked Josie into the garden, then stroked her goodbye. The puppies were busy playing and jumping up for her teats, but Josie ignored them. She was very distressed and agitated and she started to cry and whimper as I held her and comforted her for as long as I was allowed. She looked at me with her beautiful brown eyes and I knew that she knew I was going to abandon her. As I left the house, I heard her howling. I cried silently all the way back home. I comforted myself with the thought that at least she would have her puppies for a little while longer to snuggle up to at night. Would Abishai and Jodiah be kind to her? They had often visited our house with their kids, who were the same age as us, so I hoped that they would love my Jo.

It was far worse than saying goodbye to Adriano. I was sad to see him at the airport though, and we had a goodbye kiss. There were a few other friends there, too, and seeing their faces, I felt an acute pang. The loss was real. I knew that we wouldn't be coming back. This was it.

CHAPTER 10: Rebel – The Philippines, 1992

I was invited to Spain, where the authorities were building a case. I flew to Madrid, gave a statement to the police there and stayed one night on my own in a crumby hotel. I told them what my family and I had seen and heard in Spain during our travels there. When I got back, I received the details of the trip to the Philippines. The editor of the magazine who was flying me out there was a persistent young man called Crisanto. He had been given my number by someone in the Cult Information Centre in London. There had been considerable cult activity in the country, Crisanto explained, and it was rumoured for years that David Berg had lived in the Philippines, in carefully guarded secrecy in a compound with a tight inner circle of followers.

Crisanto explained that, as well as his magazine wanting to do this double-page spread exposé, a number of TV channels would also like to interview me. Would I be willing to do TV interviews? I was pleased that I would have another opportunity to speak out, to call out the abuse, the lies and the manipulation.

My hosts were delightful. I was put up in a five-star hotel and assigned an interpreter, a woman a few years older than me, called Analyn. Once the interviews for the magazine article had been given, and photos taken, it was published and within days my interpreter's phone was ringing non-stop for interview requests. I was happy to oblige but I wasn't prepared for the reality of it. To everyone's surprise, the full PR machine of the cult had swung into action, and they invited me and the magazine to come to their compound to see how wonderful it was for ourselves. They also said that it was only fair that they should have a chance to answer my accusations. On the seventh day of my stay, the Family invited the magazine representatives and me to 'Heaven's School', a compound, on what I thought was a semi-private visit.

The day before I was due to go, I began to feel scared. I looked at my interpreter.

'Are you OK, Faith? You don't have to accept their invitation if you don't want to . . .'

I wrung my hands, pacing the room. Less than two years ago, a rebuke from one of the adults would have left me rooted to the spot in terror. Then, I had been fully under the Family's control, both physically and mentally, and now, I had been invited into the lion's den on my own.

'I'll do it,' I said. The next day, my interpreter and I took a train along with a crew of a cameraman and a photographer. As we arrived at our destination and got off the train, I saw that the station was full of Family members, some whom I recognised. They looked at me menacingly, some speaking into big brick mobile phones, others in groups of two or three holding hands in a circle, fervently praying. I was suddenly so terrified that my legs turned to jelly and almost gave way beneath me. I clung to my interpreter. 'You are doing so well, Faith, these people are horrible, and you are so brave to confront them! You don't have to go through with this,' she said. I managed to gather myself and we went on.

When we arrived at the compound, the hall there was filled with my peers – the second-generation Family members, the ones I was trying to save – and about thirty adult disciples, all of whom had been primed to hate me. I recognised many of them, including the adults. Seeker! There was Seeker, whom I had last seen in Mexico.

The Family had their own camera crew, and had set up a long table, the kind I'd seen in big press conferences on TV. Apparently, I was going to be seated in the middle between four cult members.

We were given seats in the main hall and the obligatory guitars came out. Two teen boys played the guitar as four pretty girls, dressed in long flowy skirts with waist-long hair, sang some songs and did their dance routines with beaming smiles and bright eyes. For me, this was not unusual, but for my interpreter and the cameramen, it seemed utterly bizarre. When the singing was over, the kids sat down, their beaming smiles and bright eyes turning to stony hate.

Seeker motioned me. 'Faith, come up here to the podium.' My interpreter, a petite, softly spoken lady, got up and stood between Seeker and me. 'No!' she said. 'I will not allow this; you will not surround Faith and intimidate her in this way. She can have her turn and then you can answer her charges after.' Seeker tried to intimidate my interpreter but she stood her ground and I was grateful to her. I got up and sat at the table, cameras in my face.

'The fact is, what you see here is a dangerous cult that is unfit to be responsible for minors,' I said.

'Liar!' the teens roared.

'I know that you know that everything I'm saying is true.' I pointed at them. 'You are having to endure the victor programme, you are not getting an education here, not to mention Grandpa's teachings about sex with adults and children, I happen to know for a fact that most of you have endured some form of sexual abuse.'

'Liar! Liar!'

'You can shout with conviction because we have been brought up to not see it as abuse but as sharing love.' I put my mouth closer to the mic. They shouted even

171

louder. 'You! Thad!' I recognised Thad in the audience. Fifteen at the time, the same age as Dinah, they had become friends in the teen home in Mexico because of their shared love of guitar-playing. 'You were there, in Mexico with my sister Dinah, in the same home as Paul and Pandita who were thirteen and eleven and were openly sharing with adults there!' He went pale, ducked behind some adults and left the room.

'You are being exploited here; your lives are being wasted. I wonder how many of you even know where your parents are?' They all fell about laughing and jeering. The teens were the loudest.

They continued to drown me out with their hateful shouting. I was shocked and then it dawned at me that this was the first time they had ever been given permission to vent anger. Under no other circumstance would any of these youngsters have been allowed to express their emotions and if they had, they would have been severely punished.

The adult disciples continued to shout abuse at me. They filmed all of this. When there was a pause, they asked me a question: 'Do tell us about these allegations you make . . .' but as soon as I started to answer, they drowned me out with their shouting. I looked at my interpreter, sitting in the audience. She looked grave. I looked at the teens. They looked vacant, filled with hate, and I wondered if I had done the right thing. My interpreter got up and motioned me to come down from the podium. Seeker, along with three others, got up and sat behind the table on the podium and began to assassinate my character.

'The truth is that Faith is just an angry young person. She is bitter that her life hasn't turned out the way she planned so she is venting her frustration on us. Faith's family weren't really in the Family, at all,' he said. 'Everything she is saying is a fabrication. All the abuse Faith is alleging happened within her own family. Her sister even died because of her parents' neglect,' he said.

That was a low blow. I was gutted. My mind could not comprehend how this group of people, supposedly 'my Family', could spout such barefaced lies.

When the press conference was over, some of the youngsters came right up to me, surrounding me menacingly to tell me what a liar I was.

'You are such a liar, Faith, you are trying to destroy our way of life.' They looked at me with disgust and contempt. Seeker appeared and rescued me. I looked into his eyes and saw a glimmer of humanity.

'Seeker,' I said my lips quivering a little.

'C'mon, Faith, let's go for a walk, just you and me, let's talk.'

For the next ten minutes I gave him examples of incidents, quoted Mo letters, and reminded him of practices of things we both knew were part of our way of life in the Family. For a short moment, I thought I might persuade him to acknowledge the truth, but he refused. My interpreter and the camera crew watched from a distance, anxiously waiting for me. I could see they were worried. Finally, I said goodbye to Seeker. I felt shell-shocked and completely drained afterwards.

Later, at the hotel after a long hot shower, I poured myself a drink from the mini bar and switched on the TV. The news was on, and there I was, on every channel. The same footage of me being shouted at and trying to defend myself being played over and over again. Frustratingly, I couldn't understand what the newscasters were saying because it was all in Filipino.

When I heard that River Phoenix had died outside an LA nightclub in October, I was upset and it affected me more than I cared to admit. I thought River and his siblings, along with Rose McGowan, were comparatively lucky because their parents had come to their senses before they were teenagers. Their parents did not agree with the flirty fishing and sharing doctrines and had had the courage to leave, taking all their kids with them. It was no wonder then that they had a better chance of making a success of their lives. Even so, whilst I was in the Family, River was proof that it was possible to survive and thrive in the outside world, to have a second chance. He was proof that what the shepherds told us about the kids who left (that we would all become drug addicts, prostitutes and dropouts) were lies to control us and keep us prisoners. So when I saw what had happened on the news, I was shocked and a nasty gloom descended on me. I knew they would be using River's death to scare the crap out of everyone and keep them captive.

When I got back from the Philippines, I hit a low ebb. I was depressed from the moment I woke up to the end of the day. I was filled with a feeling of bleak emptiness, and nihilistic thoughts filled my head. With my friend Sacha, and some of my other friends, I began to experiment with trips, mushrooms, LSD and microdots. I found that I was willing to jump in and try almost anything that would alter my mind and my perception of the world. I was astounded by these experiences and I found that my depression would lift temporarily after a trip. I was in awe by how connected I felt to nature, how my mind would expand. But the depression would always return after a few weeks. I felt it was there to stay.

Despite my depression, I felt somewhat encouraged in the months that followed by the trickle of young people who were starting to leave the cult. Amongst them were a couple of girls I had lived with in the Holloway home in London. Mum welcomed them into our home. They slept on mattresses on the floor in my room. They were so young! Just sixteen and seventeen. I wondered how on earth they were going to cope. They wanted to live in London, so Mum helped them to connect with Social Services there.

A few months later and now living in London, the girls called me. 'We're making soooooo much money, Faith! Ha-ha-ha-ha! Oh my God, we're doing exotic dancing and we're making, like, three hundred pounds a day!'

'What is exotic dancing?' I asked.

'Well, we answered an advert in the newspaper for exotic dancers and were asked to come to an interview and to bring along a bikini. We just have to writhe around a bit to the music, take off our bikinis and then when our set is over, we take a pint jug to all the punters so they can put tips in it!' they said. 'It's so easy! You should try it, Faith. You can do it! You'd make much more money than cleaning your college!'

'No thanks, girls. I think I'd rather clean the toilets than have a bunch of dirty old men ogling me.'

A few weeks later, the phone rang: 'Faith! You've gotta come clubbing with us! We've discovered these pills and they make you feel *amazing!* C'mon Faithy . . . don't be a bore!' The thought of going to a club in central London with the girls did not appeal to me in my depressed state. 'Next time . . .' I said. The girls didn't give up and later that autumn, I agreed. I was feeling so low that I thought perhaps it would jolt me out of my black mood. I took a train to Victoria and then the tube to Oval. The club was called Paradise Club. It was an old warehouse in a dodgy part of town. I met them in a bar close to the club – I could hear the thumping music from streets away.

We joined the queue, the girls chattering away, dolled up to the nines. At the door, three menacing-looking bouncers in tight black T-shirts and jeans eyed us and waved us in. The club was dingy and dark with the odd lamp here and there in the corners. The sofas in the seating area were old and crusty and the bar mainly served bottles of water with a small section of the fridge dedicated to bottled beer. Odd, I thought. House music blared. The place began to fill up.

'Here, Faith! Take this!' Priscilla handed me a pill with a dove stamped on it.

'What is it and what does it do?' I said, popping it into my mouth and washing it down with a sip of water from the bottle she handed me.

'It's called Ecstasy . . . you'll see!' she said, giggling and handing them out like sweets to the rest of our posse of ravers, all young people who had recently left the cult.

What a weird little crew we were. So naïve, so clueless, so unworldly and lacking in street smarts. At first, nothing happened, and I couldn't really get into the music. It seemed a bit repetitive to me. Then suddenly, the lights on the dancefloor came on and the music got louder. By now I noticed that the club was packed. There were all sorts of young people here. Some boys and girls were in jeans and trainers, others were all dressed up in club gear. The atmosphere became electric and people started to hoot and cheer, blow whistles and jump up and down, dancing to the music. 'Everyone is coming up on their Es, Faith!' Priscilla laughed, her eyes like saucers. Suddenly I felt this huge rush come over my entire body and mind. It was like nothing I had ever felt before.

'Priscilla! Priscilla!' I yelled above the thumping music. 'What's going on? I feel like I'm going to be sick!'

'Chill out, Faith!' She smiled. 'You're just rushing, go with it! Here, come here. Let me stroke your back. There!'

She wrapped her arms around my waist and held me tight as we swayed to the music. Once the initial rushing subsided, I started to notice the music and it began to make sense.

I loved the feeling of connectedness it gave me, I felt pure joy, a rushing and opening of my heart, a rising-up. I joined everyone else on the dancefloor. I looked at my fellow dancers, smiling and laughing. 'Are you having a good time?' a random girl asked me.

'Yes!' I beamed and offered her my hand.

She took it and pulled me in for a hug. We held each other. She ran her fingers through my hair, lifting it away from my neck and then blew on my neck. A lovely moment of innocence and pure love with a total stranger, like I never even imagined was possible, and yet here I was, in a dingy club in a dodgy part of London, off my head on Ecstasy along with everyone else in this club, a deep feeling of togetherness uniting us all. All the normal social barriers disappeared. We danced for hours, and later we sat on the sofas in a big huggy pile, friends and strangers, chatting, giving each other massages, offering water to each other, all with no sexual undertones. So began a new adventure for me. In the weeks and months after that I went back countless times, and my suicidal depression completely vanished. I realised after that night that there is so much more that life has to offer; that, in fact, life is a huge adventure, a place of new and wonderful discoveries. I became determined to open my mind, to find out everything I could about what it meant to be a human. I partied hard into the winter of 1992, through all of 1993 and 1994, and into 1995.

Sometimes, Mum would babysit for Dinah's boys, and the two of us would go out together. Dinah and I would go to gay clubs: I loved the atmosphere at Heaven, tucked away in the arches behind Embankment station, and we spent the night dancing with gay boys and girls and drag queens, high on Ecstasy and the giddy hedonism of London. But I started to notice that my comedowns from the Es began to get worse and worse. My partying would often last for a couple of days and on those occasions, it would take me all week to recover. I told Vicky, my Crystal Palace friend, about my partying. At first, she didn't approve but soon we began to go raving together. We had an absolute blast, but I always knew that eventually I'd have to pay for it with a horrible comedown that left me feeling depressed and lethargic. A small upside was that it was nothing like the suicidal depression of the past. I smoked copious amounts of weed in the hopes of taking the edge off, but it didn't always work.

Mum made it clear that she was fed up with my partying. I would disappear for days and I was camping out in the dining room because there was no space for me. Mum had found a five-bedroomed house and Dinah had returned and was sharing a room with her two toddlers. It was time to move out. I had found a job as a receptionist in the City at a Mexican bank. It was a mind-numbingly dull job, but all the broadsheet and tabloid papers would be delivered every morning. By 11 a.m. I had read them all from cover to cover. I'm going to die of boredom, I thought. I knew I needed to go to university to get more qualifications or I would have to put up with tedious jobs all my life. I started to look into my options but felt utterly inadequate. I had no clue what I wanted to do, and Mum was no help. After some enquiries I was told that I didn't have enough qualifications to do a degree but that I could do an HND, which would give me enough points to continue on for two more years to convert into a degree as a mature student. In the end, I decided to study retail management because I found a course on Bond Street in London, a train ride away. I was interested in business, too. In the meantime, I moved out of home and shared a flat with Sacha, one of my grungy girlfriends.

I continued to work at the bank, partying at the weekends, and waited for the start of my course: September 1995. It was then that I decided that I would change my life. I would abandon all the campaigning and concentrate on me, to figure out who I was and what I wanted. I'd focus on getting an education and exploring life. Having a good time and forgetting the miserable past. I would leave the campaigning to others so I could forge my own future free from the shackles of my childhood memories.

CHAPTER 11: Pieces of Eight – Summer 1986

The first few days in Spain were cold. We stayed in a pension just outside Madrid, a stopover whilst my parents made arrangements for where to go next. Mum and Dad were bickering a lot about where that should be. The idea was to 'springboard' from Europe into the mission field; Dad was set on us going to India. Before we did that, he suggested we should all stay for a few months in the Costa del Sol whilst he and Mum made a plan. As they bickered and sniped, I tuned them out. I was preoccupied with trying to keep myself together while I felt as though my world was falling apart.

I gathered from the snatches I overheard that Mum was worried about burning through money and concerned about Dad's idea to take us all to Gibraltar to convert his inheritance into gold. The Mo letters were full of warnings about systemite banking and about how gold was the only safe investment when the end times were looming.

In my bed in the pension that first night I felt frightened, hollow and lonely. I couldn't sleep a wink and my ears picked up every little noise. The sound of the boiler, my brother's breathing, Bev muttering something in her sleep. Am I the only one in the world awake? I wondered. What's going to happen to us? I thought of Shiloh, I thought of Josie, our old house, I thought of Adriano, of the swimming pool in Las Cabinas, and my heart ached. Now here we were, on the other side of the world with no home of our own and it was cold, grey and rainy. We hadn't bought any new clothes for the trip and everything we had was summery and lightweight. Even my pyjamas were made from thin cotton.

I couldn't sleep that whole first night and felt filled with an aching emptiness. Everything was so unfamiliar. We had lived in the tropics my whole life so springtime in Madrid felt chilly and unwelcoming. There were high buildings everywhere and there was a lot of traffic, even at night. Mum let Maria get into bed with her. Maria always got extra attention and love, I thought to myself, as I pulled the starched sheets and the itchy pink blanket up to my neck. The rest of us were always left to get on with it. Finally, as it started to dawn and light began to peek through the curtains, I heard the lulling sound of truck engines outside. Must be the bin men, I thought, as I fell asleep.

The idea of India was exciting, but I wasn't looking forward to the next few months stuck here. But once we left the city and moved to a holiday villa on the outskirts of Nerja, a town on the Costa Del Sol, I felt better about it. The weather grew hotter and hotter. We were a ten-minute walk from the beach and the villa was very nice. It was set in a holiday compound. The buildings were all painted white, and there were several lovely shared pools we could choose from. Mum and Dad encouraged us to play out, and we roved around for whole days, lying on the beach and hanging out with the English daughter of a local shopkeeper, who sometimes shared her weekly Jumbo Toblerone treat with Bev and me. We had never had chocolate like that back at home! I spent three months in bikini bottoms and flip-flops, and only came home to eat.

Dinah, being older, was allowed to venture further afield. She made friends with some Swedish teenage girls holidaying with their parents and Dad gave her money to go out to the clubs. Often, we wouldn't see her for days.

We had a few visitors during that time. An extremely tall Dutch man with a thin pointy nose and a Moroccan woman. Daddy met this hippy couple when he was out witnessing and invited them to stay with us for a while. He was heavily into t'ai chi and cut a very funny figure as he practised. I thought he looked like a praying mantis. They weren't part of the Family, but Mummy and Daddy welcomed them in and spent long evenings witnessing to them. After five days or so, we started itching like crazy all over. The woman told us that the seawater at dawn would cure the itching, so one morning, she woke Bev and me up whilst it was still dark. We trooped down to the beach, bleary-eyed, and dutifully bathed. They left us then, headed for Istanbul, but the itching got worse and worse. We went to the doctor and he said our skin was just dry and to slather it with moisturiser.

The other visitors during our time in Spain were Family members, an American woman and a South American man. The woman had two daughters and the man was her second husband, but not the girls' father. The first day they arrived, we spent the day together at the villa; Mummy cooked a big lunch and we took the girls to play at the beach for a while. When we got back, the adults were still chatting with Family music playing in the background. Carlos, the man, came up to Bev, me and his stepdaughter Cindy, who was twelve. 'Hello honey.' He sidled up to Cindy and kissed her full on the lips, hooking his long, hairy arm over her bare shoulder, and linking hands with her. He cast a lustful look in our direction as we stood there, shocked and rooted to the spot in fear.

'Do you like to share, girls?' he asked Bev and me.

'No,' I said, quickly, clutching Bev's hand.

'Cindy and I share all the time, don't we, sweetie? You show Daddy the love of God, don't you? You should try it, girls . . .' He laughed as he wandered off.

Cindy looked down at the floor and blushed. I felt sorry for Cindy and I could see that Bev did too.

After they had left, we told Mummy about it. She was folding washing in the utility room.

'Carlos told Bev and me that he shares with Cindy, like, all the time . . .'

There was a silence. 'Urgh, that's disgusting. That's terrible . . .' Mum said. She carried on balling up the socks and folding the pillowcases and didn't meet my eye. I sloped off, out of the room. It was clear the conversation was over.

About six weeks into our stay in Nerja, Mum announced to our surprise that Isabella, the young Frenchwoman who had stayed with us in Costa Rica (and whom I had seen having sex with Dad), was coming to stay with baby Gabriella who was now a toddler. Baby Gabriella was only a few months younger than Maria. I quite liked Isabella so was happy we'd get to see her again, although I wondered to myself if she and Dad would be sharing.

Bev seemed more upset by the idea of us opening our house to this young woman whom Dad had impregnated. She was upset that Dad had been busy sharing with her, bringing her into our house, whilst Shiloh was so ill. She was cross with Mummy, too, for being so accommodating. Her disapproval subsided a little soon after they arrived because little Gabriella was quite cute and so obviously our sister. She was a sensitive child, always crying for her mother, and she seemed more vulnerable than Maria, despite having a far heavier build. When we picked her up, we joked that Gabriella was twice as heavy.

Her hair was not as thick as Maria's so she got away without having to endure the elaborate hairstyles that Bev and I would give poor long-suffering Maria. She would patiently sit as one of us would enthusiastically brush, part, and pull her beautiful thick dark locks into tight pigtails or French plaits. Gabriella had a sadness about her and was hard to comfort. 'Maman!' she would cry. 'Maman!' Gabriella had no English so we spoke to her mainly in Spanish, although she and her mum talked in French. Isabella helped around the house and was sweet and unassuming. I felt ashamed for her at the memory of me walking into Mummy and Daddy's bedroom that time and finding them at it.

Dad seemed disinterested in Isabella second time around, and although he tolerated her presence, it was Mummy who made her feel welcome. He showed little interest in Gabriella, aside from remarking that 'she looks just like her sisters!' She cried any time he tried to pick her up, reaching out her chubby little arms to her mum. After a few weeks, Isabella moved on, headed for one of the bigger city communes. We never saw her again.

One afternoon, Bev and I heard what sounded like construction machinery. Curious, we wandered off with our freshly made mugs of tea to investigate. 'They must be building a new villa,' we said as we walked up the lane. We saw two men working with a small digger, pickaxes and spades dotted around. We walked towards the plot.

After a few minutes of standing there, watching the men working and sipping our tea, the man in the digger looked over and started gesticulating wildly at us.

'What's his problem?' said Bev. The man carried on until suddenly, he stopped the digger and jumped out, rushing towards us. In a gruff Spanish voice he shouted, 'This is a building site . . . Get out of here! Scram!' His shirt was unbuttoned showing a skinny, hairy chest. He had a big moustache and an angry face. 'This is private property, *chiquillas*, get away before you get into trouble!'

He was so aggressive, speaking to us as if we were criminals. Bev, to my horror said, 'No! You can't tell us what to do, we are standing on the pavement!'

'Shut up!' he said. '*A que te pego una ostia! Joder!*'

Bev sassed back: 'No! I won't shut up, you shut up!'

He walked right up to her and slapped her face, hard, and as he hit her, she spilt her boiling mug of tea all over his arms and belly. He totally lost it and started shouting and swearing at the top of his lungs. Dinah must have heard the commotion from her bedroom because I saw her running at full speed towards us, a look of fury on her face as she witnessed this Spaniard shouting and swearing at us at the top of his lungs. He made a move to slap Bev's face again and next thing I saw was Dinah's foot connecting with his chest. She had used one of the tae-kwon-do kicks she had practised in the garden for so many years back in Costa Rica. He stumbled back and at the same time Dinah slipped on the loose earth and fell on her back. By now, the man was wild with fury. He grabbed a pickaxe that was lying around, raised it above his head in a move to plunge it into Dinah, on her back on the floor. The other worker started to freak out, running towards his co-worker shouting, '*No lo hagas, Miguel! Estas loco? Por Dios, hombre! No lo hagas!* (Don't do it, Miguel! Are you crazy? For God's sake, man, don't do it!)

By now I had started screaming hysterically, and I saw Mum rushing over to the scene. Miguel finally put the pickaxe down as the other builder continued to berate him.

I pulled Dinah up and we scrambled off, heading towards Mum, who was rushing towards us, white as a sheet. Mum said, 'What on earth has just happened?' Dinah and Bev tried to explain above my uncontrolled screaming. 'Be quiet, Faith! Stop it at once!' I continued screaming, beside myself. 'Take control of yourself right now!' said Mum. I ignored her and carried on. I couldn't stop. Mum slapped me across the cheek and held my face between her hands. 'Pull yourself together, Faith!' she said.

It brought me to my senses and I was able to stop screaming. As I sat quietly on my bed later that day, I pondered what had happened to me. Why had I lost control of myself? I felt a bit ashamed and embarrassed. It had taken Mummy slapping my face, something she had only done once before, to make me stop screaming. I made a vow never to lose control of myself again.

A week later, Mummy and Daddy sent me, Bev and Dinah off to stay in a Family home in Malaga for a few weeks. They thought the change of scene would do us good. We had got used to sleeping in and coming and going as we pleased. It had felt like a long holiday.

'You need more fellowship time, a bit of discipline,' Mummy said.

Dad dropped us off at the bus terminal and we got the bus on our own to Malaga. The coastal road was nauseatingly winding, and everyone got travel sick and threw up on the way. As the bus was air-conditioned, the air was being recycled and the entire bus stank of sick, which made me feel even worse. After we had thrown up all our breakfast, Bev and I continued dry retching the entire journey. It was awful. When we arrived, we stumbled out of the chilly bus into the fierce hot July sun. There stood a young, tall blond American man with long hair waiting at the terminal.

'God bless you, girls! You must be Dinah, Faith and Beverly. I'm Micah.' He reached out and kissed and hugged us, as was the custom in our group. He stank of BO. Micah cheerfully chatted away to we three rather green and pasty-looking girls and led us to a waiting van. 'Praise the Lord! Hallelujah! We're very happy that you have come to fellowship with us.' My toes curled a little bit and I hoped to goodness that creepy Carlos, his wife and Cindy and her sister were not in that home. He ushered us into a little van and off we went to a large house in the suburbs. It had a terrace outside and a big garden. There were five bedrooms, each one occupied by an entire family, mostly little kids under the age of ten and their parents.

We were given a spot on the floor of the living room and were provided with roll-up mats and sleeping bags. 'We are having an area fellowship tomorrow, girls, so there will be even more people here. Your father tells us you are good musicians?'

'We sing sometimes,' Dinah mumbled unenthusiastically.

'Thank you, Jesus!' he said. 'The Lord has blessed you with musical talent! You can join me in leading fellowship! Dinner is at six and you can pitch in with the clean-up afterwards.'

The next morning, at 6 a.m., we were woken up by Micah's dulcet tones singing the revelry. What? Nooooo, I thought. Micah stood in the middle of the floor where we were sleeping, strumming away and singing with all his heart:

'It's a new morning! A new morning! Yeah! A new morning for Jee-sus, a new morning for Jesus!' I opened up a crusty eye to see a bad-tempered-looking Dinah pulling the pillow around her ears.

'The sun is shining, the sun is shining, yeah! It's shinning for you-ooo, it's shining for you!'

After weeks of waking up at 11 a.m., it was a shock. We got dressed and did devotions for what felt like eternity; the shepherds took turns to read out the Mo letter of the day. It was 'Diamonds of Dust', one of the classics, known as the 'oldie goldies':

'You reflect the light of the Lord . . . Even the smallest speck of dust can sparkle like a diamond . . . each one reflecting in his own way the light of God . . . The less there is of you, the more the light shines through . . .' I barely listened, I knew it so well, and my mind wandered off into a daydream. The shepherdess paused the reading. 'C'mon, children! Let's sing "Diamonds of Dust"! We have been practising that song, haven't we?' The little kids jumped up, Micah picked up the guitar and we all started to sing:

'Oh, to be a diamond of dust . . . just floating by. In the morning sunlight you see me, reflecting the light . . .'

The little kids waved their hands in the air. 'Praise the Lord!' said the shepherdess. 'What have we been memorising, children?'

'If you think, think, think, you're gonna sink, sink, sink because you stink, stink, stink!' they yelled enthusiastically.

'Amen!' said all the adults in unison.

We ate breakfast and were allocated chores. Bev, Dinah and I were tasked with entertaining the children and cleaning the bathrooms. We helped prepare the evening meal and sang along to the adults' guitars later. One of them let Dinah play his guitar and they were all impressed by our musicality. A couple of the women danced, swishing their skirts to 'Gypsies Led by Abraham'. Then Micah broke out in tongues. 'Arabarashandara! Shondo laberondo!' he said with his eyes closed; his arms shot up into the air as all the other grownups joined him. Although we were used to this kind of performance, we always found it excruciatingly embarrassing. The three of us kept our eyes closed, feigning a prayerful attitude, every now and then peeking open an eye only to have to stifle our giggles when our eyes met.

Earlier on, whilst helping in the kitchen, I had noticed the sharing schedule pinned up on the noticeboard. I was grateful there had been no discussion of the sharing during that particular fellowship meeting, as it was quite common for fellowships to end up with some sort of sharing activity. I had made the mistake of falling asleep on a bed in one of the rooms in a home in Costa Rica after one such fellowship, to be woken up by Uncle Thomas and Aunty Hepzibah on the same bed as me, humping away. I scooched myself further into the corner, covering my head with the bedspread.

After the fellowship, we stayed two more nights, then headed back to the bus stop to catch a ride back to Nerja. It reminded me how boring and restrictive life in the communes was. We were lucky to be living as a family for now, I could see that.

One day in August, Daddy announced that we were going to take a family trip to Gibraltar. 'We are going to Gibraltar, children, and we are going to buy gold Krugerrands! They are very big coins made of pure gold! I want to buy many of them to take to the mission field but there is a silly rule that says we are not allowed to take more than a couple out of Gibraltar, which is British territory. You children can hide them in your pants and socks when we cross the border! Isn't that exciting?'

It took Dad most of the afternoon of the day we got there to buy the gold. In the meantime we were having fun and amused ourselves looking at the monkeys and taking in the sights in the park nearby. It was a sunny day, and we played tag and ate the picnic we had packed. Dad emerged from the shop after an hour and handed Mummy a canvas bag.

'C'mon, kids, let's go into that café and order some ice creams, then we can take a trip to the toilet so you can hide the coins in your clothes!' said Mummy excitedly. 'They are worth thousands of dollars, children, so we need to make sure they are safe,' she said. 'Socks, pants, pockets . . . We will stuff them in, kids. When we cross the border, stay calm.'

We were all happy to sit in the café and eat ice cream. Such a novelty! But I was worried one of us might give something away and get us all into trouble. Afterwards, we trooped into Marks & Spencer's and Mummy bought Weetabix, chocolate, biscuits and other goodies and gave us a bag each. 'We will blend in with all the tourists, children!' she said. 'How exciting!'

Because Dad's plan to buy a car had been a disaster (he had bought a dud from two dodgy-looking locals in Nerja – a brown Citroën that conked out after less than a week), we went to Gibraltar and back on one of the air-conditioned buses. We sat tight on the coach, with our cargo tucked inside our undergarments. I was sweating profusely, terrified we might get searched as we drove towards the border with Spain. We were all unusually quiet on the bus as the customs staff waved us through.

'That was easy, children!' Dad said unsubtly as the bus joined the *autopista*, headed back towards Nerja. Mummy shushed him. I slid my hand into the cup of my training bra to check the Krugerrand was still there. I could feel the one in my sock, nestled in the arch of my foot, and the one in my knickers, tucked inside my knicker elastic, but the one on my chest had warmed to body temperature and I couldn't feel it, so I was worrying it had dropped out.

We stayed in Nerja for another few weeks and then set off for Greece, our final European stop-off before India. Daddy gave us local coins mixed in with the gold coins and this time we were to smuggle them onto an aeroplane.

Daddy had rented us a cramped apartment on the top floor of a block of flats in Athens city centre. It was a disappointment, and Dinah, Bev and I were bored senseless. We were still itching; it had even spread to Dad. We were all being driven nuts by our itchy skin and Maria was scratching so much she started to develop sores. We spent our days helping Mummy with housework and wandering aimlessly around the neighbourhood. It was early September and the weather was beginning to get cooler. I was struck by the kiosks dotted around everywhere selling souvenirs with gods and goddesses, some of them with huge phalluses or even engaging in sex. There were pornographic magazines on public display, and I was fascinated and curious.

Mum took a trip to the local doctor's surgery. Mummy said the doctor didn't speak English but he took one look at Maria's hands and said 'Psora'. He picked up a book and showed her a picture of a mite. We had scabies. Mummy was horrified.

The doctor prescribed a strong topical ointment for the whole family, which stung terribly. We all hated it. He also instructed Mummy to wash our sheets and every item of clothing every night for a few weeks until she was sure the mites had gone. For those first few weeks we seemed to be forever airing and folding sheets and clothes, which was a challenge in our small apartment. It felt even more claustrophobic because we were all on top of each other, unable to escape from the sound of Dinah's new bazooka. Daddy was always out witnessing, or so he said, or arranging visas at the embassy most of the day, so he didn't have to deal with a bunch of bored kids. He left all that to Mum, as was usual.

After a few weeks, Mummy began to look into ways to dissipate the bickering and tension that was on the increase. Petra was the first to make a friend – the daughter of an Iranian family living in the same block. They were the same age, and although neither of them spoke the same language, they played happily for hours in the little girl's apartment. Mummy decided we needed to do the same. She made contact with the shepherds locally and suggested that I could go to stay in one of the Family houses nearby where there were other children my age. I was so bored that I figured anything was better than day after day shut up in the dull apartment. Besides, it would be fun to meet other kids my age.

We arrived at the home, which was on the other side of Athens, and were introduced to Stephanos, the home shepherd, a tall Greek-American man. He and his wife Malita had ten children. Aziel, the eldest boy who was my age, explained that his mom was in London with his sister India, who was twelve. 'Mom has gone to England with India and baby Jasper. India is looking after Jasper whilst Mom does ES-ing [escort work] so we can raise money to go to the mission field,' he said to me matter-of-factly.

'Really?' I said. 'Why London?'

'Oh, there are lots of rich Arabs there!'

'Oh,' I said.

'She's coming back soon and then we're heading to India,' said Azi.

'We're heading to India too!' I said. I'm glad our Mummy hasn't gone to London to do ES-ing, I thought gratefully. It was upsetting enough to think that Mummy had shared with numerous brothers and done flirty fishing, but somehow ES-ing felt worse to me. It wasn't the first time I'd heard about it though, it was fairly commonplace in Family communities.

The rhythm of the days in the Athens home was like the one in Malaga. There were two other couples and their infants and toddlers in the home. We older kids went out more, witnessing. I would head out with a selection of Stephanos and Malita's kids and Stephanos would drive us and park up in a dense tourist spot. Storm, the third sibling, was eleven years old and he was a brilliant guitarist. We practised a few songs together back at home and then Stephanos would walk us round the tourist restaurants in the Plaka district, near the Acropolis. People loved seeing a troupe of cute kids singing their little hearts out in harmony, doing little dance routines and playing instruments. We would go around the tables with a little basket asking for tips. Sometimes we made quite a lot of money busking. We were all competent musicians and the tourists seemed to love the Von-Trapp-like vision we must have presented. I enjoyed these outings and the positive attention we got, and Stephanos seemed pleased with our takings. Sometimes I wished we would be treated to an ice cream or a drink but we were taught that sugar was the Devil's poison and would rot our teeth, so treats were out, although once in a while we were allowed a *souvlaki*, which was delicious.

Although I quite liked Stephanos, I soon learnt he had a fierce temper, and was a strict disciplinarian. Once, I was invited to join Azi, Storm and the younger children on a visit to a Greek 'king' – one of Malita's 'big fish' and a friend of our group. 'We're going to see Uncle Alexander!' Storm told me excitedly. 'Uncle Ali gives us ice cream and has a huge house with a pool, Faith, make sure you bring your swimsuit!' We had a wonderful, rare day of pure fun around the pool. No chores, no witnessing, no looking after the little ones. It was heavenly. To my dismay, though, the joy was short-lived. When we got back, Stephanos screamed at us for having left the breakfast bowls on the table earlier in the day. He lined all seven of the offending children up except me and beat them in turn. He beat them hard, with intent. As I heard their cries, I felt crushed and embarrassed. My heart went out to Azi, who was thirteen like me. He was berated especially harshly for 'being a bad example to the younger children and especially to Faith who is new in the home'.

The violence in all Family homes seemed arbitrary and always felt disproportionate. Toddlers were beaten if they wouldn't nap on schedule, and the minutest slip-ups were punished as huge transgressions. This was disturbing, but it was not the worst thing I witnessed in this particular home in Athens. A young mother who lived there, Philomela, would openly abuse her toddler son, playing with his penis, sometimes performing oral sex on him when he was restless. She would do it in communal rooms, and nobody reacted, although she seemed to invite us to notice: 'Look at how excited he is! It's so sweet!'

We made comments under our breath amongst us kids that it was disgusting, that she was sick in the head . . . but we kept very quiet about criticising her openly around the adults because we knew that 'Grandpa says this is good for children, how dare you be so prideful to question it,' would be the default answer. None of us wanted to risk a spanking.

When Malita, Azi's mother, came back from London, I was struck by her incredible beauty. She was Syrian American with huge brown eyes, olive skin and long, wavy black hair. She had the body of a movie star, despite having had ten children. She wandered about the Athens home in her lacy bra and knickers, without a stretch mark in sight. I was in awe of her. She was a big personality, with a loud, cheerful, breezy voice. It was clear that the children utterly adored her. She was fun and affectionate. She would spontaneously pick up the guitar sometimes and sing: 'Forever young! Forever young! May you stay, forever young.' That's not a family song, I thought. I guess it's OK for her to sing systemite songs. I wished so much that I could sing systemite songs.

I also met India, Azi's eldest sister, for the first time. A year younger than me, she was stand-offish and seemed to be jealous over her brothers, whom I had become quite tight with. In time, she became a little more friendly and one day she snuck me into her parents' room. 'Let me show you my Mommy's sexy nighties,' she said. She opened up a drawer and pulled out some lace-trimmed satin negligees in a range of colours, and some beautiful silky bras and knickers. We stroked them approvingly. 'Mommy lets me wear them sometimes,' she boasted.

Being around another mummy made me miss my own. One day, Stephanos announced: 'Faith, your dad telephoned me today that he will be picking you up because everything is arranged for you to go to the mission field! Praise the Lord! Are you excited, honey?'

I nodded but felt a little sad saying goodbye to my friends. I wondered if I would ever see them again.

CHAPTER 12: The Day of the Demons – Bromley, Autumn 1998

I met Levi in a pub in Leicester Square one summer evening in 1994 after a three-day E bender with one of the girls who had left the Family. She was one of the exotic dancer crew and like me, loved to party hard. It was twelve noon on a Sunday by the time we left the after-party in a huge detached house in north London. A DJ was playing banging house music and the place was crowded with people still off of their faces from the club. Most were still at it. Coke and hash spliffs were being passed around and a big muscled bouncer sat holding a huge bag of Es on his lap, surrounded by a bunch of young girls gurning away. We were broke by now and made our way to the tube station. We jumped the barrier and made our way back to Patience's flat in Kilburn.

After dozing for a couple of hours we decided we might as well go to the pub and knock back a few drinks before I made my way back to my flat in Crystal Palace. We went to the cashpoint to wring out the last of our money and jumped back on the tube. It was a big touristy pub in Leicester Square, the Bear and Staff. Not the kind of place we would usually hang out. Levi was striking; I noticed him immediately, standing at the bar. He was very tall, six foot three, and a good few years older than me, with long dark hair, an ankle-length leather coat and cowboy boots. Under the coat, he had on a loud silk shirt and a waistcoat. I could see he was a bit pissed, because he was swaying lightly to the music that was playing: 'London Calling' by The Clash.

We got talking and he told me he'd spent the day at an art fair. 'Let me show you my drawings,' he said, taking them out of his waistcoat pocket. They were sketches made in black ink and they were brilliant.

'Wow!' I said. 'You're a good artist! I really like this one . . .' I pointed to an intricate drawing of a corkscrew.

'Thank you! I use this ballpoint pen,' he said, taking a biro out of his waistcoat pocket.

'Did you sell many?'

'Oh, no. I don't sell my work. I draw as a hobby. I just came out with my mate to admire other artists' work. Hey, Dave, meet Faith!' He called his mate over. 'My mate here is also an artist. We come down to London every few months to go to art fairs or galleries and then we go on a pub crawl. Can I buy you a drink?'

We talked for a couple of hours about art and music. He told me he wrote poetry, and he loved Bowie and punk, especially The Damned and Stiff Little Fingers.

He was so knowledgeable and so much more interesting than the boys in Crystal Palace who only wanted to talk about cars. This is the first guy I've met that hasn't bored me to tears, I thought.

It was getting late and I needed to get home as I had to go to work the next day. 'It's been great chatting with you, Levi, why don't you give me your phone number and I'll give you a call? Maybe you can show me around some art galleries one day.'

He looked stunned. After gathering himself he said: 'Of course! That would be great!' and reached into his waistcoat pocket for the biro and wrote his name and number in beautiful writing. It was the start of a four-year relationship.

As I got to know Levi, he told me about his life. His mother had died suddenly of a brain haemorrhage when he was thirteen and he couldn't focus on his schoolwork after that, so was thrown out of his posh day school and put into a local comprehensive. His father, a wealthy watercress farmer in Hampshire, married his 'lady friend', a woman he'd been having an affair with, weeks after his mother's death. Levi was a sensitive little boy and he missed his mother terribly, but his father didn't seem to notice and carried on as usual, flying his light aircraft above his fields and driving his vintage cars. Levi had begged his father to allow him to go to art school but his father refused to entertain the idea. 'You will be taking over the watercress business, my boy, and you will start from the bottom up!' Levi described how as a teenager he would get up at the crack of dawn to go down to his father's cress beds with the other workers to wade in the freezing water and to cut cress. Two years before I met Levi, when he was twenty-seven, his father had shot his second wife, then turned the gun on himself. The family decided to sell the cress beds and surrounding land, keeping only the houses, which had been rented out to long-standing tenants.

Although he had inherited early, Levi continued to work for a pharmaceutical company, making pills in a factory. It suited him. It was well paid and he worked four days on and four days off; on his days off he spent time drawing, drinking, reading, playing his guitar and writing songs and poetry.

The first time I went to his flat, I noticed that each step leading up to the top floor was piled high with mainly unopened envelopes. The living room had an old, battered Chesterfield sofa and last year's Halloween decorations were still hanging askew from the ceiling, which was covered in real cobwebs. Ashtrays were piled high with fag butts and empty bottles of cider and cherry cola were scattered around here and there. There were stacks of books and magazines. He had a twelve-string guitar and a couple of electric guitars. I was amazed to see his poetry, songs and art everywhere: behind a pile of CDs stacked on the floor; on top of the Yamaha amp; on the floor in the bedroom and hallway. He had sketches pinned to the walls, and half-written poems in his elaborate font on scraps of paper everywhere. I picked one up, and dusted it off:

This World of Mine

I can only hope I settle whence I came
And I can only wish it always will remain
This Palace Evergreen that's never been defiled or
deflowered so
It can only be revered
Of all the Worlds that I could own, it would be fine
If I could only own this World of Mine
How I Love this World of Mine.
If I could promise you that someday I'd make good
And rise triumphantly like the way I should
Then I could offer you a seat beside the throne looking
down upon
Fields that we could call our own
And every day be just like was the one before
Decay and decadence no more
No, we'd have closed and locked that door
So won't you walk with me among the autumn leaves
Before the night draws in and winter brings the freeze
And we can revel in the revelry of past, hoping praying
that

This palace evergreen will last
Of all the dreams I could fulfil this most is dear
That it will be with us next year, and year then after
year
As I watch and wait for what befalls this earth
My one inheritance might reach me with a curse
For what becomes of her will surely fate us all, so please
feel for me
And pray the enchanted wood won't fall
Of all the Worlds that I could own it would be fine
If I could own this world of mine
How I love this world of mine
How I love this world

Levi Stone 5.2.89

I was moved and the words resonated with me. 'This is beautiful,' I said.

'Oh that one . . .' he said. 'It's a song.'

'Play it for me!' I said.

He nervously picked up the twelve-string and began to sing.

Levi liked to drink. A lot. He would become morose and melancholic or just plain annoying, pontificating about this or that nonsense, which I found incredibly boring and frustrating. It wasn't long before I introduced him to weed. A heavy smoker, he took to it like a duck to water and when we smoked, he usually switched from cider to water. It made him much better company.

Levi loved fine dining and he took me to the most amazing restaurants in central London. We would dress up, both in tight black jeans, which he accessorised with a studded belt, a flowing scarf, a silk shirt, a Fedora hat with his long hair in a ponytail, his black-and-white skull-and-crossbone-adorned cowboy boots and his trademark waistcoat. I loved his eccentric looks and ways and I didn't give a hoot when people looked us up and down. I wore heels and the satin camisole tops that were fashionable in the nineties. 'Let's make sure these people treat us right, sweet,' he would say as the maître d' walked towards us, slightly suspicious. He'd go to shake his hand and palm him £20. The change in the maître d's demeanour was instant and we would always have a little chuckle about it over the dinner as we were fawned over by waiters. He always ordered double gin and tonics to start and fine wine for dinner. 'Have whatever you like, babe.'

'It's too much, Maw-Maw!' (My pet name for him.)

'Don't worry, I'll polish off what you can't.'

We went to gigs and to galleries, we wandered around Camden Town, Carnaby Street and the King's Road. He would buy me expensive gifts and treated me like a princess. In 1996 he took me back to Costa Rica for a holiday. My dad had been living there for many years and by now had what he loved to call 'a success-ful laundromat business'. He would set up anonymous companies and allow dodgy Americans to use them to launder illegal gambling money. He had come back to England for a short visit, so I took Levi to meet him.

'Dad, meet Levi! He's taking me back to Costa Rica on holiday!' Dad turned to Levi and with a stupid grin on his face said: 'Why are you taking her there? It's like taking a sandwich to a banquet!' Levi was mortified and didn't know where to look. My heart filled with hurt and hate.

On his four days off, Levi would come to stay with me at my flat, which I continued to share with Sacha. We would spend hours smoking weed, cooking elab-orate meals and watching movies. We took magic mushrooms and LSD and sometimes Levi would come raving with us. We would take Es and he'd watch me dance the night away. He wasn't one for dancing and never got into house music like me. This carried on for years and I loved it. I had started my course at the Lon-don College of Printing, just off Oxford Street. I would phone him most evenings. Once or twice when he was working weekends I would ring for a chat. 'Mawskin,' he would say (his pet name for me). 'Get off the sofa for a minute . . .'

'Why?' I replied.

'I'm sending you on a treasure hunt.'

Intrigued, I would follow his instructions as he sent me on a wild goose chase around the flat, to pick up little notes giving clues, cordless phone in hand. Finally on the bookshelf, a note: 'Pick up the book on guitars and open it.' I opened the book and out dropped a £20 note. 'So you can go to the pub with your girlfriends, sweet.'

One day I got a call from Dinah who was living with her two boys and the rest of my siblings at Mum's. 'Guess what, Faith, I met this couple at the pub, and they own a Mexican restaurant just down the road from your flat! They offered to pay us £70 to do a few sets in Spanish on Saturday nights. Easy money, Faith. Can you see if Levi will lend us his gear?'

I could do with making a few extra quid, I thought. I had been supplementing my student loan and grant by pulling pints at the local pub, the Cricketers. Levi had a few electric guitars, a bass, keyboards, a drum machine, microphones and stands and a huge amp, which he wouldn't touch for weeks on end.

Levi was delighted with the idea and on his next four days off, he drove down from Hampshire with all his gear. We lugged everything up the stairs to my top-floor flat, a conversion in one of those huge old Victorian houses. The carpets were threadbare and the walls were covered in woodchip, but I loved it because it was very spacious and airy with big sash windows. It was near the town centre on a quiet leafy road and my bedroom was in what used to be the loft. Dinah was like a kid in a candy shop when she saw Levi's kit. She was a talented instrumentalist and played the bass, guitar, keyboards, the drums, and anything else she could lay her hands on.

Once everything was set up, she started coming over to practise regularly. We'd plug in the bass and guitar and fire up the amp. We picked a number of typical Latin American songs and practised away for hours. On one such practice session the doorbell started ringing frantically. I peered out the window to see a fancy black Mercedes parked outside. Worried, I sprinted down the communal stairs and opened the enormous oak door. Outside stood an irate, very well-dressed stocky lady in her late forties with short blond hair. 'What the hell are you girls doing up there?' she said in a rough south London accent.

'Pardon?' I said. 'What do you mean?'

'Don't give me that! I've had nothing but complaints from the tenant in the flat beneath you. He says you're making a hell of a racket! I'm the owner of these properties!'

'Oh, I'm so sorry!' I said wide-eyed. 'The tenant downstairs has never said a word to me, I had no idea!' She looked at me suspiciously. 'We're just practising our songs, we're going to be singing at Las Maracas this weekend . . . come!' I said beckoning her in. 'Come and see!' Her face softened a fraction and she followed me in. 'This is my sister Dinah,' I said, introducing her to Dinah who still had the bass strapped around her shoulders and was fiddling with the keyboard.

'Nice to meet you,' said Dinah, smiling sweetly. The landlady looked surprised and stood there with her arms crossed.

'Let's sing her the song we've been practising, Dinah, and then she can advise us about the volume . . .' I said resourcefully. Before she could say anything, we had started singing. A huge smile crept over her face and she uncrossed her arms. When we had finished, she clapped.

'Well done, girls, that was super! I tell you what, you continue to practise but turn that blessed amp down, OK?'

'Oh sure!' I said. 'I'm really sorry you had to come by . . .'

'Yes, well . . . just mind the volume,' she said as she turned to leave.

I saw her out of the flat and when I closed the door, I heard her banging on the door of the tenant below. He got a ticking-off for not speaking to me first before dragging her out.

We had fun singing at Las Maracas. We had our regular Saturday slot for a number of months. Levi would often come with us and sit on a table nearby and cheer us on. Afterwards, he would order food, beer and tequila chasers. 'Maw-Maw, you've spent at least three times what we've just earned,' I would say.

'Worth every penny, sweet. Worth every penny!'

My course was almost over after two years and I started to fret about what I was going to do next. I saw a job advertised in the local paper: 'Salesperson Wanted. £10K basic plus commission up to £30K a year', which having been a poor student for so long seemed like a fortune. It was a high-end leather furniture shop in the retail park a twenty-minute drive from my flat. I thought I would give it a go. I was delighted when I got the job, and was to start in September. I found I was a natural saleswoman, smashing my targets with a knack of upselling all the add-ons: ottomans, coffee tables, lamps, and cushions. I started making good commission. During the January sales I won 'Top Dog' status and my pay packet was huge. I couldn't believe my eyes; I had never had so much money in all my life. I gave some to Mummy and to each of my siblings. I took Levi out to a fancy restaurant and bought him some expensive gifts: 'My treat, Maw-Maw,' I beamed with pride.

On the nights Levi wasn't staying at mine, I struggled to get to sleep. A rising feeling of panic would settle on me. Normally, weed would take the edge off and help me to sleep, but it wouldn't always work. I began to feel real fear, as if I were spiralling out of control. In desperation,

I went back to an old self-soothing habit: reciting the Lord's Prayer. It helped me, and I began to question the way I had cut myself off completely from God, turning my back on all of it.

I started to toy with the idea of opening my life again to God. But even as I entertained the thought, I felt furious with myself. A voice inside me asked: 'Are you really going to put yourself through this shit again?' But I would remember the connection to *my* Jesus that I had felt as a little girl, and all the times I had prayed and had believed that he'd saved me. After a year of mulling this over, and fully accepting that my romantic relationship with Levi was drawing to an end, I decided I would speak to God directly again, and see what happened.

One evening when I was alone in my bed, I thought this was as good a time as any. The prayer was a childish one: 'OK God, if you're there, I have a feeling that I need you in my life, that I need to open up to you. If you're there, I'll say sorry for the bad things I've done, but there's a caveat. If nothing happens you can forget I even said this prayer, I'll take it all back . . . would you come to me again, God?'

I reached over, switched off the lamp and fell asleep. The next morning, I woke up and I knew that something was different. Something had shifted, opened. The connection I had felt as a little girl had returned.

The next Sunday, to my Mum's amazement, I decided to go along with her to church. She had been a regular member of the congregation for years by then, and I knew little about it, except that it was definitely not for me, ever . . . or so I had thought until then. The church was evangelical, a fundamentalist Christian church. Although I had berated her for swapping 'one cult for another', I could see that she was happy and that her faith seemed to give her real comfort and purpose. She was delighted when I said I wanted to join her that day. Standing in the church during the service, I was quiet, taking it all in.

I found I cried a lot in church, but it felt like a relief. I kept going back from time to time. During the prayers and the singing, I became aware that what I was feeling was love, a love so different and intense from any other love I had felt. I could only compare it to taking Ecstasy, but without the comedowns. I thought that this must be the same thing that Mum and Dad experienced when they converted to Christianity back in the early sixties and the same thing that the grown-ups in the Family would tell us stories about. About how they asked Jesus into their heart and then suddenly they felt peace and love and knew they had been 'saved'. I was confused. How could people who had experienced an ecstatic conversion so pure and joyful be controlled and manipulated into doing such evil things?

The love I felt was gentle and all-encompassing, but I also felt raw and vulnerable. I listened to some of the preaching, but some of it enraged me. The anti-gay, anti-sex before marriage, anti-masturbation, and elitist rhetoric fuelled by the literal interpreting of the scriptures made me bristle: 'He that believeth not the Son shall not see Life but the wrath of God abideth on him' (John 3:36). I asked myself what kind of God would condemn to eternal hell and damnation perfectly decent people from other religions who have never even heard of Jesus?

But still, there was something so healing about this new 'Father God' that the preacher spoke of. At first, the two words together made me bristle, but I came to understand that this Father God was a true father. He was not 'Grandpa', or Dad, with his self-serving moral relativism.

I stopped taking psychedelics and Ecstasy and partying so hard. Levi found it difficult to understand why I had been drawn back into faith again. I struggled to explain it to him. We were growing apart, anyway, and I saw him less and less. We ended our relationship and remained close friends.

I felt good about my decision to give up on the crazy partying and found I didn't miss it. I was doing well at work but I was feeling increasingly anxious and fearful. Mum suggested that I go to see the pastor at church to talk about it and to see if he might be able to help. I was sceptical, but thought it was worth a shot. I'd go in and ask for prayer with something minor, I thought, to see how he reacted to that. I had low-level hay fever that was irritating my eyes, so I settled on that.

It was a sunny midweek afternoon when I went to see the pastor, a middle-aged, portly man wearing glasses. He was very reserved, conservatively dressed in a long-sleeved buttoned-up shirt and trousers. I was wearing jeans and a T-shirt, my cigarettes and lighter in my canvas bag, to steady my nerves. He welcomed me in, and I sat down in his office, lined with religious books. Mum had explained to me that he had written books on 'deliverance'. She thought that perhaps I was plagued by demons, and that he could help get rid of them. This sounded unlikely, bordering on bonkers, to me, but I was curious and figured I had nothing to lose.

He greeted me and motioned to the sofa. He turned his office chair and sat opposite. He used his words sparingly and got straight to the point: 'What's been bothering you, Faith?' he asked.

I told him about my eyes but found myself stammering a bit and sounding unconvincing. He knew Mum well and knew about our background, so he knew we had been in a cult.

'Have you ever been hypnotised?' he asked, and as he said those words my mouth opened involuntarily and out of it came a terrible animalistic stream of noise, spewing from deep within me.

'Mmmmmraaaaahhhwwwaaaaaaaraaaaaaaaaa.' Then it stopped. I was deeply embarrassed. 'I beg your pardon, pastor, I have no idea what that was all about!' I blushed furiously.

'It's perfectly normal,' he said. 'There is nothing to be sorry for. Now, let me pray for you.' He put one hand on my head and the other on my sternum. I felt safe with him. I closed my eyes and he began to pray. 'Open your eyes please, Faith.' Looking straight into my eyes he said, 'Whatever you are, in this young woman, come out now in the name of Jesus . . .'

My hands started to tingle, and I began to wail. I couldn't stop. I had no control, I felt my hands move into strange positions, like a puppet, and all this noise came out of me, nonsensical and urgent. I was powerless to stop it. Strangest of all, I wasn't frightened, or distressed; it felt strangely natural. It lasted for about forty-five minutes, and had the momentum of a process, of something being moved through.

When it was over, I sank back into the sofa, exhausted. What in the *fuck* was that all about? I thought. I felt empty, incredibly calm, and open. I understood in that moment how such intensity and openness could easily inspire radical change, could move a person to take up a new path, to leave reason and common sense behind . . .

to take leave of their senses, and leap, landing in a parallel universe, ripe and ready for indoctrination.

I thanked the pastor and left the church, sparking up a cigarette on my way out. I decided I would commit to reading books on the subject of Christianity, to see if I could study the Bible with new eyes. I wouldn't leap, but I would use my logic and my reason to learn more, to give me more context. I made up my mind that I would keep an open mind. After all, isn't it more important to ask the questions than to know the answers? I resolved to try to reconcile my cynical self with the young woman who felt and knew the love of God: my own God.

CHAPTER 13: The Mission Field – India, 1987

A wall of heat and humidity hit us as we stepped off the plane in Bombay. Even in the airport, the culture shock was immense. Emerging from passport control with our bags, we were surrounded by thin men in dirty lungis (wraps of muslin worn in place of trousers). On their torsos they wore filthy, faded T-shirts, some of which looked as if they were intended for children. The men's feet were almost uniformly cracked and filthy in worn and ill-fitting sandals. The airport was crowded and chaotic, and when Mum, Bev and I went to the ladies' we were shocked to find homeless women in saris sleeping in many of the stalls. Some of the Indian women shouted at them in their language to clear out, and they emerged from the stinking metal cubicles, adjusting their saris and yawning. As soon as we made it back to Dad, who was waiting with the rest of our siblings, the tallest and thinnest of the baggage carriers picked up our heaviest suitcase and, with surprising strength, hefted it onto his head, fixing his large, serious eyes on Bev as he hoisted it over his shoulders. Two other men, with twig-like arms, grasped our other bags. We sped off towards the taxi rank and struggled to keep pace with them, weaving in and out of the families, beggars and travellers who were milling about the concourse. I was worried they might steal our things. All of our worldly possessions were in those bags. They led us to the taxis, and the tall man approached a driver, a small man with a moustache and battered-looking minivan, and spoke to him. He gestured to us to come and we piled into it, the men tying our suitcases to the roof of the van with ropes.

We were bound for the 'reception home' in the centre of Bombay, and as we weaved towards the city, passing slums that stretched to either side of the highway as far as we could see. I felt frightened. If this was the mission field, I was not prepared for it. As we slowed down, approaching the city, I noticed the smells: human shit; cow dung, wafts of incense and a humidity that made it seem as if the city itself was sweating. India stank like nothing I had experienced before. Whenever the minivan slowed, children would run up to the windows to implore us, shouting through the open upper halves of the windows. 'Maaa . . . Maaaa!' they said, 'Rupee! Rupee!' There were children holding babies with runny noses, scrawny toddlers and older children miming eating, to show us they were hungry. All looked sickly and malnourished with eyes that were at once glazed and fierce.

We were put up in a 'family room' at the reception home and told that we'd be moving on in a few days' time. We were expected in Madras. There was no air-conditioning in the reception home, and I found it impossible to sleep. I could hear crows – there were a lot of them living near the home – feeding on the overflowing rubbish bins that were stacked in the alleyway between the home and the apartment block next door. 'I miss home,' Bev said that first night.

'What does it say in Two Corinthians, chapter four, verse seventeen, children?' said Mummy.

'For our light affliction, which is but for a moment, worketh for us a far more exceeding and eternal weight of glory,' we dutifully chimed.

Dad seemed irritable. He was sweating and his nerves were on edge. Mummy tried to cheer us all up. 'Don't worry, kids! We will be moving to a much nicer place than this and guess what? We will be buying our own blankets, plates and cups!' she said. The home shepherds had explained to Mum and Dad that we would need our own for the journey to come, as each family arriving in the mission field was expected to have a few basic provisions to take from home to home. I wondered how many of our gold coins we'd need to spend.

Those first few days in Bombay passed in a blur. On one of those days we were taken to a big air-conditioned jewellery shop downtown, where we exchanged our remaining Krugerrands for gold bangles and rings. Bev and I were given stacks of them. They were small and we had to push them hard over our hands to get them on. Mum had a stack on each forearm, too. They made a lovely shimmering sound as we moved.

The routine in the reception home reminded me of life in the babe's ranch: the timings were the same, and we were all expected at devotions, and were allotted specific chores and responsibilities. We only stayed three nights, then caught a coach down to Madras, where we were due to spend a few weeks before travelling to our final destination, Bangalore.

The home in Madras was huge and spotlessly clean. I noticed the smell of disinfectant immediately. We were to take our shoes off before coming inside and, the home shepherds explained, whenever we had been out, we would need to shower and put on clean indoor clothes, which for the women consisted of nothing more than a sarong tied under the arms, a pair of knickers and flip-flops. Even though we were exhausted the first night we arrived, the rule applied, so we all showered before collapsing into our beds. We all shared a room, Mum, Dad, Dinah Bev, Michael, Petra, Maria and me. We woke up the first morning to sweltering heat and the sound of heavy rain, and what sounded like a voice saying, 'Paper; paper; paper; paper,' over and over again. I looked out of the window. We were in a ground-floor bedroom, and Michael pointed to the grass, which was covered in the pulsating bodies of hundreds of toads. 'Ink,' he said. 'Paper,' they said back. This kept us amused for some time. Apparently, although the monsoon season was over, heavy rains were not unusual during the winter, and the toads were annual visitors, stopping by on their migration route.

The rain was a relief from the stifling stillness of the heat and humidity, but although it seemed to 'wash' the streets, it also flooded the sewers, and many of the gutters nearby became open latrines. So, although the strict hygiene rules of the home had seemed extreme at first, as soon as we began to explore, we could see that the rules were in place for good reason. Whatever the weather, the streets were filthy. In addition to the blocked drains, open sewers had been dug into the ground all over the city, and often overflowed. I noticed that people coughed and spat on the pavement and would blow their noses into their hands, then carry on with their business. We were told that we were not to drink tap water or buy freshly cut fruit from street vendors. Only bottled soda drinks and chai were allowed (the latter having been boiled at a high temperature). I liked the chai; it was sweet and fragrant.

There was a lot to admire, too, as we began to explore. Bev and I loved staring at the women in bright saris with long coils of thick dark hair, twisted in plaits smoothed with coconut oil. They smelled so lovely as they went by. Jasmine blossom seemed to grow everywhere, its scent heady and strange. Mum and Dad took us to the market to buy woven blankets. We each chose one, brightly coloured, thin but intricately woven, soft and light. She bought us all a 'Punjabi' to wear – baggy drawstring trousers with a tunic top. Bev's was orange and I chose one that was bright pink. It was airy and light to wear. We also bought a couple of colourful sarongs each, a pair of flip-flops and a pair of typical 'outdoor' Indian sandals. All of this we paid for using the bangles we wore. Over the eighteen months we were in India, my bangles depleted month by month until my arms were bare.

Wandering about, there were more shocks. We saw men and women, their faces and bodies deformed with leprosy, begging and wandering the streets. It was a disease we had heard about in the Bible. Mummy explained it had been eradicated in most of the world, but that here, it was still a problem. Petra said: 'We can pray and ask Jesus to heal them . . .'

'Yes we can!' Mummy said.

When we finally arrived at Bangalore, we had been in India for almost a month. We quickly settled into the rhythm of the home there. The shepherds, Steven and Violet, were an English couple with three teenage sons of similar ages to Bev and me. Our favourite part of the daily schedule was 'get out' time, which was our allotted daily exercise. The home was next to a field, and we teenagers all headed out there at 3 p.m. every day to play baseball or badminton. I looked forward to that time. It kept me going during 'JJT' (Jesus job time) when we were expected to clean the house from top to bottom. If I wasn't cleaning, I'd be sent out witnessing (selling tapes and posters in the sweltering heat with a grown-up), which was a real novelty at the beginning as there were so many sounds, smells and sights. I far preferred this to cleaning or to childcare responsibility, when I'd need to wrack my brains for 'lesson' ideas. Mainly I just sang with the children when it was my turn.

At one point one of the 'aunties' who came to stay, Rula, who was married to an American, Paul, introduced a stringent new hygiene regime after the whole house had come down with diarrhoea (it was not the first time this had happened). Rula had all sorts of health problems including countless allergies. She was fastidious to the point of obsessiveness about cleaning and one afternoon instructed me and Bev to scrub the grouting on the bathroom floor with caustic soda; we were to go over the grouting on the tiles with a toothbrush. A daunting task. A few minutes in, Bev felt a burning sensation on her knees. She stood up and I saw that her skin was peeling away. We went to tell Mum, who was angry, and told us that caustic soda could cause permanent damage to our eyes. She took the tub of powder from us and told us not to use it. We resolved to ignore Aunty Rula next time she instructed me to use a particular product. We'd just pretend; it was safer all round.

We soon got used to our living arrangements, surrounded by a constantly shifting mixture of people, families with children of various ages who would come and go, occupying the various rooms. There was one childless couple from Canada. She was unable to be a mother, one of the other aunties explained to me, because she had herpes, caught when she was flirty fishing. She had a separate toilet to herself. STIs were rife in the Family and were openly talked about in the homes and in the Mo letters. There were hygiene rules around this and often the smell of Dettol would permeate the Homes. The aunties would sit in a bucket with a solution of Dettol and warm water to alleviate their symptoms.

The house was huge with two stories. There were four bedrooms and three bathrooms on each floor. Large landings separated the bedrooms and bathrooms. Children under eleven would share their parents' rooms, but the upstairs landing was the teen girls' bedroom. This meant that we would see the adults comings and goings after lights out. Often, you would hear them making a racket, moaning and grunting sounds escaping from doors which were sometimes left ajar. Afterwards, uncles and aunties would walk out stark naked to the toilet and sometimes the grown-ups would swap rooms. At first this was a shock to my siblings and me, but everyone, including my parents, acted as if this was perfectly normal and in time, we got used to it too. 'It's sharing night tonight; I checked the sharing schedule in Aunty Violet and Uncle Stephen's room,' one of the teens would announce. In this home, the sharing schedule was in the home shepherds' room.

I would make a mental note to put my spare pillow over my ears and eyes on sharing night so I could get some sleep. At least I'm sleeping on the landing now, I thought. For a few weeks my floor mat had been moved to Uncle Mark and Aunty Lilly's room. They had five kids under ten. One night, I collapsed onto my mat after a long day out witnessing in the boiling heat, only to be woken up twice. The first time, I was just nodding off when I felt a scampering, crawling feeling running up my back. I jumped up and to my horror a winged cockroach the size of a large juicy medjool date ran out of my bed. I didn't scream for fear of waking the kids and getting into trouble. The second time, I was woken from a deep sleep by the sounds of giggling and moaning. I looked up to see Uncle Mark and Aunty Tina, one of the single mums, bouncing away on the bed. That's it, I thought. I was furious and exhausted. I got up from the floor and dragged my mat, sheet and pillow out onto the landing.

One day, during devotions, Uncle Stephen said he had some very exciting news. Grandpa had sent word to the homes in India that he wanted to see all his 'precious girls' dance for him. We would be filmed performing dances with veils 'to make Grandpa happy'. 'What a privilege, what an honour, girls!' he said enthusiastically. All the women said 'Amen,' and 'Praise the Lord!' The little girls and teens got excited too. 'We're going to dress up and dance? Yay!' they said, innocently clapping and jumping up and down. I shot a look of horror over to Mummy and then at Bev. We knew what 'dancing for Grandpa' meant. Mum didn't look too enthusiastic and Bev had gone as white as a sheet.

After devotions, Bev and I looked for Mum. 'There is no way we're going to do those dances! we said, resolute.

'I know, girls, I will speak to the shepherds, it's not compulsory.' Bev and I covertly followed Mum as she made her way to Aunty Violet and Uncle Stephen's bedroom. She knocked and entered, leaving the door ajar. 'Violet, I will not be joining in with the dances and neither will my girls. They don't want to and it's not for me either.'

'Oh, Rachel!' said Aunty Violet in a surprised and sweet voice. 'Grandpa will be so disappointed! He loves your family and he knows you're here!'

'Oh. . .' said Mummy, confused and surprised. 'OK, I'll pray about it,' she said.

Bev and I scuttled off to the toilet for a chat. 'Poor Mummy, she admires Grandpa,' I said. 'He must know about us because of Shiloh writing to him – supposedly he met her in heaven, remember?'

Over the next few days, boxes of beautiful silky materials and props arrived. It was such a novelty! All the women and girls were allowed to abandon their chores and crowded around the boxes, pulling out the lovely fabrics and wrapping them around their bodies. 'You don't need to see the dressing-up clothes, Faith and Bev,' said one teen girl spitefully, pushing between us and the box. 'You two are not going to dance, you are not joining in.' We felt left out and sad as we watched the girls excitedly choosing their songs and planning their dance routines. They were lavished with praise and allowed to practise putting make-up on. Make-up! What a special treat. Wearing make-up was considered worldly and we teens certainly were not allowed anywhere near it. 'Don't worry about what you're going to wear too much!' said Aunty Violet with a sweet smile as she happily watched the girls, from as young as five, trying on the different coloured diaphanous veils. 'They won't be staying on for long, you are meant to take them off!' Everyone laughed.

After a week of this, Bev and I caved into peer pressure and said we would join in but that we would be keeping our knickers on. Aunty Violet said, 'Wow, girls! You're so revolutionary! Praise the Lord!' The large living room was set up with lights and for a few days one of the uncles filmed all the females in the home, including Mummy, performing the veiled dances.

During our time in the Bangalore home, my siblings and I grew to love Mary, an Indian woman who cleaned and cooked for us, and her daughter Victoria. We sat helping as they rolled chapatis in the kitchen and delighted in their delicious curries and the paneer and chutney sandwiches they made us when we went out witnessing. One day during devotions, Aunty Violet announced that Mary and Victoria would be fired because of hygiene rules. They lived in the slums and they were worried they would bring back diseases to the home. There had been several bouts of fever and diarrhoea in the home. Every month, someone or other would be sick. I watched sadly as Mary and Victoria left the house that morning, a look of shock and distress on their faces.

The Bangalore home was far less boring than other Family homes we had lived in, because of all the other teens around. There were regular reminders, however, that vigilance was essential for survival. The demerit chart, which lived on the noticeboard in the kitchen, was a constant reminder of that. Any adult could get us to 'chalk up a demerit' next to our names on the chart.

If we got more than seven in a week, we were eligible for a spanking.

Sometimes we got to accompany a grown-up to the meat market. This was in the Muslim part of town. I would watch, fascinated, as the birds of prey would circle around, waiting for the butcher to throw up into the air a scrap of unwanted gristle or offal, and the bird would swoop down, catching it in mid-air.

A few months in, we looked out of the window of the home to see three or four local men grappling with something in the field. We went out to investigate it and they shouted at us to keep back. We saw them hold it up then, and one of them cut it with a machete. It was a cobra. After they had killed it, we went over to look. We joked with one another that we saw it moving still and one of the boys said they'd heard a grown-up say that if you kill a snake, its mate would come back to avenge its death. I stared at the bloody mess where its head had been severed and wondered if it had been living there all along, right there in our baseball field.

Inside the home, there were dangers, too. One of the American uncles in the home was a particularly brazen feeler-upper. He would come up behind me or any other teen girl unlucky enough to be doing the washing-up and put his hands under our sarongs on our braless breasts or between our legs. He would have no qualms about doing this when there were other people in the room, including other aunties and uncles, saying something like: 'Wow honey, you have a beautiful body.' We'd squirm out from under him and he'd guffaw and say, 'Don't be so churchy! You're being unrevolutionary, sweetie.' We never felt able to get angry or indignant for fear of being made to chalk up a demerit, but he made my skin crawl.

Uncle Mark, Aunty Lilly and their five kids were among the stream of other visitors to the Bangalore home. They stayed for a few weeks and then disappeared who knows where. Some of the other permanent resident families included the Allens and the Morrisons, along with Steven and Violet, the shepherds, whose two children, Diego and Noah, were in their early teens. Steven also had a younger daughter, Olive, whose mother we liked to call 'Wahappen' (this was her catchphrase, used mostly whenever some action or other kicked off). Her real name was something like Patricia. They weren't officially a 'thrupple' – Steven and Wahappen were no longer together, but they all got along and Wahappen lived in the home with them. Sal Morrison was a bear of a man, African American. He was usually cheerful but incredibly strict and I would give him a wide berth. His wife, Praise, was a very large blonde. An American woman and mother to five of his eight children (now pregnant with her sixth). I liked Sal's two eldest children from his first marriage, Matty, a year older than me, and Hope, who was one year younger. Their mother had backslidden, leaving the cult, and Sal had 'rescued Hope and Matty from the system', he told us, to 'keep them in the will of God, in His Family.'

One morning, to my delight, Stephanos and Malita showed up with all ten of their kids. I was happy to see Azi, Storm and India again. 'You made it to the mission field!' I said as I hugged them. I spent a week down in the quarantine room (the utility room, repurposed with mattresses on the floor) with Azi shortly after he arrived as we both had high temperatures and diarrhoea. They didn't stay long after that and I was sad to see them go.

Upstairs in the Bangalore home was the kitchen, living room, dining room and balconies looking out to some flat fields, with shacks dotted around and behind the house and a stream with enormous boulders. Sometimes when it was my turn to look after and 'teach' the little kids, a task that I found incredibly boring, I would take them to the balcony and we counted the colourful lizards sunning themselves on the rocks.

There was also a 'thrupple' with eight children in the Bangalore home. A Swedish couple, Matthew and Jan, who were travelling with Jan's second husband, Jeremy. Jeremy was much younger than Uncle Matt and Aunty Jan. The children used to make fun of him. 'He breast-feeds off of Mom then she burps him and he falls asleep after. Just like baby Oli!' they would giggle. Bev and I looked at each other, disgusted.

I often found myself paired up to go witnessing with Uncle Chris. He was an Englishman with a dry sense of humour, dark brown hair and blue eyes, married to Aunty Laila and quite eccentric. We considered him one of the 'fun' uncles. There were one or two of those in most homes, uncles or aunties that you could relax with a little and sometimes even joke and tease with. I liked Uncle Chris, despite his penchant for wandering around naked, his long penis flapping about. Sometimes when we'd go out witnessing, he would say, 'Hey Faith, what do you fancy today? *Chana batura*, or *biryani*?'

'Oh! Are we going to a restaurant?'

'Shall we?' he would tease.

'Yes please!' He didn't like fancy restaurants. He would love to go into the local ones, noisy and full of people. 'Remember, no raw salads or veg or fruit, OK? I don't want us to get sick!'

One of those days out witnessing with Uncle Chris, I chose to wear my only Western outfit, a long pink cotton dress, instead of my Punjabi suit. We had been bouncing along around Bangalore in the back of rickshaws for several hours, moving from office to office, shop to shop, selling posters and tapes.

We got out whenever we saw a row of shops, or stalls, or a park, picking our way around the beggars, cows, bicycles and rickshaws. We'd wave the rickshaw off and pick up another one when we were done. It was tiring work. Standing up all day and calling in on shops and offices, struggling to sell tapes and posters. I found it embarrassing and mind-numbingly boring, even though people as a general rule were warm and welcoming towards us. Often, they offered us chai and sweets. Regretfully, we were not allowed to accept the sweets, but we were allowed the chai because it was piping hot and free of bugs.

Sometimes we would go to residential areas and knock on the doors of some very big houses. I would be a bit wary to begin with because these houses usually had a huge scary and colourful sculpture of a demon on the front of the house above the front door. The servants would open the door and call to the man or lady of the house who would be absolutely delighted to receive us. 'Come in! Welcome, welcome!' they would say enthusiastically. I loved going to people's homes. I realised these were wealthy Indians and a far cry from the people living in the slums that we would see as we passed by in a rickshaw. We would take our sandals off and walk into the cool house with light tiled floors. The smell of sandalwood, incense or jasmine hung in the air. My eyes would greedily take in the colourful wool rugs, curtains and cushions and exotic wood bookshelves and tables. I would be fascinated by the tapestries and paintings. How

I longed to see what was written in those books! We were always offered chai and the occupants of the house would listen politely as the adult I was with tried to witness to them about Jesus and sell them tapes or posters. After an hour or so, they would either politely decline or buy something from us.

On our way out of these many houses, I would surreptitiously slow down so I could get a good look at the puja (prayer) room. The puja room would house the chosen god of the household and a colourful statue of Shiva, Ganesh, Krishna or some other minor god would be lovingly placed above a mini altar. Garlands of jasmine or colourful flowers hung around their necks and red paste or yellow turmeric was smudged on their foreheads. Offerings of exotic fruit would surround it and incense filled the air. These scenes always gave me a delicious frisson of fear, compounded by the scary demon I'd look at once more on our way out.

'They are worshipping demons and that is why we pray after we leave each house, to rebuke and cast off any "hitchhiking" demons we might have picked up,' the grown-up with me would say before starting to pray. I found this confusing. How could such nice people be worshipping demons?

These wealthy and polite Indians would ask me where I went to school and what I was studying, which was excruciating. I mumbled that I was doing a correspondence course. They were often confused by this and sometimes looked concerned. I hated that feeling and hated the fact that we were there to sell to them. I wanted just to talk to people, to meet them without having to witness to them all the time.

On one of these trips with Uncle Chris, a mortifying event took place. We were standing in the street walking along to the next row of shops when suddenly I turned to notice a huge cow walking towards me at a disconcerting speed. Before I had time to move, it had scooped up my dress way past my ears with its horns, bruising the back of my legs and my bottom on the way up. 'Mooo!' bellowed the cow. I was terrified. Surpassing my terror, however, was the excruciating embarrassment I felt as my dress came down and I noticed a bunch of local men ogling, pointing and laughing at me. Fortunately, my dress had a belt around the waist but I was wearing a particularly skimpy pair of Western knickers. My legs were shaking. I heard laughter from some of the men around me, a ripple that seemed to sweep through the crowd. It felt as if it lasted forever, but after thirty seconds or so, Uncle Chris noticed what was happening and shooed the cow away. 'Hey, hey, hey!' he waved his arms furiously and when the cow had wandered off, he turned to me: 'Ha–ha–ha–ha–haa! Faith, that was funny!' he laughed heartily. I blushed furiously, wishing the ground would swallow me up.

'You'll be paying more attention to what's going on in the streets from now on, won't you?' he said with a twinkle in his eye. 'Oh, I have been in India for six years now, Faith, and I can tell you some funny crazy stories. Are you OK, sweetie? Are you hurt?' he asked, noticing I was quiet.

'Not really hurt, Uncle Chris. A bit bruised and embarrassed, that's all.'

'Ah, poor girl!' he said and put his arm around me. 'I tell you what. Why don't we get a nice cold Thumbs Up?' he said trying to cheer me up, but I needed more than a cola.

We hadn't been in Bangalore long when Dad told the shepherds he had got word that the rest of his inheritance was to be released. He told them he must return to Costa Rica to collect it and that he would be gifting it to the Family. In reality, we knew that Dad's inheritance was tied up in the house and that his brother was dead set against him taking control of it as he (and our grandfather) had wanted to preserve it for us, knowing Arturo as they did, and understanding he was likely to squander it. Truth was, after a few short months, Dad was bored by life in the mission field.

'I can't take it, Macha,' Bev overheard him say to Mum. 'You are stronger than me. You stay here with the kids.' His time was not his own. The strict routine of life in the home meant he wasn't able to disappear off on his weekend-long 'witnessing' trips. He got irritated with all the extra children around and he needed his own space. The truth was, it was stifling being confined with his wife and children for the first time in years, and he wanted out. I wasn't particularly sad to see him go; it just seemed like another one of those things.

Not long after that, Mummy and my other siblings were moved to another home on the opposite side of town. I was to stay in the original house to 'be a blessing', whatever that meant. I was sad to be separated, but I accepted it as the way things were. In the Family, parents and teenage children were often split up.

Although I missed my mum and siblings, I had bigger worries, so didn't think about it too much. The home shepherds had decided to draft a 'teen sharing schedule'. I was fortunate that I was nominated to share with Jack who, mercifully, I liked. A year older than me, he was always in trouble for trying to be cool. He was charming and funny, and all the aunties and little kids loved him. He always managed to get them to cut his hair so he could style it in the fashionable 'duck ass' style of the eighties. Sometimes, he would even turn up his collar and roll up his sleeves, a nod to worldliness that most wouldn't have dared to attempt. He was an unusually talented guitarist and was one of the chief systemite music smugglers. Often, the grown-ups were pretty clueless ex-hippies who had no idea of fashion, but every now and then, you would get a clued-up super-controlling, dogmatic and self-righteous grown-up who would not hesitate to rebuke him, dishing out demerits if he or she thought that Jack was trying to be worldly.

The adults thought the teen sharing night was cute. The aunties got all excited, busying themselves by preparing a couple of the bedrooms for us with candles and soft music. I felt a mixture of embarrassment, dread and excitement when the appointed evening arrived. All the teen couples were given a big talking-to beforehand. 'Teens,' Uncle Stephen exhorted us, 'you can do anything you like except "going all the way". We don't want any of the girls getting pregnant, is that clear?'

'Yes, Uncle Stephen,' we said.

We started kissing, which was nice. I fancied Jack and he fancied me. We fumbled at one another's underwear. In the back of my mind, I tried to remember the rules. I didn't want to get pregnant. But even as I thought this, it was as if my body was on autopilot. Jack undressed me and took off his shorts, and he was inside me, and we were moving together, and then after a few minutes it was over.

'Oh no! What have we done!' We looked at each other in horror. 'Swear to me, Jack. You won't tell. Swear it! No one needs to know!' I said, as I got dressed.

He looked sheepishly back at me. 'OK. We won't tell anyone Faith . . .' he promised. We both knew that if one of us broke and confessed, we would be in very big trouble.

It was Jack who broke. He ratted on us after a few days, and we were hauled up in front of the shepherds. For an hour they lectured us on obedience, taking correction without justifying ourselves, and not confessing immediately, which was, in effect, lying, covering up and being deceitful. 'Who is the Father of Lies?' Aunty Violet asked, eyes like thunder. I quaked in my flip-flops.

'The enemy, the Devil,' we replied, thoroughly humiliated.

'So when you are deceitful, what are you doing, exactly?' she asked.

'Worshipping the Devil,' we squirmed.

'You have broken the Family rules!' Uncle Stephen bellowed.

I didn't look at Jack the whole time. I was furious. I would never snitch on anyone like that and I couldn't understand or forgive him for being so spineless. They put us in 'Spiritual Quarantine'. This meant we were confined to separate rooms and put on silence restriction for three days. We were given a huge Mo letter reading list and our meals were brought in by an adult. We were told to search our hearts, to repent and to change.

My anger fermented in those three days, but it was also crushingly boring. I was given lots of scripture and passages from Mo letters to memorise. I was made to write extra-long entries into my daily 'OHR' (open heart report). I wrote what I thought would please the shepherds, or at least get them off my back, and Jack did the same (we compared notes later). I was not put on the sharing schedule for a month after that and I was very pleased as I didn't fancy any of the other boys. A month later, I was put on it again, this time one week with Matty, and the next week with Noah, who was Aunty Violet and Uncle Stephen's son. I didn't fancy either of them and I panicked when I saw my name written next to theirs. The boys made no secret that they were looking forward to it and would smile and wink at me. We girls were used to their flirting and pestering. At the end of a long working day, we were usually all herded into the big shower room with everyone, boys and girls, stripping down to nothing and showering together, so they had had plenty of opportunity to look.

I asked to speak to Aunty Violet.

'Please, Aunty Violet. I don't want to be on the sharing schedule. I don't want to share with Matty and Noah. Please?'

She was not happy at all and looked thoroughly disappointed.

'Why are you being so selfish, Faith? I think you need to go away and pray about it for a couple of days and ask the Lord to give you the grace,' she said.

I meekly obeyed and stressed for two days straight, getting more and more anxious as my first date was getting closer. I wished Mummy were around.

The day of reckoning came and I told Aunty Violet that I hadn't changed my mind. She was angry with me. 'Well, I won't force you, Faith. But I'm extremely disappointed in you.' The boys were cross and hurt.

To my surprise, Aunty Violet and Uncle Stephen and their kids were moved on to another home immediately after this. I got away without further punishment and some new home shepherds took over: Aunty Virginia and Uncle Peter. Talk of the teen sharing schedule died down.

The months came and went. The days dragged on. I was used to the routine by now, going out into the towns and villages selling music and video tapes during the week, cleaning, cooking for the entire home of over fifty people (I was usually paired up with another teen for this job). I was kept busy, looking after children, selling posters in the parks and singing at orphanages and schools. The children there loved it when we came to sing and they were fascinated by our Western looks and accents. Not much younger than us, some of the bolder ones would crowd around us and try to touch our faces and hair. These events were interspersed with bouts of severe diarrhoea. Once I was cleaning the fridge and the most severe cramps overtook me and everything went black and yellow. I fainted. When I came to, I rushed to the toilet. I spent the next three days in quarantine suffering from fever, cramps and constant shivering.

The home was always rammed to the gunnels with different families coming and going. I became very skilled at quickly reading them, gauging their moods, learning their quirks and working out which ones to avoid. I took extra care around the tired, angry, jealous, envious and strict aunties who would make you run around doing jobs for them (these were usually the mums with umpteen kids). Many of these aunties were particularly cruel to teen girls because their husbands openly letched over our pretty young bodies. I was warier still of their husbands, both the ones who groped and the angry ones who doled out demerits at the slightest provocation.

The new home shepherdess, Aunty Virginia, who was also the teen shepherdess, had it in for me and took a particularly dim view of what she had made up her mind was my 'haughty and rebellious spirit'. She and her husband were French with thick accents. He was lecherous and gropey. She took me to one side and said that she and the other home shepherds had been praying about my 'attitude', deciding I needed a change of spirit, a total change of heart. She explained I needed to be 'broken', to become 'more yielded'. My stomach flipped.

I was given a huge boring reading list with chapters and chapters to memorise. I was also told that I was to ask the Lord to give me a brand-new name, befitting, she said, of a 'brand new creature'.

I knew what she was getting at. The recent Mo letters were full of adults and teens going through similar 'breakings' and being made to change their names from archaic biblical names like Jericho and Kenaz to names like 'Peace' and 'Meekness'. Families were being broken up increasingly, too, and moved to different homes, countries or towns.

'Mummy chose my name because it was the name of Grandpa's daughter,' I tried to reason with Virginia. 'She told me that the Lord gave her and my Dad that name for me. So now I'm confused. Are you saying He lied?'

'This is exactly what I'm talking about, Faith. You talk back, refuse correction and always try to justify yourself!' she shouted at me. 'You are long overdue a breaking. I want to see true repentance from you. I want to see a meek, loving and yielded spirit coming from you. I want to see you totally broken and made into a new creature. Amen?'

'Amen,' I said.

'You have a week. Next Friday we'll meet to see what name the Lord has revealed to you.'

She instructed me to write my OHR every night for her to inspect, revealing exactly what I had done, hour by hour, what I had prayed for, and any thoughts I had that were significant. I was to record the number of glasses of water I had, what Mo letters in my list I had read and even if I'd had a bowel movement (BMs, we called them) that day – always a nerve wracking event, as we were under no circumstances allowed to lock the bathroom door, and were only allowed three sheets of toilet paper to wipe with. That Friday, she inspected my diary, saying a brief 'Good' when she saw I had completed it. She asked me about my name, and I said no name had come, even though I had asked the Lord for it. She went red in the face.

'You have one more week. If the name hasn't come, I will call you Dove. That will be your name.'

Dove? I thought. There is nothing Dove-like about me! I was furious but kept my head down and didn't show it. I understood she wanted to erase me. They wanted to wipe me out, to make me a 'new creature'. What bothered me, what I found most distressing, was that I was being forced to do something which I knew was false and fake. I wished Mummy were there to talk to. But even if she had been, I knew there was nothing she could do. Mummy was no longer in charge of us, I knew that. I had heard through the grapevine that Dinah, who had been sent to Madras not long after we arrived in India, was going through 'breakings' too, and that her name had been changed to Joan.

In a strange twist of fate, I was saved by the bell – events intervened before that next Friday, and the battle over my name was forgotten.

Midweek, the shepherds called a home council meeting. This was odd because it wasn't the usual regular one. The home shepherds made an announcement: our 'contact' at the Indian visa department had been found out. Apparently, the Family had been buying visa renewals from this person, under the counter, for years, and he had been caught. We were to buy tickets immediately using our flee fund (every family was allowed to keep a certain amount of money for emergencies such as this one) and head back to the West. 'The Lord has called us back, for a new generation of Western sheep need us to show them the way.' I found this very confusing. We had been told that we were to stay in the 'mission fields of the East' until Jesus came back. The home shepherds were worried the authorities (the systemites) would start a persecution campaign. Aunty Virginia soon forgot about me as she busied herself, making sure that the home doubled down on 'security.' We needed to be extra vigilant and all witnessing activity ceased. We were to be 100 per cent packed and ready to move at a moment's notice.

A few days later, I was informed to pick up my little suitcase and get ready to leave. I was to be reunited with Mummy and the rest of my siblings. Dinah was going to join us as well. I was super-excited about seeing my mum and siblings again after what seemed like years. I was also wondering what country we would be sent to. Would we go back to Costa Rica? Or would we go to my mum's country – England?

That Sunday, I arrived at the home on the other side of Bangalore, where Mummy was living with Bev, Michael, Petra and Maria. I could barely contain my excitement. I changed out of my outside clothes and rushed to hug them. Dinah was there already having arrived from Madras the evening before. I gave her a big hug. 'Guess what?' said Bev, falling over herself with excitement. 'Dinah is pregnant!'

'What?' I said, looking at Dinah and then at Mum. Mum smiled. A shadow passed over Dinah's face. She had just turned nineteen. I was over the moon and hugged her. She smiled weakly. 'Let's sing!' I said picking up the guitar. The other kids in the home gathered round. Dinah picked up the other guitar and we spent the next hour singing away, laughing and joking.

'Where are we going to next, Mummy?' I asked.

'We're going to Mexico!' she said.

'Why Mexico?'

'It's a wonderful mission field, your father and I spent some time there in the early days and I'm very excited because we have received clearance from the national shepherds in Mexico to come.'

'Is Dad going to meet us there?'

'Yes, he will join us once we're settled,' said Mum. 'Next week, we're going to take the overnight train from Bangalore to New Delhi. We're booked in a first-class carriage, kids. It's going to take three days! Then, we will stay in the reception home in New Delhi for three days and we'll be given a lift to the airport. We will be taking an Aeroflot flight from New Delhi to Moscow where we will stay the night in a hotel. Then we will catch a flight to Dublin, then from Dublin to Havana in Cuba and from Havana to Mexico City. Isn't that wonderful, kids?'

We jumped up and down, excited about the adventure ahead of us.

A couple of days later we were packed up and dropped off at the train station. We each had a suitcase plus a spare one containing our blankets, sheets and a couple of Maria's stuffed toys: Pepe the Moose, a present from Daddy, bought in Spain, along with Pummies and Mousie, who was her favourite. She carried him around everywhere. The fact that she was able to hold on to them was a bit of a miracle. She came close to losing them a few times when the home shepherds started to complain that 'no child should have any personal toys; all toys should be shared'. They had reminded Mummy that 'children should be working, reading the Word and redeeming the time, not goofing off'. In their view, anything that encouraged children to escape into a world of imagination and fantasy was spiritually dangerous. Mummy ignored the admonishment and looked after Maria's toys.

At the train station, Mummy showed her tickets in the office and to her concern, we were shown to a second-class carriage. Apparently, the wrong tickets had been booked. We were shown into a filthy section of the train and given a carriage with two bunk beds which doubled up as seats.

Mum's face fell, but she soon recovered her cheerful demeanour. 'OK, kids! I brought some Dettol and some cloths. Let's clean down the carriage and bunks.' We placed our cases in the case compartment.

'Dinah can have one top bunk; I will have a bottom bunk and share with Maria. Bev and Faith share another bunk and Michael and Petra the other.'

It was a squeeze and the bickering and complaining began. 'Three nights? Mum! There's not enough space!'

'Stop murmuring and complaining, kids, we have to make the best of it.'

The carriages were next to each other and we had to share a toilet with the rest of the packed train, which you could get to by way of the corridor. It was just a hole in the floor with a latched door and a small sink. It stank. The rest of the passengers in the train looked at us with open curiosity. By now we were used to being stared at, so we just carried on as if we were the only people in the train.

We kept our carriage door closed the first day but soon it got too hot, so our door remained open except at night. The train station was packed, noisy and chaotic. Vendors would come up to our windows trying to sell us fruit and snacks. We were not allowed to eat anything unless it was a bottled drink or pre-packaged biscuits or the food that Mummy had prepared for us, for fear of getting sick. Monkeys and children roamed about the train, begging and stealing.

We stared out the window for hours taking in the Indian countryside. Each time we stopped at a train station, it was the same drill with the vendors. Sometimes the passengers would get off and buy stuff from the station, but we stayed put. Going to the toilet was tricky and scary. Mummy said we were to go 'two by two' to keep an eye out for each other. There would sometimes be a queue and people would look at us curiously. On one of these trips there was only a lady waiting. Suddenly, an enormous winged cockroach scuttled into view. Bev and I froze but the lady crouched down, picked it up and carefully placed it outside the ledge of the window. 'Maybe she thinks the cockroach is someone's ancestor,' I whispered to Bev.

The first night was very uncomfortable but the rocking of the train soon lulled us to sleep. Dinah had had morning sickness all day and spent the entire day lying on her top bunk. She was pale and wan and couldn't keep any food down. She was thoroughly miserable. In the morning, we had biscuits and a drink and made trips to the toilet. Boredom had set in. The only respite were the rare moments when Dinah's morning sickness would subside, and we got the guitar out to amuse ourselves by singing. This drew a crowd of curious passengers from the other carriages who crowded around our door. Two young men clapped particularly enthusiastically and introduced themselves to Mummy. They spoke good English and explained that they were university students going home for their holidays. They were curious to see an English lady travelling in a second-class carriage with her six children.

'Can we sit with you for a while?' they asked. Bev and I felt uncomfortable, but Mum welcomed them in. They chatted merrily away with Mum but I noticed that one of the young men looked a bit sweaty and unwell. He told Mum that he was recovering from a bout of sickness.

After a few hours they left and went back to their carriage. That night, I got a raging fever and tossed and turned in the bunk, much to Bev's annoyance. We were all starting to get very irritable. A few days earlier I had bitten off part of the quick on my fingernail and it had become infected. Dinah's morning sickness worsened, and my fever raged; I shivered and sweated for the rest of the train journey. When well enough, I would look out of the window, fascinated by the changing landscape. By the time we were approaching Delhi, my fever had broken, and I began to feel better. Mummy kept soaking my infected finger in Dettol and eventually I healed.

When we arrived at the train station, there were a couple of 'brothers' waiting for us. They greeted us with the usual 'Hi! God Bless You!' and ushered us to a waiting minivan. This is different, I thought. New Delhi, being in the north of India, was much colder than the south. The streets were wide, and it seemed a bit more modern. For one, we were in a minivan and not a rickshaw.

When we arrived, we all showered, which was a relief after three nights on a stinking filthy train. Once we had cleaned up, we were introduced to the rest of the home members. Dinah, Bev and I were delighted that one of the Family's best musicians, an American known as 'Singing Sam', was in the home. He was one of the musicians that we teens thought was cool. He had a great voice and also, in the 'early days', he had sung with *Os Meninos de Deus* (The Children of God), a Brazilian band whose music was very cool. So cool it got banned by Grandpa for being too worldly. This was music that had featured on the teen contraband tapes.

'I see you have a guitar, girls!' said Sam in his loud voice. 'Let's jam!' We spent the next couple of hours playing with Singing Sam and some other musicians in the home and we loved it.

Two days later, we were in the minivan again and on our way to the airport. My fever returned with a vengeance and Dinah was miserable. By now she was beginning to look a little skeletal. We checked in and got on the Aeroflot aeroplane. The cabin crew were starkly different to the Indians we had grown used to. They were unsmiling and unfriendly. We were in third class and it wasn't until three hours after take-off that we were finally offered water in a paper cup, boiled eggs, hard butterless brown bread and some sort of sausage. Everyone except Dinah and me forced it down as they were so hungry. I gratefully gulped down the water.

When we arrived at Moscow airport, it was cold. There was snow on the side of the tarmac, and we alighted a transporter tram that was waiting for us. Maria was clutching Mousie and the transporter taxied us into the airport.

'We are in Russia, kids!' said Mummy. 'As you know, your grandpa was Russian, but he was from St Petersburg. My grandparents had to escape from Russia with nothing but a few jewels and the clothes on their backs when the revolution broke out and the communists took over in 1918!'

'How scary, Mummy. Poor Grandpa,' said Dinah.

'Grandpa wouldn't have remembered much, I don't think, because he was just five years old, but my grandma, Lala, used to tell me stories about Russia when I was a little girl. Lala spoke perfect Russian but she was actually French. And my grandpa was a 'white Russian' who was high up in the government. One of my great-uncles was an advisor to the vice-Czar and that is why they had to escape, to make their home in England. I remember family gatherings when I was little, my father jabbering away in Russian with relatives and friends. My mother, an English lady, used to sit there looking rather bored,' she said.

The airport was enormous with a clinical feel. The walls and floor were granite and the staff in the airport looked severe. Suddenly, little Maria started to cry.

'What's the matter, darling?' said Mummy.

We all surrounded her, worried. 'Mousie! Mousie!' she wailed. She had dropped Mousie. Bev, Mike, Petra and I scoured the area to see if we could find the toy. Maria's sad brown eyes were filled with tears as she patiently waited with Mummy and Dinah. Our search was fruitless. 'Oh, you poor darling! You must've dropped Mousie when we were climbing on to the transit tram on the tarmac!' said Mummy. We all felt very sorry for Maria and tried to comfort her by reminding her that she still had Pepe the Moose and Pummies – they were safely tucked away in the blanket suitcase.

We passed through the metal detectors and it began to beep furiously when Bev went through. The guards looked at her angrily. Bev looked scared as the female guard roughly patted her down. She went through again. It beeped again. The air became tense and you could have cut it with a knife. Bev turned out her pockets and out fell a few scraps of yellow foil from some old biscuit wrapper we must have had on the train. She went through the detector once more. This time no bleeping and we all laughed, relieved. Even the guards cracked a slight smile.

We were to stay in the airport hotel for one night to catch a flight to Dublin in the early hours of the morning. That evening, we were given another meal of boiled eggs, sausage and butterless thick, heavy brown bread.

'Yuck, Mum!' we complained. By now we were bordering on mutiny. My siblings and I bickered and complained. Everyone was tired, hungry and thoroughly bad-tempered. Dinah was always being sick, my fever would wax and wane and my nose became more and more sore. Mummy was as stoic as ever.

'Don't worry, kids! We'll be there soon!' she would say as cheerfully as she could.

We peeled our exhausted bodies out of bed at an ungodly hour and made our way down to breakfast before catching the flight. We were too tired to complain, and ate the boiled eggs, sausage and nasty brown butterless bread without a word. We boarded the plane and were in Dublin airport seven hours later. By then I was practically delirious.

Despite being ill, it was a relief to be in Dublin; it was such a contrast to Moscow. There were shops stacked with food, chocolates, books and magazines and the shop and café staff seemed friendly. We trooped to the loos and Dinah and I had a furious row about something or other.

'Girls! Stop it at once!' said Mum, losing her temper. 'I know you're both unwell, but you are the oldest! Behave yourselves. Stop fighting, wash your hands and faces and then we can go to Woolworths and I'll buy us all some Cadbury's chocolate. Wouldn't that be nice?'

We all cheered up and felt instantly better once we were munching away on naughty 'Devil's poison' chocolate as Mummy looked up at the monitor, waiting for our next flight to show up. 'Just think, Bev. England is just a hop and skip away and then we could see Grandma!'

'There we are!' Mum finally exclaimed. 'Aeroflot 224 – Dublin to Havana! C'mon, kids!'

We got up, re-energised by the sugar rush, and filed onto the plane. Seven hours later, we landed in Havana. It was exciting looking out of the window at the tropical scene below as we came in to land. The humidity and heat hit us as soon as we got off the plane and walked the short distance to the ramshackle airport. It was nice to be in the sunshine and warmth after the cold of New Delhi and Moscow.

The poverty was very apparent. There was a little café in the airport serving delicious fresh tropical fruit drinks. We were allowed to pick which fruit we fancied, and it would be made right there on the spot. 'The water from the tap is safe to drink here, kids,' said Mum. We drank our smoothies gratefully. When Bev and I went to the ladies, we held our noses. It stank of urine and the walls were covered in swear words and drawings of penises, boobs and vaginas. We giggled at them. Soon it was time to board the final plane for what Mum called 'a short hop to Mexico City'.

CHAPTER 14: Love – London, 1999

After the strange experience with the pastor and having broken up with Levi, I felt different. Going to clubs, taking party drugs and getting wasted no longer had the same appeal. My job was going well. I was making what felt like lots of money selling sofas and working out a lot at the gym in the evenings. Levi and I were still friends. We met up to go to the pub, or to gigs, but I was happy being single. I went on a few dates, had a fling or two and the odd one-night stand, which left me feeling flat. The fantasy, I found, was always far better than the reality.

One midweek day, Petra called me after work. I had a little flat by now, where I lived on my own, and I was sitting on the sofa watching TV.

'Faith, please – I need your help. I left my satchel in the Black Sheep bar last night. Please, please, will you be a sport and drive over to pick it up? Can you get it, please? I called them; I know it's there. You just need to ask for a guy called Nick.'

'I just sat down, Petra.'

261

'Please Faith! I'll owe you.'

I drove to the bar, which was one I knew fairly well. It was small and dingy and they sometimes had indie band nights there. There were three or four people inside. The barman said Nick wasn't there and no one had left a satchel, so I drove off.

I rang Petra, annoyed. 'Nick wasn't there and there was no satchel. You sent me on a wild goose chase.'

'Oh please, Faith,' said Petra. 'I beg you, please with flowers on top, go back there tomorrow, I swear Nick will be there with my satchel!'

'Absolutely not!' I said. 'Get it yourself!' I slammed the phone down.

It rang again. 'Please Faith, please, please,' Petra begged. 'I don't have a car and it'll take me forty-five minutes on the bus there and forty-five minutes on the bus back. It will take you ten minutes. Please, Faith . . .'

I gave in.

Whilst I was standing at the bar and Nick the barman was looking for Petra's bag, the guy next to me struck up a conversation. He was short and slim, in his late twenties with a moustache. It was the 'So, what do you do?' sort of conversation. Here we go, I thought. I told him I was in sales.

'Ditto,' he said, and introduced himself as Caspar. 'What do you sell?' he said.

'Oh, I sell luxury leather sofas . . .'

'I had money for a sofa earlier this year, but I've gone and spent it all over Christmas!' he laughed.

My ears pricked up. 'Really? We do interest-free finance . . .' Wouldn't it be funny if I ended up making a sale, I thought.

'How much commission do you make?'

'I make 2.5 per cent commission on the sofas; my average sale is £3,500 and I sell quite a lot of those in a month.'

'I make 17 per cent,' he said.

'That's a lot. What do you sell?'

'Advertising space in trade magazines. In fact, I'm looking to build up my team. Are you interested in finding out more? We're looking for people to join the company. You could make some serious money . . . the average sale is anything between £5,000 and £10,000. But you have flexibility to negotiate with your buyer and bring the price down pretty much as you see fit. When you get the hang of it, it's easy to sell . . .'

We swapped numbers. The barman reappeared with Petra's satchel.

Back home, I thought about the 17 per cent. I was getting bored at the sofa shop, so maybe it was time for a new challenge. I called the number the next day and arranged an interview. I had a few savings to tide me over until my commission came through in the new job.

My new office was in Farringdon, central London. The air in the open-plan office was thick with cigarette smoke. There was a big whiteboard and a huge bell next to it. On the whiteboard were sums of money and people's names on it: Annie £5,000, Caspar £3,400, JJ £8,500, Pat £750. I could hear cold-call salespeople delivering their pitches in orchestra, punctuated by the 'click-clack' of Rolodexes being spun intermittently. Caspar the guy who I'd met in the bar, interviewed me and offered me the job on the spot. I accepted, thinking, Why not?, despite a niggling worry that there was no basic salary. Instead, the company subbed you £250 a week, which you paid back out of your commission. Any extra commission would be mine.

I arrived on my first day having never made a telephone sale in my life. I was cocky and overconfident; having been the top dog at the sofa shop, I thought I'd get the hang of selling on the phone in no time. Caspar greeted me enthusiastically. Standing next to him was a fair-haired man who was about four years older than me, I guessed. 'This is Jules, he's starting today too. He's just come back from Hong Kong and he's between jobs – we met when we worked together selling ad space for the *FT* a good few years ago, when he was fresh out of uni, didn't we, Jules? He knows a bit about how it works.'

Jules offered me his hand, and I shook it. 'Hi, I'm Faith,' I said. I looked at him; he was tall and athletic with sparkly blue eyes and perfect teeth. A thought popped into my head, unbidden: Oh, I recognise you! You're the man I'm going to marry! I felt it as a certainty, like a fact I already knew. A strange thing to think, as I hadn't given marriage or children any thought, except to scoff at the idea of them. But the thought was fleeting.

'There are your desks, guys,' said Caspar to Jules and me, pointing to two desks next to each other. Each member of the team was given letters in the phone directory to target. I was tasked with cold-calling companies whose names began with the letters M, N, O and P. It was hard work. Without the face-to-face interaction, selling on the phone was foreign to me. I was totally out of my comfort zone and I found it hard to sound natural on the phone. I worried that the person on the other end of the line, usually the marketing director of whatever company I was pitching to, would know that I was a fake with a script in front of me. I sold nothing the first two weeks, whilst next to me, Jules made it look easy. I watched him and listened carefully. Jules was well-spoken and enunciated his words carefully. He took control of the conversation and asked lots of questions. He would pick up the phone with such confidence and always asked for the deal. It felt as if the bell rang continuously to mark other people's wins, including Jules's. There was a lot of whooping and high-fiving. I went home feeling dejected.

Jules seemed so natural with it. He bonded with the rest of the team with such ease. The team was a mishmash. Cockney wideboys, university dropouts, people between jobs like Jules, and old-timers who had been there for years. Caspar explained the culture was 'work hard and play even harder' with a dash of friendly competition thrown in. On Friday, once the commission had been decided, the sales-people would get to cash their commission or advance cheques at the local Barclays branch. That first week, Jules walked out of the bank with £800 in cash. I cashed my £250 advance and thought, One day soon, I'll be walking out with big money. I just have to be patient. Jules invited me along with the rest of the team to the pub.

'C'mon, Faith, Geórgios is putting his credit card behind the bar!'

Geórgios was the owner of the agency. In his mid-forties, he was friendly and once a month on a Friday, he would treat the entire team to drinks. That evening, Jules got busy chatting with one of the other young women. I noticed they were quite flirtatious with each other. Ah, OK, well, that's fine then, I thought, bringing the shutters down hard on my heart.

After four weeks I still hadn't made any sales and the stress was starting to get to me. Before I had started my new job, I had booked a holiday to go back to see Dinah and my dad, who were back in Costa Rica. I was beginning to feel pissed off and frightened at work. I was losing confidence in myself and my ability to succeed. I felt as if I'd lost my touch. After making it through the first part of my third week with no sales, I quietly put down the phone and walked out of the office. In the corridor, my eyes filled with tears. I wanted to control myself for long enough to make it up to the roof, where I knew I could be alone. I felt panicked about the basic advance the company had subbed me, which I knew I'd have to pay back, worried about how I'd pay my rent, and more than anything, frustrated that it seemed so easy for other people. I climbed the steps and let the tears roll down my cheeks. Turning around to sit on the top step, to my utter horror, I saw Jules had followed me up. I was mortified. I covered my face. By now, the floodgates had opened and I couldn't control myself any longer.

'Oh, Faith!' Jules said as he sat down next to me. I sobbed, by now not caring what he thought of me. Make-up streamed down my cheeks and my nose was running.

'I'm frightened that I'm never going to make it here, Jules. I'm worried I'll run out of money, I'm worried about my rent, paying back the basic.'

He sat down next to me and put his arm around my shoulders, drawing me in. I cried like a baby. We were quiet for a while.

'Hey, Faith, I promise you'll crack it. It will click for you! It took me six weeks before I made any sales at the *FT*! It wasn't long after that that I became the top seller and earned the right to have my name printed in the paper. I still have a copy of it. "For enquiries about advertising, contact Jules Morgan",' he said with a funny voice. 'You're only three weeks in! The trick is not to be afraid of the other person at the end of the phone . . . I'll teach you how to do it. Next time I'm on a call, you can listen to what's going on.'

I didn't want to quit. I knew I had done much harder things than selling on the phone. I had sold tapes and posters on the streets, in houses and in offices in multiple countries. I had sung in orphanages, old people's homes and on TV. I had busked in restaurants in Mexico and Greece, I had busked in Leicester Square and Covent Garden, I had 'provisioned' food in restaurants and markets, I had overcome my fear and confronted the cult, given interviews on TV, radio and for newspapers and magazines, and testified in court cases. Surely, I could sell advertising space over the phone?

When the time came to take my holiday, I told my manager and the rest of the team that I'd be back in three weeks' time. Jules walked me to the train station on my last day.

'Hope you have a good time, Faith!' he said.

'Cheers, Jules!' I said and turned to wave.

He took my hand and said, 'Come here! Give me a hug.'

I was taken aback. 'Er . . . OK!' I said and put my arms around his neck as he pulled me in. He hugged me and then gave me a big kiss on the lips.

'Bye!' he said.

I smiled and walked off. 'Bye, Jules!'

On the train, I thought: what was that about? The hug, the kiss? No way. I'm not going there. He's into Tracy in the other office, I'm sure of it. I can't deal with any more emotional upheaval.

Dinah was there to welcome me at the airport. We were so happy to see each other. She had decided to take her boys back to Costa Rica to live near Dad. He had promised he would get her a job with some rich gringos he was working with. ('Gringo' is a slang word used in Latin America for Americans. It is the combination of two words: 'green' and 'go', 'green' referring to the colour of the American army's uniform). She jumped at the opportunity because she had never really adjusted to life in England.

Dinah explained that Dad was working as a consultant for some American businessmen who had set up an offshore gambling operation, whereby gamblers in the US could place bets over the internet or by phone. As it was a

legal operation in Costa Rica and because of Dad's connections, he could set up anonymous societies and bank
accounts on their behalf, taking commissions as payment.
Some of my dad's associates, Dinah said, were decidedly
unsavoury characters, and Dad was gathering to himself
a bunch of 'hangers on', mostly young women. I cringed.

Dinah was living in a simple little cottage in a quiet
neighbourhood. It was lovely to see her and her boys –
they had grown so much. By now, Robert was ten and
Tito was eight, and they were attending the local school.
In stark contrast, Dad was renting a surprisingly lavish and
tastefully furnished suite at a five-star hotel downtown.

Dad was happy to see me. 'My beautiful girrll!' he
said, throwing his arms out wide. 'I pray for you every
day, sweetheart!' In his suite, I noticed a large turntable
and a shelf filled with his classical record collection. I
wondered how it had survived. He told me one of my
uncles had looked after them for him. He showed me
through the art he had collected, which hung on the
walls of his suite. On the mantelpiece were some beauti-
fully framed black and white photos of my grandparents
when they were young, a photo of my grandfather in
his sixties with John F. Kennedy, and another of my dad
in his thirties shaking the King of Spain's hand.

'Dad, what was Grandpa doing with JFK?' I asked.

'Oh, your grandfather was part of the welcoming com-
mittee when Kennedy came to the university where your

grandfather worked,' he said proudly. I was impressed and wondered why he and Mum were so willing to throw everything away – the advantages of his connections in the 'systemite' world which could have meant opportunities for their six children.

'Dad,' I said as we stood looking at the pictures, 'do you realise the hell the Family put us through? Did you realise how abusive it was, and how hard it is for us kids to now get our lives together? You had so many opportunities and connections which you could've passed on to us, but you denied us and now we're all scratching around, trying to adjust to normal life and to make ends meet.'

He looked stunned but quickly recovered: 'We were serving the Lord and I'm still serving the Lord. Maybe some mistakes were made along the way but I'm winning souls for Jesus every day!' He picked out his little black book of souls. It was similar to the one I recognised from my childhood: leather-bound and elegant. He waved it in front of me. I felt angry at his wilful blindness and unwillingness to acknowledge the pain that his decisions had visited upon us. I also realised that it was futile to expect any kind of remorse or apology from him. The hypocrisy was stunning: one minute he was supposed to be a 'missionary' and now here he was doing shady deals with dodgy people and hanging out with lowlifes. Somehow, everything was squared in his mind because, as far as he was concerned, he was still winning souls for Jesus and recording each one in his little black book.

I looked at my father and wondered whether he was sick in the head. He used to brag that his parents didn't know what to do about him because he was such a 'black sheep'. 'I was thrown out of every private school they put me in!' he told us, gleefully.

My parents met in the early sixties in Washington DC when they were both working for airlines. Mummy told me that, for as long as she could remember, her dream had been to visit India. She had found out that 'nice English girls with nice English accents were very well-paid secretaries' in the United States and decided this would be the quickest way for her to save up. But she didn't make it to India until much later, with us. She met my Dad in Washington DC where he was working for a South American airline, and 'playboying around'. Apparently, my grandfather had pulled some strings and got him the job, hoping it would be the start of a career for him. Instead, he partied like crazy. Mum didn't stand a chance. He was tall, dark and handsome and very charming. She quickly fell pregnant and didn't want to go through with it but he begged her to marry him as he was a Catholic.

Dad then took his English fiancée back to his country. At first his parents were horrified. He was supposed to marry a good Catholic girl from his own country and from a certain pool of 'señoritas de sociedad' with the right

surnames. Equally, my grandparents in England were horrified that their daughter was marrying a South American
from a banana republic. The snobbery on both sides was
breathtaking. In the end, my dad's parents embraced my
mum with deep affection, even though she refused a big
Catholic wedding on the grounds that she was an atheist. She did, however, throw herself into learning to speak
Spanish. My mum's parents never accepted my father.
They thought he was an irresponsible so-and-so, and they
were right.

Amongst the pictures on Dad's mantlepiece was one
of an attractive young woman in a skimpy dress. It was
next to a picture of my mum.

'Who's that, Dad?' I asked.

'Oh, that is Cindy, my girlfriend. Well, she's *one* of my
girlfriends.' I made a derisive sound. He shrugged. 'I have
lots of girlfriends, Faith. Only a fool has one girlfriend. I
hate women anyway; they are only good for two things:
the bed and the kitchen, ha-ha-ha-ha-ha-haa!'

'Dad!' I said. 'I am a woman!'

'Well, I still hate women and I certainly don't trust
them, they are all conniving trying to get money, always .
. . even your mother threw me out of the house.'

'I'm a woman, Dad . . . how could you say that to me?'

'Yeah. I love you, darling, but all women are conniving
. . .' he said. 'You can't help it, I understand that . . . but
you're not to be trusted.'

I felt as if I was seeing it in full technicolour for the first time. This was my dad – a selfish misogynist. I could see he had put Dinah in danger, too, when she had moved out there to be near him, a single mother desperately in need of care and protection. I concluded that my dad was most probably sick in the head.

I decided to stay at Dinah's after that night. I didn't want to be around Dad much. He did take us both out for dinner a couple of times the following week, but when I asked for the $50 I needed to pay taxes at the airport the afternoon before my flight, he said simply, 'No. Don't come to me for money, you make your own way.'

'Dad,' I said, panic rising, 'it's Sunday. None of the exchange banks are open. I didn't know until now I'd have to pay taxes in dollars at the airport. I've only just found out!' There was no way I could 'make my own way' to $50, but he was adamant that he wasn't going to help.

'See what I mean?' Dinah said to me later. 'He's sick. He happily doles hundreds of dollars in front of me to his girlfriend after refusing to pay me for work I've done for him so I can feed my boys.' I was disgusted by his mean-ness and asked Dinah why on earth she was prepared to put up with his cruelty.

'I can't get another job out here, Faith, because I don't have my baccalaureate,' she said. 'Companies don't hire you unless you have that basic qualification . . .'

I felt sorry for Dinah. She was a bright and talented girl who had been used and abused and witnessed her big sister dying at the age of thirteen. She had been taken out of high school and dragged around the world. She had suffered much more than I had and I knew I had got away very lightly compared to her.

That night, my Uncle Emilio's children, my cousins who were not much older than me, threw me a party to say goodbye. I told them about the $50 dollars. I had the money in Costa Rican colones, I explained, but they wouldn't take it. 'Please, here, from us,' they said, and handed it to me. My dad had always been so dismissive about his family and had made no effort to maintain contact with them, but I had been touched to meet them, and to discover that they were good people and that we got on.

Back in London, I returned to the office. Jules looked surprised to see me as I came in. He said the team had made a wager that I wouldn't be back. By the end of the week, though, still no sales. The following Monday, I was called into the boss's office and asked to sit down.

'We don't think this is working out for you, Faith, I'm really sorry, but I think you're going to have to leave.'

Rather than feeling resigned, it was as if his words lit a fuse under me. I was determined to prove him wrong.

'You have got to be kidding. You need to give me another week to prove myself,' I said.

'OK,' he said, 'I tell you what we'll do. I'll move you to another team to pitch for a different publication. Maybe you'll find that one easier to sell.'

I pitched like crazy that week, with new determination. I finally got through to the marketing director at a large recruitment company. I noticed that I felt more confident, as if I was owning the conversation. I finished my pitch and she said, 'How much did you say it was for half a page?'

'£5,000.' There was a long pause.

'Can you do it for £4,500?'

My heart was thumping by now. I said, 'I'll have to check with my line manager.' I put her on hold and counted to ten.

'Yes, we can do that. I'll send the paperwork over now.'

The relief was enormous. I knew then that I had cracked it. Jules was right. I literally felt it click. My sales manager was delighted. He rang the bell for an extra-long time and made a huge fuss. The rest of the team congratulated and high-fived me.

'What did I tell you, Faith?' said Jules. 'Five weeks before your first sale. You beat me by a week, what a star!' I was pleased as punch. 'Hey, fancy staying behind in the office with me for a couple of hours this evening? I'm pitching to the marketing director of a large energy company in the USA and I've been told by his secretary that he's expected to be at his desk. I'm going to sell him a double-page spread for $20,000.' He grinned from ear to ear.

'Oh yeah?' I said, teasing. 'Bet you discount like crazy,' I laughed.

'I bet I won't . . .'

'OK then, I'll hang around and watch as you discount to close the deal . . .'

A couple of hours later, I watched as Jules got through to the marketing director of the American energy company. After twenty-five minutes of pitching, he was closing: 'Great, Rod! I'll send you over the paperwork now. Are you next to your fax machine? OK, here goes . . .'

Five minutes later the fax machine in the sales manager's office rang and bleeped, spitting out the sales order with a price tag of $20,000 and a big bold signature on it. Jules picked it up: 'What did I tell you?!' he chuckled, his big blue eyes twinkling cheekily.

'Oh my God, Jules! You've just made $3,400!'

'Right!' he said. 'Dinner's on me, let's celebrate!'

At the restaurant, Jules and I toasted his win. We talked a little about our families, but I kept very quiet about my weird upbringing. Towards the end of the evening, as we said goodbye and parted ways, I realised that I hadn't been bored for a second. We chatted with ease and I found Jules interesting. He was open-minded, curious and thoughtful.

A few weeks later on a Friday afternoon, Jules and Caspar invited me to come along to the pub for a drink. After a couple of hours, Jules invited Caspar and me back to his apartment in Windsor. 'Let's go back to mine and get stoned!' he said.

'Sounds like an excellent idea!' said Caspar.

'Cool! I'm in!' We sat around smoking weed, listening to music, eating biscuits and drinking tea and laughing. At around 7 p.m., Caspar announced that he was off. 'I might as well get on the same train as you, Caspar,' I said. He got up to go to the loo.

Jules turned to me and said, 'Would you like to stay, and come out to dinner with me, Faith?'

I was taken aback but it felt natural. I liked him, this nicely spoken English boy with sandy hair and manners that reminded me a little bit of Mum's.

'OK! That'll be nice! You've only got one bedroom though . . .' I said, testing. I didn't want him to think that I would be sleeping with him.

'Don't worry, I'll sleep on the futon down here and you can have my bed.' We had a great time at dinner. We had the munchies and were giggly from the weed.

When we got home, we had a smoke and listened to 'Timeless' by Goldie. We kissed.

'I'm ready to hit the sack!' I said after a while. Jules showed me to his bedroom and gave me a clean towel. 'Cheers, Jules – goodnight!'

Ten minutes later I was lying in Jules's bed, my mind going over the day. After a while, Jules called up: 'Faith? Do you want some company?'

Company would be nice, I thought. But I don't want him to think he's going to have sex with me! I shouted down: 'Jules, company would be nice but you must promise not to try to seduce me. If you can promise me that, then yes, company would be nice.' Up he came and, true to his word, we slept in each other's arms and he didn't try a thing.

The next morning, Jules brought me up a cup of mint tea. 'We ran out of teabags and milk,' he said. 'Let's hang out today!'

'OK!' I showered, got dressed and borrowed his spare toothbrush, a bit self-conscious that I didn't have my make-up with me, except a lip gloss. We went to the local shop, bought tea, milk, biscuits and some pasta. We carried on smoking and chatting that day. We spent the day in a stoned haze, drinking tea and listening to music. We laughed our heads off that Saturday. By now, all self-consciousness had flown out of the window and we were both comfortable and relaxed. At one point I wandered up to him, eyes like saucers, and said, 'Hey Jules, I think we should be friends forever! Don't you think that's a great idea?'

'Yes!' he said. 'I think that's a fab idea!'

'You should meet my mum and my siblings. We're all a bit crazy . . .' I said.

Later that afternoon, snuggling on the sofa watching a movie, one thing led to another. I hadn't intended to sleep with Jules that day. I liked him a lot, and I didn't want it to be a mistake and ruin things, particularly as we worked together. But it was so natural that it almost felt as if we were getting to know each other again; that somehow there was a connection that had existed longer than the few weeks we had known each other, which was being rekindled. From that moment we were joined at the hip. It was crazy: there's me, the independent, hard-hearted cynic, somehow not feeling frustrated or smothered when he'd call ten minutes after we'd left each other, or when he'd ring up on an evening we had agreed not to see each other and ask if he could come over, making an hour-long drive to arrive at 11 p.m.

The first time he came to the house in Crystal Palace, I could tell that Mum was delighted. Jules was charming and polite. She had always said to me that Levi was unsuitable. Mum had made two roast chickens. The table was chaotic. Petra, Bev and Maria were there. Bev started a food fight with Maria. Mum was mortified, and Jules seemed baffled by it all. I rolled my eyes. 'Cut it out, show-offs!' I yelled. 'Jules, meet my family. Family, meet Jules . . .'

Since my rediscovered faith in Christianity, I had not wanted to witness (the thought of it made me shudder) to people, despite this being something I was encouraged to do by the church I attended from time to time. But Jules was inherently curious about my faith; he was constantly asking questions, like: did I believe in the miracles? Did I believe Christianity was the only way to God? What was it about my experience that made it so real for me? I told him that he should find out for himself, read books, do his own searching, because I didn't want to influence him. Whatever conclusions he came to would need to be genuine and authentic and not because he loved me. The last thing I wanted to do was to spout scripture at him; I'd had a lifetime's worth of that, and trying to turn what I felt into a religious sales pitch felt false in light of the deeply spiritual experience I'd had. Anyway, Jules would have seen through it in an instant.

Over many long and deep conversations, I told him about my family, my childhood, the cult, everything.

Jules told me about his time in Hong Kong, how he was interested in Eastern religions. He had practised kung fu for six years and regularly practised qigong. He was fascinated by the *I Ching*, (The Book of Changes), an ancient text that predates Christ by around a 1,000 years. He told me that it could be used for divination and he had had surprising results when he'd tried it. By holding a question in one's mind and throwing coins or drawing straws, one would be guided to certain parts of the text within the book which would relate in some way to the question that was being asked. Jules didn't come across as superstitious or 'woo-woo' in any way, more like an explorer wanting to try things out to see what happened. He told me that he'd been lazy about throwing the coins one day and had simply held a question in his mind and 'cut' the book, opening it to a random page and plopping his finger down on the text. What he had read had shocked him a bit, due to how relevant the text was to the question he had posed.

Once, when he was staying over, I went out to the loo, and when I got back, I found Jules with my open Bible on his lap, his eyes wide with surprise.

'What's wrong?' I asked.

He explained he had decided to try a spot of divination as an experiment, and had thought, If there is any power in this book, it will show me something. He turned the Bible over to me, pointing at the text his finger had hit. Hebrews 11:1. 'Now faith is the substance of things hoped for, the evidence of things not seen.'

'Faith, that's what it showed me. Faith. Of all the sentences I could have found.'

That started Jules's own spiritual exploration into Christianity. He started going to church, always asking questions.

Jules proposed three months after we started dating. We were watching *EastEnders* in his flat and he turned it off and got down on one knee. I waited about thirty seconds before I said yes. It was the thirty seconds it took to override my instinct based on a fear that I'd be trapped and that it might be unwise to trust this man, whom I hadn't known long. Something in me recognised this as bad logic. It was the best decision I have ever made and one I have never regretted for a moment.

I met Jules's parents a few times before the wedding. They welcomed me with open arms and treated me with such kindness when I cautiously began to share a little about my background and how I grew up. They were delighted that their now thirty-year-old son was so happy and looked as if he was about to settle down. Mum arranged the wedding reception on a shoestring, although much to my surprise, Dad sent a contribution too, and although he couldn't come, he invited Jules and me to Costa Rica after our honeymoon in Tunisia, which we had booked for November. Dinah and her boys flew over from Costa Rica for the wedding, and all of my other siblings were there. Mum and my sisters cooked all the food and a friend of Jules's DJ'd. It was a joyful day, but I trembled as I walked down the aisle on my own with my lilies. I knew, though, in my heart, that it was the start of something good.

We bought a two-up-two-down on the same road as the church where we got married. I felt excited and hopeful about this new phase of my life.

CHAPTER 15: Sweet Fifteen – Mexico, Spring 1988

We arrived at Mexico City airport utterly exhausted, and sat patiently in the arrivals lounge, waiting for a long time for the local shepherds whom we were expecting to pick us up. Michael piped up, 'Just think, we were three days and nights on a train and then a total of eighteen hours in the air and that's not counting the layovers and overnight stay in Moscow . . .' By now, my fever had gone but I felt as if I was walking like an astronaut, feet sometimes not quite touching the ground.

The hours stretched on. Mum was getting worried, walking from one side of the lounge to the other, asking the staff questions. Finally, she came over to speak to us: 'Stay right here, kids. I'm going to use the payphone two lounges away.'

Half an hour later she was back.

'We were supposed to be picked up by now; I think the wires have been crossed somehow and the message didn't get through. The phone number for the home here is not working.'

'What are we going to do, Mum?'

I felt sorry for Mummy. She looked exhausted and frightened.

'Let's pray that someone comes soon, otherwise we will have to book flights back to Costa Rica. The only problem is that there is nowhere to go because your father sold the house and there is almost no money left. He spent it all whilst we were in India.'

Mum looked angry. The rest of us were just too tired to care by now. Just as she was getting up to see about flights a slim man with a moustache and glasses walked towards us.

'Rachel!'

'Jorge!' said Mummy, getting up to give him a hug. '*Dios te bendiga!*' (God bless you.)

'Sorry I'm here so late,' said Jorge in English. 'I was only given the message half an hour ago.'

Poor Mummy was so relieved to see him. He greeted us all warmly: 'I know most of you already although you won't remember me, you were too little!' he said. We piled into his truck and one hour later we were in the San Ángel home. 'I got Mirna and Tatiana to get some bedding ready for you with mattresses on the floor and we have cleared out a room for you. When we get home, you can shower, have a snack and go straight to sleep. You must all be exhausted.' It sounded like heaven. 'Praise the Lord you made it here safely!' said Jorge.

The first morning in San Ángel, we trooped down for breakfast and were greeted by friendly faces. The little children gathered around looking at us. 'God bless you!' greetings from our new 'family' rang in the air. They hugged and kissed us as if we were long-lost relatives. We were all 'one family, one wife', and there was a sense of familiarity and, to an extent, affection. It was nice to feel welcome. I recognised one or two faces, Jorge being one of them. He had come to visit us back in Costa Rica when I was very little and I vaguely remembered his face, except that he had been much younger and even skinnier, with long hair. I remembered he had worn a polyester paisley shirt and flared trousers. Now, he had filled out a little; was softer round the edges. He's good-looking . . . for an uncle, I thought.

I took in my surroundings. The house was large and carpeted. There were five bedrooms upstairs and the garage on the ground floor had two bedrooms annexed to it; downstairs there was a large living room/diner with open stairs leading to a landing where the bedrooms and bathrooms were. The kitchen was large and bright with tiled flooring. The daily schedule was pinned to the fridge with names against jobs such as cooking, laundry, bathrooms, vacuuming, toddlers, YCs (younger children), OCs (older children). No demerit chart or sharing schedule, I thought to myself, relieved.

As was usual in Family homes, this home was packed with adults, children, and a couple of teens. The teens introduced themselves: Theresa, my age; Paul, a year older than me; and Josh, also my age.

'Have some cereal!' said a tall young woman with a baby hanging off her hip. Her face was practically covered by huge 1980s glasses. Her skin was milky white, her hair was long, brown and limp. She wore it parted in the middle, a demure fashion which many of the aunties and even some of the teens stuck to. Bev and I used to giggle and call it the 'Hi, God Bless You' style. We all knew that Grandpa liked his women to have long hair. It was 'unrevolutionary' for sisters to cut their hair and worldly to have it cut or coloured in any kind of fashionable style. As such, it was forbidden. A fringe, however, was allowed and I used to ask one of the aunties to cut mine for me. Back in India, I had walked in on Aunty Violet as she cut her own hair. She was Italian-American and her hair was long, dark, thick and glossy. She was hunched over, head upside down, as she cut into her hair with a pair of scissors. She noticed me watching.

'Hello, sweetie,' she said. 'I'm giving my hair a little trim, turning it into a "shag". Your hair is very much like mine. Would you like me to trim yours too?'

'Yes, please, Aunty Violet!'

I turned my head upside down and she cut into the tips. 'Not too much, honey. Our hair is our crowning glory and Grandpa wants us to keep it long. As nature intended!'

I had also somehow managed to keep hold of a pair of tweezers, which I had guarded with my life since I was eleven years old. I kept them very well hidden in my flee bag and secretly plucked my eyebrows when I was quite sure I was alone. I was very self-conscious about my monobrow and I didn't want to be accused of being vain or wordly and get them confiscated from me.

'Wow!' my siblings and I said in unison as we sat down at the breakfast table. 'Cereal from a packet!'

'Yes! The provisioning team gets all kinds of things in the supermarket . . .' said Aunty Mirna, who spoke with a strong American accent. She introduced herself as 'one of Jorge's wives. Tatiana, his other wife, is just over there,' she said, pointing to a heavily pregnant lady with a shock of blond hair, 'but she is now together with Josiah.' She indicated a tall tanned man with dark brown hair and very blue eyes, talking to Jorge in the kitchen. A little blond girl clung to his long leg, whining.

'I will be with you in a minute, Marie-Claire!' he said in a strong South American accent.

A foursome, I thought, I guess that's new. Mirna explained that, together, they were the home shepherds. Between them, Jorge, Mirna, Tatiana and Josiah had nine children and another on the way.

We were soon put to work, given different jobs around the house. Bev and I were put in charge of entertaining the younger kids. The witnessing was different here in Mexico, we soon found out. Rather than going from house to house or business to business selling tapes and posters, here in Mexico, we witnessed at the weekends. Those who could play the guitar well would lead the rest of the crew in singing and dancing. A grown-up would drive us in a minivan and take us from fancy restaurant to fancy restaurant. The adult would ask the restaurant owner if we could sing and sell tapes to the lunchtime diners. The restaurant owners were mostly very happy to welcome a bunch of cute teens and pre-teens of all colours to sing in English and in Spanish. We soon learned that there were some favourite songs which we sung over and over. 'La Bamba' always went down a storm.

Once our singing set was over, we went in little teams of two from table to table trying to sell our tapes and post-ers. Our mouths would water at the amazing Mexican food spread across the tables which, of course, we weren't allowed to buy. It's not like it would've even occurred to us to ask. We never had any money and were never given any from the sales we made. We were to hand it all in to the grown-up who had taken us 'witnessing' that day.

We did our best to ignore the food and smiled sweetly to the diners who were usually very kind and friendly to us, even if they didn't always buy our wares. Mexicans, I noticed, were lovely, generous, humorous and good-na-tured people. This seemed to me to have rubbed off on the adults in the home. I think I am going to like being in Mexico, I thought happily.

I felt more part of a 'family' in the Mexico home than I had anywhere else. One day, one of the heavily pregnant aunties was about to give birth. Mirna was a midwife and she asked me if I wanted to watch the birth.

'Aunty Yvonne would be very happy for you to attend, if you'd like to!' she said. I was delighted and nervous. I helped bring in towels and hot water and watched Aunty Yvonne as she laboured. Then the moment for the birth came. 'The baby is crowning!' said Mirna excitedly. 'Come close, Faith! Isn't this a miracle?' I watched, mesmerised, as the baby's head crowned and then, out it plopped. I was astounded and knew that I had just witnessed something absolutely incredible.

We soon fell into the rhythm of the home. We found out more about the other homes in Mexico City and beyond. We heard that 'Road Trips', also known as 'Faith Trips', were very common in the Family in Mexico. Teams of between five and ten or so would take a minivan down to Acapulco or other beach resorts with no money and just enough food for the drive. A hotel or apartment would be 'provisioned' and so would all our meals and drinks.

Once there, we would hit the restaurants and sing and sell. Then we would provision a meal and after that, we would go from hotel to hotel looking for somewhere to sleep. It was exhausting work, which we were expected to do without 'murmuring, griping or bellyaching'. We were expected to have a 'cheerful, grateful and humble spirit' and to always 'be yielded to do the Lord's work'. On these trips, I watched the tourists having a wonderful time, swimming in the sea, eating delicious food and partying, and wondered again, Why can't we just be normal? Why couldn't we just relax and have fun like everyone else? One small blessing was that we got to provision our food. We would sing for the restaurant owner and then ask for food. It was terribly embarrassing and humiliating. But more often than not, the owner would generously wave us in and provide us with delicious Mexican food.

Uncle Jorge was extra nice to me and complimented my 'many talents'. He was fun and funny and would make me laugh. He wasn't like the other uncles, I thought. He was cool and treated me like a grown-up. He often called me 'linda' ('pretty'), a term of endearment in Spanish and often gave me extra-long hugs, stroking my hair. 'Que linda!' ('How lovely!') he would say to me and smile. I loved the attention. It made such a change to always having to be on guard in case I put a foot wrong and got into trouble! I think I might be getting a secret crush on Uncle Jorge, I thought.

One time, when no one was around, he laughed at something I said. 'Que linda, Faithy!' he gently cupped my face and gave me a light peck on the lips. My tummy flipped, but I was also shocked. I'm only fourteen and he's forty! I thought. I knew he wasn't allowed to flirt with me like that because the rules about teens and adults sharing had changed six months before. Even when you reached fifteen, you were only allowed to share with other teens, but anyone over twenty-one had to stick to adults only. The 'persecution' had seen to that, with systemite police coming close to raiding some Family homes, the fear being that they would take the children away. The new rules didn't stop the grown-ups from breaking them, though.

The 25 April 1988 was a Saturday, and also my birthday. I asked the singing team leader if I could be excused from going witnessing that day, for a birthday treat. Both Mum and Jorge heard me trying to weasel out of going out, but they insisted I still had to. I sulked, grabbed my guitar and got into the van, but this witnessing trip was cut short. We only sang in one restaurant instead of the usual four.

When we pulled into the garage, we were told to go back upstairs. There was a huge cry of 'Surprise!' when I walked into the living room, trailed by the other teens and kids. I couldn't believe it! A surprise party just for me! The teens and older kids from the other homes in the city had been invited to drop in after their witnessing trips for party food and games. Mum and Jorge stood there smiling broadly as I took in the decorations and delicious snacks laid out on the table, a huge chocolate cake the crowning glory. In all, there were about thirty teens and kids. The adults and little children came down to join in too. We even got to listen to systemite music! The speakers blared with 'Rock Around the Clock'. It hadn't been long since Grandpa had said that we teens could learn to dance the Sock Hop during Dance Night and said we could play 1950s music.

We played games, danced and ate. All the adults had smiles on their faces as they watched us dance; some even joined in. Jorge asked me to dance. He was a good dancer, and I was happy he asked me, but then I looked over to see Aunty Tatiana sitting on a sofa, hand on her heavily pregnant belly, looking back in our direction. If looks could kill, I would've been dead. I was shocked and felt dirty, ashamed and puzzled. What had I done wrong?

It wasn't long after my fifteenth birthday that my family was separated again. I stayed in San Ángel, while Dinah and Bev were sent to another home on the other side of town and Mum, Dad, Michael, Petra and Maria were sent to a home in Cuernavaca. These moves were all done very matter-of-factly and were no big deal to us anymore. We had grown used to the separations.

After the party, Jorge started to find moments to be alone with me. He gave me extra special attention. 'You're fifteen now, Faithy! A big girl . . . you can start sharing with the other teens if you want to . . . I wish I could share with you . . .' he would say, starry-eyed, and squeeze my hand. I swallowed hard, frightened.

'We're not allowed to because the rules have changed now!' I said, secretly relieved that the pressure was off. Or so I thought.

'I know, but it's such a shame because I think you are beautiful, and I would love to share with you . . .'

'Yes, well . . . we can at least hold hands and we can still have a crush on each other. That would be nice,' I replied, innocently.

I was so flattered and touched that he thought that little goofy, chubby, ugly duckling me was beautiful.

'*Bella,*' he would say and kiss me gently on the lips, when no one was looking.

He would come into the girls' room to say goodnight. The teen and pre-teen girls shared a room with three bunkbeds. Some slept on the floor. His daughters would jump up to hug him. I was on the top bunk and one day, he switched the lights out and said, 'Let's pray.'

He had positioned himself next to my bunk and as he prayed, he slipped his hand under the covers and started stroking my legs. I felt a mixture of fear, disgust and sexual arousal. It was disturbing and exciting at the same time. This started to happen every night and his touching and kissing got bolder and bolder.

One Saturday, when it was his turn to drive the singing team, after we got home and drove into the garage he said: 'Faith, stay back with me for a little while and help me get these bags in the house.' The others rushed inside. When we were alone, he grabbed me and started kissing me passionately and feeling me up.

'I want to share with you, Faith,' he whispered in my ears as he kissed my neck. 'I have the faith to share with you even if the rules have changed. I always shared with the teen girls before the rules changed . . .'

I understood that having 'the faith' for something meant he had the courage to do it, the belief that the Lord allows us to do what we like as long as it's done 'in love'. I felt frightened, disgusted, overpowered and powerless. I didn't want to 'share' with him. Of that I was instantly sure as his tongue forced its way into my mouth, and I certainly didn't want to break the rules and get us all into trouble. I knew that for breaking such an important rule, I could be sent to a detention camp and Jorge could be separated from his wives and children. Besides, he was forty. It was one thing to have a teenage crush, to steal a kiss or a hug from time to time; it was quite another to have full-blown sex with a man who was old enough to be my father. The thought was frightening and a complete turn-off.

A couple of weeks later, Jorge announced we were going on a road trip to Puerto Vallarta to witness to the tourists. The team would be him, Tatiana, his first wife who was eight months pregnant, a single 'brother' called Manuel, three of Jorge's eldest daughters – Theresa, eleven, Meek, ten, Lilly, eight – and me.

The day arrived and we got up really early as it was a ten-hour drive from Mexico City to Puerto Vallarta. We packed some sandwiches, an overnight bag and two guitars. Jorge and I would play and the children were to perform their cute little dance routine. The three girls were Tatiana's daughters and like her, they were cute with very blond hair. The trip was exhausting and even though I was a bit wary of Aunty Tatiana, I felt sorry for her and her big belly. The journey was long, hot and dusty and winding. We finally arrived in the late afternoon, exhausted. It was around 5:30 p.m. and we had yet to provision a hotel.

We sat by the side of the beach eating the last of our sandwiches and watched the sun go down. Then we hit the road again. We went from resort to hotel, resort to hotel. We would pile in and Jorge would ask for the manager. There we were, a heavily pregnant 'gringa', three little blond girls, two men and a Latina teenage girl. Time after the time the manager would say, 'So sorry, we don't have free rooms,' or 'I'm not able to give free rooms'. By 10 p.m. we were desperate. The children and Tatiana were absolutely exhausted. Finally, just as we began to worry that we all might have to sleep in the car for the night, a friendly manager agreed to give us two rooms for two nights. What a relief!

The resort was lovely. The rooms were more like apartments: a living room with a sofa bed, a camping cot and a kitchenette with a balcony with views to the sea, and a large bedroom with a huge double bed and en suite. The smaller room was given to Tatiana where she shared the bed with her eldest daughter and Manuel slept on the cot in the living area.

I was put in Jorge's apartment. He would share the bed with eight-year-old Lily, I would sleep on the sofa bed and ten-year-old Meek would have the cot. We all fell asleep immediately.

The next morning, the manager invited us to have some breakfast from the buffet. What a treat! After breakfast, we hit the restaurants, singing and selling our wares. By late afternoon, we were all tired. It was hard work, performing and selling in the hot weather. When we got back to the resort we were allowed to go for a swim in the pool. Tatiana went for a nap, Manuel went for a walk and Jorge and I swam with the girls. He sidled up to me in the pool when the girls were distracted and started to touch me all over.

'Faith, I want you to share with me tonight. I will call you into my room when Lily and Meek are asleep. Don't fall asleep, OK?'

'OK . . .' I replied. A jolt of fear coursed through me.

Although I was very frightened, I was also excited at the same time. It was the thrill of doing something that I knew wasn't allowed. We were being disobedient. Worse. A grown-up was encouraging me to be disobedient and then to lie by keeping a secret, and I believed Jesus would know about it.

'You must promise to keep this a total secret. If you tell anyone, they will rip me away from the girls and the rest of my family and you will be sent to the detention camp. OK?'

I agreed. I had a crush on Jorge and I thought I was so grown up even though I had just turned fifteen. I felt flattered that I had what I thought was some kind of power over an all-powerful grown-up.

That night, we provisioned a meal from one of the local restaurants and it was late before we got back to the resort and went into our respective rooms. Meek and Lily were fast asleep in no time. I lay in bed and the anticipation of what I was about to do filled me with absolute terror. When Jorge opened the door and whispered for me to come in, I got out of bed and walked towards the room. I started to shake uncontrollably.

'Hello *linda*,' he said and pulled me into the room, closing the door. I was shaking so much that my teeth began to chatter.

'But . . . but . . . Lily is sleeping on the bed . . .' I said.

'She won't wake up, don't worry,' he said sitting on the bed and pulling me over. 'Let's pray,' he said as he felt me up and down, hands under my nightie, running over my breasts, legs and crotch. I continued to shake and tried to control my teeth chattering. I was embarrassed by my reaction.

'Jesus, we have the faith to share together, whatever is done in love is without sin, in Jesus's name, Amen.'

He pulled me onto the bed; as I continued to shake, he parted my legs and got on top of me and started to rub his dick up and down my private parts.

'You're shaking, are you OK?' he said as he continued to rub. I wondered why he hadn't noticed before.

'Yes . . .' I said, teeth still chattering. By now I was starting to wish I were somewhere else. I wished I could take it all back. But it was too late and I knew there would be no going back.

Then he was inside of me. Two minutes later it was all over and I was still shaking.

'God bless you, *linda*,' he said, giving me a peck on the cheek.

I got up and went to the toilet to wash – his sperm was all over my legs where he had pulled out. I was still shaking as I washed. When I got into bed I felt totally disgusted, ashamed and guilty.

'This is all your fault,' I said to myself as I curled up into the foetal position, hugging myself. The next morning the same routine, singing, selling, but this time we had to find somewhere else to sleep. Again, the provisioning was very hard but eventually someone gave us a room where we all bundled in. We were given cots and spare blankets. The next morning, we got up early and made the long journey home.

Over the next few days, I rationalised what had happened. I told myself it's no big deal, I was mature, it wasn't my first time, and I did have a crush on him. Jorge carried on touching me up at every opportunity. He would pull me into a bathroom to kiss and grope me. He would screw me in his bedroom when I was minding his baby, push me into the garage to screw me. Every time, I would freeze. It would be over in a matter of minutes and I never felt any pleasure. The fear of being caught and the certainty that it would be all my fault saw to that.

'We must be extremely careful, *linda*, that no one ever finds out or we will be in big trouble.'

'Don't worry, I won't tell,' I reassured him.

All the while this was going on, there were lots of adults, kids and teens milling about the home, following the daily schedule, and all the while, we dodged and ducked and dived, pretending nothing was going on. Families would come and go but there would almost always be between thirty and fifty people in the home. One day, Jorge said he thought Josiah, Tatiana's second husband, was getting suspicious.

'I'm very worried, *linda*, I think he's getting suspicious and I'm worried he might tell Tatiana and then Mirna will find out and we could all be in so much trouble. I've seen the way he looks at you, you're so beautiful . . .' he said, flattering me. Jorge would bring this up often so I started to pay attention to Josiah looking at me. One day it occurred to me that if I were to get him to break the rules too and sleep with me, he wouldn't tell of his suspicions about Jorge. Jorge thought that was a brilliant idea.

'Tatiana, Mirna and I have to go to the United States to fix some paperwork in two weeks' time so Josiah will be alone,' he said.

The day of Jorge, Tatiana and Mirna's departure came. I flirted with Josiah all day and that night, when I knew the kids would be asleep, I knocked on his bedroom door. He looked delighted to see me there and let me in. He sat on the side of the bed and I simply went up to him, put my arms around his neck, hopped onto his lap and let him screw me. When it was over, I just got up and went to the loo. I didn't feel bad. I felt in control. I gave no thought to how Tatiana might feel if she found out, having just given birth to his baby. I felt I was doing what needed to be done to protect Jorge and to protect myself.

Jorge was proud of me when he came back and I told him what I had done.

'We'll be going on another road trip to Acapulco soon!' he announced. 'This time though, we will be staying in one of Ricardo's hotels!'

Ricardo was a very wealthy 'king'. He was a 'fish' and was very good friends with Jorge. There were quite a number of us who went along; we sang and sold in restaurants and again, I longed to just be normal.

Ricardo was in his late thirties. He was portly with curly black hair and a moustache. He welcomed us graciously and was very happy to see us. In the evening he welcomed us to his restaurant and said: 'Order whatever you like!' His waiters ran around us trying to impress their patrón.

The next day, Jorge said to me, '*Linda*, Ricardo would like to take you out to dinner, just you and him. This is a good opportunity for you to witness to him and you can take your guitar. He likes to be sung to.'

'On my own?' I asked.

'Yes, but I made it clear that he can't share with you and that you must be back by ten p.m.' I was relieved.

That entire day, Jorge looked worried. He came up to me a few times saying: 'Don't worry, *linda*. He'll have you back by ten,' and then: 'He knows the rules have changed and we can't share with teen girls anymore. He's been used to sharing with the teen girls . . .' he trailed off.

In my innocence I wasn't worried because I trusted Jorge. I knew Jorge and he had a close relationship because Ricardo owned the home we lived in in Mexico City as well as the van we used to go out witnessing in.

Ricardo picked me up in his fancy Mercedes and took me for a drive. He did most of the talking, showing me landmarks and pointing at hotels or condominiums that belonged to him. Then we drove out of the touristy area up into the surrounding hills. Higher and higher the car climbed. The air became chilly so he wound up the windows. Then he pulled into a *mirador* (stopping place). It was quiet and no one was around. I started to feel nervous. He pointed across the bay. 'Look,' he said, pointing to twinkling lights on the other side of the bay. 'Over there is the famous Pyramid Hotel.' Then he went quiet. I started to feel worried and creeped out in the silence as he looked out into the bay. He seemed to be thinking, his eyes moving this way and that. I have no reason to be nervous, I thought. He's been nice this whole time . . .

'Why don't I sing to you now!' I said, distracting him.

'OK,' he said. I got out of the car and took my guitar from the back seat. I sat back down in the front seat next to him and began singing all the songs I knew. He never said a word, just kept staring out to the sea. I was running out of songs and was getting tired. I could tell it was almost 10 p.m.

Finally he said: 'That was lovely, *linda*. Let's go eat.'

He started the engine. 'But Jorge said you were taking me back at ten,' I said.

'Oh, don't worry about Jorge, he'll be fine.'

He took me back down the valley and stopped outside a fancy restaurant in the main boulevard. The area was packed with happy people dining and strolling. He ordered for me: a fizzy drink and *cabrito* (a goat dish) and lots of accoutrements, then dessert.

He chatted away and I just listened and nodded. It was gone midnight by the time he drove me back to the hotel. When I arrived, Jorge was waiting in lobby. He was pale, his eyes looked slightly panicked and I felt that his hands were clammy on my shoulders.

'What happened, *linda*?' he said, worried.

'Nothing.' I said. I told him about the evening.

'Oh, thank God, I was very worried. You'd better get to bed now,' he said.

Back in Mexico City, life resumed as normal and that included sharing. The adults, Jorge included, swapped bedrooms regularly and openly. This was not unusual and was simply part of everyday life. At first, I struggled with feelings of jealousy when Jorge matter-of-factly would tell me who he was sharing with. One day, after one such announcement, I found a quiet corner and had a word with myself: 'You need to shut off your emotions, you must harden your heart.' A steely determination came over me and I felt a new coldness.

I began to notice one of the aunties, Maria, looking at me with curiosity. My danger radar was on alert, so I made an effort to give her a wide berth. One day, the teen shepherdess announced: 'Teens, those of you fifteen and up, as you've been working so hard, we have arranged for you to have the dining room on Saturday night so you can watch a movie and have sharing time. You can take your mattresses down and we'll make you some popcorn. Please don't cum inside the girls, boys, we don't want them getting pregnant.'

The boys were over the moon. I liked Paul and Josiah, they were cute and sweet, so that's what we did. The four of us, Theresa, Paul, Josiah and I, put our mattresses downstairs, watched a movie, screwed, swapped and screwed again. It was disappointing for me that I didn't feel turned on. I felt no pleasure; it was as if I was going through the motions. I wondered if Theresa felt the same as me. The other three seemed to be enjoying themselves. What's wrong with me? I thought.

The same thing happened a few months later with another group of teens when I stayed for a few weeks in the home on the other side of town. I decided there was definitely something wrong with me, I should have been turned on by the whole idea, like the others seemed to be. But I wasn't. I felt bored and disappointed.

I noticed that Jorge was starting to avoid me. I asked him what was wrong, but he refused to discuss it. He started to blank me completely, which was hugely upsetting. When I approached him, even when there was nobody else around, he snapped: 'Don't talk to me!'

All physical niceties and contact stopped cold. I started to lose weight. I lost about 5kg, which Aunty Maria pointed out. About three weeks later, I cornered Jorge when we were alone in the kitchen, demanding to know what was going on. He told me that Maria, who disliked Jorge, was suspicious that something was going on between us and reported it to the area shepherds. He looked very worried and told me again that I must not admit anything or there would be hell to pay. The area shepherds were visiting in a week, and had asked my parents, who were living in another home two hours away, to attend this meeting. I was terrified. For an entire week, I could barely eat or sleep. The stress was terrible. Finally the day arrived. I heard the door go and Mum and Dad walked into the living room, as well as the area shepherds: Aunty Kerenina, who was part of the Caribbean crew, but was now together with Uncle Silas.

I followed Mum into the corridor as she went to the loo: 'Mum! Mummy! What's going on?' I said, terror on my face. I hadn't seen her for months. She turned around, looked at me and said, 'No. I'm not going to discuss this with you. Don't talk to me!' She walked into the bathroom and slammed the door in my face. I went to find a corner to hide and cry.

This meeting was held just between the grown-ups. Afterwards Jorge told me that I was to pack my stuff as I was being moved to Aunty Kerenina and Uncle Silas's home for the foreseeable future. He told me he had denied everything, saying I must absolutely do the same. I felt bereft and terrified and I realised I would probably never see him again. I promised I would keep my mouth shut.

Karenina and Silas's home was another big one, filled with lots of teens, new disciples and families with young kids. When I arrived, I was told the shepherds had gone away on business for a couple of weeks. One of the aunties told me they would deal with me when they came back.

For two weeks I agonised and lost more weight. Finally, they came back from the trip and the date and time was set for a meeting between the three of us. They called me into the room.

'Hello sweetie,' said Aunty Kerenina. Aunty Kerenina had beautiful thick, long chestnut hair. She always wore a smile and was one of the sweet aunties. Even so, she was a top leader in the Family so I was always on guard around her. Silas was stern. He stared at me and began to quiz me. He came straight to the point:

'Have you been having sex with Jorge?'

'No.' I looked him straight in the eye.

He didn't believe me and carried on with his questioning.

'We think you're lying to us, Faith. I think you're not telling me the truth,' he said, even more sternly. I denied it and denied it.

'Yes, I have been looking after his baby but we haven't done anything, please believe me,' I lied and lied, my heart pounding.

Silas started to get agitated and Karenina looked stern. After forty minutes of this, I felt the heat rise to my face and started to feel dizzy and unwell. I tried to hold it down. Suddenly, Aunty Kerenina noticed something was wrong. 'Honey, are you feeling unwell? You look pink and you're starting to sweat!' She leant over and felt my cheeks. They were feverish, burning.

'Silas, Faith has broken into a fever. Let's stop the meeting now,' she said.

'OK,' Silas said, and turning to me: 'Faith, we will be sending you to the teen home in Guadalajara in one week's time on the next convoy up there. I hope you're better by then.' Kerenina told me I should get into bed straight away. Three days later, I was better, and not long after that, I set off with a group of other teens on the long trip to Guadalajara.

I was only at the teen home for two weeks. During that time, when I was on garden duty, I saw that Uncle Andrew and a number of other people had arrived and were unpacking their stuff into some of the outhouses, which were cabins away from the main building. I liked Uncle Andrew and his wife Kathrina. They were one of the 'fun' couples and were the shepherds of the home on the other side of town that Dinah and Bev had been sent to.

'Where is Aunty Kathrina?' I asked him, following him into his cabin.

'They've separated us, we're learning lessons,' he said. 'Come here, honey.' He beckoned me over as he sat on the bed. As soon as I walked up to him, he pulled me towards him in between his legs and started to feel me up and down, kissing me all over. I was stunned and froze; I didn't pull away. After a few minutes he stopped.

'I'm sorry, Faith, I'm sorry I did that. Please don't tell anyone.'

It was miserable at the teen home. I kept to myself as the other teens were well into their established cliques. The routine was very rigid, every hour of the day scheduled, and we were expected to hit the restaurants in teams at the weekend to sing and sell. The weather was sweltering hot and it was exhausting. There was never a free moment. However, my time there was short-lived. After three or four weeks, I was told to pack my stuff again. This time I was going to England with my mum; we were to set off in a week's time. I was excited and hopeful but worried that Mum was angry with me.

My mind raced with questions: 'Why have I been chosen to go to England with Mum? What's going to happen to the rest of my siblings? Are they going to join us later?'

My questions were soon answered when I was reunited with Mum in the home on the other side of town, in Mexico City. 'We are all going to England, darling, except Dinah and Bev. Dinah will stay with baby

Robert in Mexico, but Bev will eventually join us. You and I will go first to pave the way.'

'Why me, Mummy?' I asked her.

'I'm worried about you, darling. I think you're better off coming with me.'

I was surprised and thrilled that Mum should choose me to be the first one to go back to her homeland.

CHAPTER 16: Mothering – 2001

I decided I wanted to have my first child before my thirtieth birthday. For that to become a reality, I would have to make further changes to my lifestyle. Party drugs were no longer on the scene but smoking and drinking were still my favourite habits. I enjoyed smoking and carried my Benson & Hedges with me everywhere. I loved the ritual of lighting up after a meal, and the mindful sensation of rolling a spliff in the evening followed by the floaty, mellow buzz of it. Aside from the desire for a baby, I had not the slightest inclination to give up even though I was plagued by guilt because of the damage I knew I was doing to my body. I explained my predicament to Mum, and she said:

'Why don't you explain that to God and then just give him permission to change your mind?' So that's what I did. I sat down before bed one night and said: 'God. I don't want to give this up, I adore it. But I give you the permission to change my mind. I give you permission.'

I kept repeating the prayer, every day for six months, galvanised by my desire to have a healthy body for my baby to grow in. One day I woke up, and I knew I was ready to stop. I called Mum: 'Mummy! I'm ready to give up now! I'm ready to give up! Will you come round and pray for me?' Mum was so pleased.

'Well done, you clever girl!' she said.

She came over, sat next to me on the sofa and laid hands on me. She said a prayer as I humbly listened and agreed. As she prayed and I agreed, I felt like a cloud had been lifted from me.

This is what it must mean to have a monkey come off your back, I thought. I never thought I would be able to give up smoking. It was my crutch. My friend. This felt like another miracle had just happened to me. A gift.

By now, I was working for a marketing agency. It was fast-paced and stressful, but I enjoyed it. At times I was managing up to seven clients and their projects at once, and twenty temps, training them to sell on behalf of my clients. There were a lot of deadlines to juggle. Jules was doing well at work, too. He had got a very well-paid job as a sales and marketing manager for an IT consultancy.

After quitting smoking, we got pregnant quickly. I knew my job wouldn't be compatible with the demands of a small baby but felt secure in that, if I needed to take time out, Jules could support us for a while, at least. Unexpectedly, when I was four months pregnant, Jules was made redundant. It was a worrying time; our baby was due and we were anxious about how we'd pay the mortgage on the property we had only just bought.

Jules was determined in his search for work and picked up short consulting contracts, but it was unsettling because, more than anything, I wanted to be there for the baby when it came. Although I could never describe my childhood as ordinary or secure, Mummy had been present in my early years. She was a stay-at-home mum and even though she was very busy, she was usually always there. I wanted to be there for my babies too.

Theo's birth was difficult. I was in a lot of pain at the end of the pregnancy because the baby was pressing against my ribs. The due date of 10 May came and went and when I still hadn't gone into labour by 20 May, they induced me. Being induced was horribly painful, but even after I'd been put on the drip, I had no contractions. The baby had decided to stay put and refused to come. My bump was wired up with a baby heart monitor and after a couple of hours it started to bleep. The nurse rushed in.

'The baby is getting distressed; we need to perform an emergency caesarean,' she said, looking worried.

I was devastated and frightened for the baby. I cried unashamedly as Mum and the nurse helped to undress me and put me into a theatre gown. I was put onto a hospital bed that was wheeled into theatre. I felt like a beached whale. To my utter mortification, I was greeted very sweetly by three young, very good-looking men.

'We're going to get you ready for your C-section, Faith, we are going to give you an epidural. Now. Let's roll you over onto your side . . . gently does it!' said one of them encouragingly. As the bed was lowered, I was rolled over; the gown opened up, as it's designed to do, exposing my entire huge behind.

Oh, the shame of it! I thought, as I cringed and sniffled. 'You must stay very still, Faith. I am going to put a needle in your back, just by your coccyx. It's very important that you stay as still as you can as I perform this procedure. You have said you want to remain conscious for the birth of your baby so you will feel nothing from the neck down after a few minutes. Are you ready?'

'I'm ready,' I whispered, and the full realisation of what was about to happen hit me.

The epidural started to take effect. The theatre was bustling with activity, with nurses and anaesthetists readying themselves for the surgeon. I spied Mum and Jules gowned up, with blue shower caps on their heads. I smiled, amused. I was rolled onto my back. By now, I was totally paralysed from the neck down and a feeling of panic began to rise within me. I am at the mercy of these strangers in this room! There is nothing I can do about it, I can't move! The drugs, and the weight of my bump pressing down onto my lungs, were making it difficult to breathe.

I realised very quickly that I had to calm my thoughts or I would lose control. I distracted myself by focusing on the movements of the medical staff around me. Then a large man in a gown walked in.

'Hello Faith, I'm going to deliver your baby now. It won't take long!' he said. Jules sat at the head of bed with me. I looked at the end of the bed where a screen obscured the view, but I could see the surgeon working. I felt tugging and pulling and suddenly, a weight lifted off and my breathing became easier. I heard a cry. My heart leaped for joy.

'Congratulations! It's a boy!' said the surgeon. The baby was wrapped in a towel and handed to Jules.

'Put him under the lamp for a few minutes, please,' Jules was instructed. After a few minutes of anxious waiting, Jules brought me the baby and put his little face right up to mine. I looked in wonder into his blue eyes and noticed he had strawberry-blond hair. I couldn't hold him as I was still paralysed and the surgeon was busy working on closing up my wound.

I felt immediately overwhelmed by a rush of love and the sense that I never wanted to let him out of my sight, ever. I quickly realised I was going to have to adapt to his timetable. After spending the first half of my life under restrictive control, I'd become used to my freedom, so it was a huge adjustment. Later, looking at his scrunched-up face as I held him in my arms in the hospital, I felt it as a fact: I must submit to this. I must be present. His needs *must* come first. The implications of this shocked me. It meant I was going to have to give up a huge amount of control to Jules, too. I was going back to work, part-time, but he would take over as the main earner. This didn't sit well with me – it made me feel vulnerable. In my twenties, I had felt in control for the first time ever, and now a little part of me felt as if I was going backwards. My husband and my son were in control now.

In the first few weeks at home with our new baby, my sole focus was on feeding him. Getting him to latch on was very tricky at the beginning and my nipples were excruciatingly sore, cracked and bleeding. Finally, we got the hang of it and Theo and I spent hour upon hour on the sofa as he suckled away. A few days later, my milk came in. I looked in the mirror at my humongous breasts. My olive skin was in stark contrast to what looked like inflated white party balloons with a couple of cracked cherries on the end, stuck to my chest. I laughed out loud. 'Jules! Check this out!' I called him over. We fell about laughing.

I tried to get Theo to stick to a schedule. Just when I thought we'd got the hang of things, it would fall apart and we'd have to start all over again. When Theo went down for a nap, I would rush into the shower and whip around the house tidying up. My days, and nights, were full of activity and it was exhausting but very rewarding. My time no longer belonged to me, it belonged to him. Once I had accepted this, I was at peace and able to enjoy it. I was overwhelmed with love for Theo. Jules was very supportive and helped me with all the chores. We bought a breast pump so he could take turns feeding him and I could have a break and go to the shops on my own.

Going back to work when Theo was eight months old was one of the most difficult things I ever had to do, even though it was only part-time. We decided to put him into a nursery. It was really hard to give him up to the nursery assistant. He cried his little eyes out and my heart was breaking. I sat in my car outside the nursery during that first hour-long 'settling' session. As I sat there anxiously waiting, I knew that I would need to learn to trust a little and cede control.

The experience of being a new mum made me think again about my own mother and the choices she had made. I looked at Theo and cried. So many conflicting emotions rose up within me. On the one hand, I was filled with compassion for my mum. She had been born just after the war in 1941. In those days, girls were taught that all they could hope to achieve in life was to find a good husband, get married, stay at home and have children. This is exactly what my mother had wanted and expected. She was taught that a woman should be loyal, supportive and follow her husband. I realised, as a married woman now myself, that on the face of it, these are good values if you are lucky enough to marry a decent, good man as I had. I asked myself, would I follow Jules, no matter what? The answer to that was an emphatic no.

Even so, becoming a mother had put me on the back foot. I realised that Mum had abdicated her personal responsibility and handed it over to my father and to the cult. This had happened over time, at first making what seemed like small bad choices and going against her better judgement until it was too late. The little compromises soon turned into huge ones. When she did that, it opened the doors of hell for herself and for us, her children. This realisation put the fear of God into me. I thought, There but for the grace of God go I, and I thanked my lucky stars that I hadn't become a perpetrator myself and that I had engineered my escape before it was too late.

I wondered how could it be that Mum had behaved so carelessly towards us, entrusting our care to people she barely knew? How could she have been so willing to let us go to stay in other homes, and to give so little thought to the consequences of the lifestyle she and my dad chose for us, moving from country to country, depriving us of a home, of an education, of a consistent group of friends? I felt judgemental, confused and angry. Even as I watched my mother with my new baby in her arms, I imagined her as she had been with us. She had been loving, strict and fun, but had made some terrible mistakes. I also marvelled at her strength. She had buried her oldest daughter two weeks before giving birth to her youngest daughter. After we left the cult, she had the courage to face up to her mistakes and sought our forgiveness. She was as supportive as she could be and always loving.

I started questioning all of my own thoughts about parenting. Why do I think what I think? And why do I believe what I believe? I interrogated each of my assumptions in turn. Did I believe I should expect absolute, unquestioning obedience from my children? Was that because Mum and Dad had drummed it into me? If so, was that a good reason to believe them? Were they good judges of right and wrong? I was aware that Mum had been wonderful in lots of ways as a mother. She was warm and fun and loving, but temporarily, I lost sight of that. I felt so overwhelmed by a fresh awareness of all of the bad logic, the self-justification and the denial that had accompanied my itinerant childhood, that it became hard to hold onto what had been good.

In my mind, I set out the kind of parent I wanted to be, defining myself in opposition to the parenting I had experienced as a child. I would discipline my children and teach them good manners but I would not beat them as I had been beaten. I would not try to control them or their thoughts. I would encourage them to develop their own thinking, their own ideas about how they wanted to live. I would offer them a stable base to build from. I would never presume other adults were trustworthy. I would never let them sleep over at a friend's house because I knew I wouldn't be able to trust other parents: a hazard of my own experience. I understood the potential cost too acutely.

When Theo was two years old, we decided to get pregnant again. I was so excited and wondered if I'd be getting a little girl this time. We went for the three-month scan and I hopped onto the examination bed. As the nurse put the jelly on my tummy, I felt a jolt of excitement and a sudden realisation hit me. I turned my head to Jules and said, 'Jules! It's going to be another boy! I know it's going to be another boy!' The nurse smiled and put the scanner on my tummy. The screen lit up and sure enough, there was my baby, and there was no doubt whatsoever that it was a boy.

I hoped and prayed I would have the privilege of experiencing a natural birth this time. My pregnancy was easier physically. I left my part-time job and started to help Jules in his business from home. I loved the freedom that this afforded me and the routine of being a mum to a toddler and being pregnant again. As my due date approached, I started to feel anxious. 'Please God, let me have my baby naturally.' One morning, my eyes flew open. 'Something is going on!' I sat up, waddled to the bathroom and stood in the bath. My waters were breaking. 'Jules! Jules, come!' Jules rushed into the bathroom. 'My waters! My waters!' He was smiling all over his face.

'Quick! Call Mum!' The contractions started slowly and began intensifying that afternoon.

'I wonder if I'll have a natural birth?' I crossed my fingers and toes. By 8 p.m. that evening, the contractions were excruciating. I couldn't believe I was capable of experiencing so much pain. Jules led me into the car and Mum jumped in the back seat.

In the hospital, I was readied for the birth and given gas and air. 'Oh, this is fun!' I said with a naughty glint in my eye to Jules and Mum and as I greedily sucked into the mask. 'Let's have a go!' said Jules enthusiastically. I passed him the mask. Mum said, 'I'll have a turn!' When the nurse came to check on me, the three of us were giggling, high as kites. It didn't last long for me, though. The contractions kept coming. I was screeching my head off and had Jules in a headlock. I was surprised at myself, at my lack of control. The second I'd recover from one contraction, the next one would arrive. At 10 p.m. that night, Jude literally flew out.

My mother-in-law had given me a yellow sun-shaped inflatable ring. 'You might need it to sit on, after the birth, my dear,' she said. I thought that was strange. Two days later, the inflatable ring came into its own. I found myself back at home on the sofa, new baby clamped to my boob and a bright yellow inflatable ring under my bum. Why the heck had I been so set on experiencing this torture and pain? I thought. Theo tried to tug the inflatable out from under me. 'It's mine! It's my toy, Mummy!' I looked at Jules, a pleading look on my face. 'Come along now, Theo,' said Jules. 'Let's play trains!'

During my pregnancy and the long hours spent feeding baby Jude, I went through another reassessment of my beliefs. It started because I caught the end of a documentary about lice. The voiceover was talking about how we can study a key event in the evolution of Homo sapiens, the loss of our primate hair, by investigating the genetics of lice. I was shocked and struck by a sudden awareness of the magnitude of my ignorance about science, particularly evolutionary theory. I had been taught that the world was made in six days, that the theory of evolution was a lie of the Devil, designed to destroy our belief in God. And despite the studying phase I went through in my late teens and early twenties, I had left evolution unexplored and hadn't given it much thought. Now, conscious of my responsibility as a mother, I wanted to know. I read voraciously, researched and learnt. I lost myself for months on end. As I learnt, I was alarmed by the intensity of my reaction to the new information. I felt freaked out by my new knowledge, and somehow bereft. It was the same feeling as when I'd found Mum in bed with Uncle Peter, as if a structure I had taken for granted had been kicked out from underneath me. I turned back to the Bible again, rereading it with fresh perspective. I came to the realisation that when it came to the Bible and questions about God and the metaphysical, I was more comfortable with the questions than the answers. To me, it seemed more honest to say, 'I don't know for sure'.

I didn't for a moment lose my personal faith, though, and for a while when the children were very little we continued going to church as a family. It was on a church weekend away that my instincts were tested. Theo was five and Jude was a toddler. There were at least twenty families there, staying in pods that connected to a central kitchen and hall. I really liked the people we had met through our new church which, although evangelical, was not fundamentalist. They were mild and pleasant, mainly middle class, and English. There were lots of guitars and singing, and sometimes socials for the adults.

One of the church dads, Rich, was married to a mother who had befriended me in the group. They were in the same pod as us. He was a senior policeman, and she was an occupational therapist. They had a young son the same age as Theo. Rich and his wife were the children's pastors, responsible for children's church. Rich constantly seemed to be on child and crèche duty – and never seemed to take a turn to join the grown-up worship, even though his wife did. We would all drop our children off at the crèche, which was set up in the room next to the main hall, whilst we went to church meetings. At the time, I felt a prickle of anxiety about it, but there were lots of other grown-up helpers around so I told myself not to be silly. The boys would cry when we left them there, but they cried at nursery, too, so I didn't think too much of it. Subconsciously, though, I was on my guard around Rich.

On the Saturday morning of the weekend in question, Jules was getting ready to go out to play golf with a few of the dads from the group. We had been told that one or two of the adults from each pod would be needed to volunteer for babysitting duties for the evening activity, so that the rest of the grown-ups could enjoy some dancing and have a few drinks. I took Jules to one side before he headed out and said: 'You watch. I swear to you, Rich will volunteer to babysit; there's something not right about him. I saw the way he looked at the children at bath time last night, I didn't like it. It was familiar to me. You mark my words: he will volunteer . . . and I'm not leaving our children with him.'

Jules said: 'Oh, please, Faith. Don't be so silly! You're being ridiculous. It's natural you're paranoid: you grew up in a cult surrounded by perverts, but you can't apply the same thinking to the rest of the world . . . you're suspicious of everyone.'

When he said that, it was like he'd woken up the tiger in me. I was pissed off and pushed back. 'No, Jules. You are wrong and I am right. I swear to you that I am right. Just you wait.'

I spent that sunny morning outside with the other mums having coffee and watching the little ones play with their toys. Theo was playing trains on the floor with two other little boys and Jude started to fuss. I picked Jude up and balanced him on his chubby feet. He clutched my fingers and I walked him a little way away from the rest of the group, singing him a song. I had a feeling someone was watching me, so I looked up. There was Rich, purposefully walking towards me. As he approached, he said with certainty: 'Hi Faith! About tonight. You two have a night off, chill out with everyone else. I don't mind being on child duty so that the rest of the adults in our pod can join in.'

My heart stopped, my tummy flipped, and my knees felt weak. 'Oh. Thanks Rich, I'll speak to Jules when he gets back . . .' I said, smiling, nausea rising. It was as if I was a child again, that feeling of being asked to do something I knew was wrong, but feeling unable to say no. My body froze. The rest of the morning went by in a blur. I was scared and didn't take my eyes off my boys for a second. I couldn't wait for Jules to get back from playing golf. Then I saw him and the gaggle of happy men walking towards us. Theo ran up to Jules, his arms outstretched. He picked him up and looked over at me. His smile faded.

I was furious. 'I want to talk to you,' I said, swiping Jude into my arms and walking back towards the pod. 'I told you! I told you! I told you that bastard was going to try and get his hands on my boys!' I ranted, pacing up and down our bedroom, ringing my hands. Jules went white.

'What do you mean? What happened?'

I was livid and terrified at the same time.

'Don't you ever question me again. I am the mother and I know. I know best! We're getting the fuck out of here and going home,' I said, sobbing.

Jules hugged me. 'I'm so sorry, Faith . . .'

We packed up and left, blaming our departure on an upset stomach.

That week, I wrote to the leaders of the church, good friends of ours, and told them of my concerns. I asked if they didn't think it odd that a man in his position should volunteer to be left alone with a bunch of children at night? Didn't he know the rules around child protection? Why would he put himself in a position where an accusation of this sort could be made against him, unless he thought it was worth the risk? I realised that this was a very serious accusation that I was making and that I probably would not be believed. But I didn't care. That man had the trust of scores of people in that church and all I could think about was the children in his care. 'There is a fox in the chicken coop,' I told Jules.

They were incredulous and very surprised and said they'd look into it. After that incident, we went to church less and less, and never left the children at the crèche. I never saw Rich again and heard that he and his wife had resigned as the children's pastors.

I thought hard, as my kids grew up, about how I wanted to talk to them about my faith in God. When they fell over, I said a prayer, asking God to heal them, and every night at bedtime, we said a little prayer. When I was little, I had found comfort in those small rituals, and I hoped that it would comfort them as it had comforted me, but I always felt it was up to them.

When Jude was eleven, sitting in the car with me one day on the way home from school, he said, 'Mummy, would you be very offended if I told you I didn't believe in God?'

I was taken aback and felt a little pang of trepidation. I checked myself.

'No, sweetheart,' I said. 'But I might feel a bit sorry for you because for me, whether God is real or not, the belief has given me a lot of comfort in my life. It's your decision, but I'd say don't close your mind. People who close their minds to things lead a narrower life.'

CHAPTER 17: Cinderella – London, Spring 1989

Alex, the home shepherd from the reception home in south London, came to collect Mum and me from Gatwick off the flight from Mexico. He was English, and Mum told him all about our travels as we crawled along the road that snaked through south-east London in his battered Vauxhall.

I was so happy to have left Mexico and the horrible business with Jorge behind me. I felt as if the spell he had cast over me had finally broken, somewhere mid-air during the flight. As the plane landed, Mum sighed as she looked out of the window and grasped my hand.

'Well, this is England, darling, welcome to the awful weather.'

I could tell from her voice she was relieved to be back – the first time in almost twenty years. We collected our luggage – Mum's battered suitcase and my nylon duffle bag, which was not even full. It was strange to think they contained all that we had. We knew to look for a man called Alex where the taxi drivers stood with their signs, and we found him quickly. I felt relieved when he hugged me; he welcomed me with no trace of flirtatiousness, but as a child. 'It is a blessing to have a new teen in our home,' he said. I was tired and rested my head against the window in the back as we drove, looking out at snatches of suburban London with its off-licences, pubs, betting shops, playing fields and launderettes.

The sky was the colour of dirty glass, and the semi-detached Victorian house, set on a quiet suburban road with a neat front garden, may as well have been Mars after the pollution, noise, grime and chaos of Mexico City and Bangalore. It was strange to find that Mummy's homeland was so quiet, so orderly.

Alex's wife Ellaria greeted us in the hall. She looked like a ghost, as if all colour had drained from within her. Her eyes were disconcertingly vacant. 'Welcome, it is our privilege to receive you from the mission fields. We have prepared a room for the two of you. You must be tired. I'll show you up.'

Mum and I couldn't believe our luck. To have a room to ourselves was unheard of. It was the first time in years we had shared a room, and the first time we had been in the same house for a year. It was lovely to have Mum to myself. We talked mainly about plans and practicalities. I made a mental note not to spoil it by revealing anything about what had happened with Jorge. We hadn't spoken about it since the horrible day when she'd come to talk to the shepherds and I decided it was best to leave it that way.

I was used to the strange, provisioned food in Family homes by now, so felt only slight disappointment at lunch when we came downstairs to find the dining table piled high with loaves of sliced white bread. Next to the bread was a bowl containing hundreds of sachets of sauce, the kind they had in fast food restaurants: blue cheese, ketchup, salad cream, tartar sauce. I was hungry and found myself eyeing a lone sachet of thousand island dressing, hoping nobody else wanted it. We queued up to take a plate. It was adults-only at the main table, so I took my food to the teens and pre-teens table, set off to one side.

At the main table two couples and my mother sat, eating cheese and tomato sandwiches. Alex led the prayer before we ate. At lunch, Ellaria sat slightly apart from the rest of the grown-ups helping themselves to the bread. The eldest of some British–Thai sisters (there were seven, all siblings from one to twelve) had told me the night before that Ellaria was sad because her two-year-old daughter Helen had died six months earlier. Ellaria was quiet because she was learning lessons, the girl told me, explaining the Lord had taken Helen to test Ellaria's faith, to help her work toward her victories. 'She had been out of the Spirit, Mama says,' the little girl explained, and Helen's death was a harsh punishment, but one she deserved. I thought of Shiloh when she told me this, and in our room later, Mum said: 'They are so cruel, so unkind. There is no compassion. That poor, poor woman, she is grieving for her child . . .'

Because this was a reception home, we knew we were on borrowed time. Alex explained to Mummy she would need to go to the council to sign on and get put on the list for a family home. This was Family policy now as there were so many of us returning from the mission fields. Family members would secure a home then invite other members to share it. She went to Lambeth town hall that first week, got put on the dole, and because we were a large family with six children (the others were to follow on once Mum sent word we were settled), we were bumped to the front of the queue and were offered a house in Brixton. Mummy refused it – she was a bit of a snob, and her upbringing in a sprawling house in rural Bedfordshire meant she had certain standards she believed should be upheld.

Life in the reception home had a familiar rhythm, although the day started a little earlier in London than it had in some of the other homes I'd lived in. We were up at 6 a.m. for 'devotions' when, as usual, one of the adults would read us a Mo letter. Then we'd sing the familiar Family songs (I got to play guitar) and we'd discuss the rota for the day.

One memorable morning, an American man, Ted, who was living in the house, and had a passion for fine dining, or at least for the idea of fine dining, decided that I should get a group of the children in the home together to rehearse a few songs. When we were ready, he would drive us to the restaurant run by the chef Albert Roux, who was in the papers at the time because of a reputational crisis involving cockroaches. Ted's big idea was that we should 'witness' to him. He was dearly hoping Mr Roux would be so moved, he'd invite us in for a slap-up meal. Four days later and excited by the idea of 'exquisite' French cuisine, we were ready. There was me on guitar and lead vocals, with three of the Thai sisters and two young English boys who were staying in the reception home. I had worked them hard and we had practised some of the songs I used to perform with my siblings in Costa Rica, and that were popular in the Family. We drove to the restaurant in high spirits, practising our harmonies. 'He's going to love it,' Ted told us. The smaller girls were excited, but I was nervous. I still found witnessing embarrassing.

Roux himself answered the door, and Ted enthusiastically propositioned him: these children had heard about his great skill and would like five minutes of his time to entertain him. He invited us in and stood listening as we sang 'Just a Little Bit of Love'. *Just a little bit of love, goes a long, long way . . .*

Roux looked embarrassed, resting awkwardly on a chair in front of us with the rest of his kitchen staff gathered behind him. When we had finished, they clapped and Mr Roux said: 'Wonderful. That was lovely. Let me offer you children a glass of water.' Then he ushered us out. The drive back to south-east London was deadly silent, Ted's disappointment clear in the hunch of his shoulders.

A week later, Mummy was offered a house in Crystal Palace, which she accepted. 'Crystal Palace is much nicer than Brixton, kids,' she said. By now, all of my siblings, Bev (now fourteen), Michael (thirteen), Petra (twelve) and Maria (six), had joined us too. Dinah, who was now twenty, was still in Mexico with her toddler, and newly pregnant with her second child. We hoped she would join us in time for the baby to come. We were relieved to all be together again, but worried too. The money from Dad's inheritance had been burned through, and we had nothing to live on.

Although there were beds for us all in the new house, Mummy sat us down one evening and told me, Bev, Michael and Petra that the local area shepherds thought it would be best if we went to live in other Family homes. My siblings were to go to the teen home, and I was destined for the north London home. I was to go immediately.

'There's nothing for you to do here,' Mummy said. I was so accustomed to moving and being apart from the rest of my family that it didn't occur to me that I had a say in the matter. What's more, as far as I was concerned, she was right: Crystal Palace was as boring as it got, and with no chance of going to a 'systemite' school, we were knocking around the house, bickering.

The Holloway home was far bigger than the reception home had been, with eight bedrooms. The house was on a main road, one of those big A roads in north London with no sense of community. The anonymity suited us. Even so, we were trained to get off the bus two stops early so we couldn't be easily followed to a Family house by nosey systemites.

Whenever I wasn't out witnessing, I was under virtual house arrest with all the chores I had to get through. The home shepherds reminded the witnessing teams before we were sent out to witness, that unless we were spreading the word of the Lord, we were never to talk to systemite strangers. I got the feeling that there was a new atmosphere of paranoia. Igor, the home shepherd and one of the more draconian of the adults in the Holloway home, exhorted us as we energetically ripped up pages out of books, chucking them into a pile for burning: 'We are the new wine, and they are the old wine. If you put the new wine in the old casks, the casks burst open – it is too strong for them. They are babes. No wonder their bottles will be broken if they see these Mo letters!' he chuckled to himself.

It was no surprise he was paranoid. Public interest and heat on the Family was growing around this time, with newspaper exposés and reports of raids on Family houses around the world drawing attention to the welfare of children within the organisation. I heard whispers about this occasionally, in hushed tones, but it was never openly discussed. Increased warnings about the dangers of 'systemite' contact from the home shepherd and other adults created an unsettled jumpiness in all of the young people at that time. We understood it was imperative we children should lay low. Discipline was stepped up. Some of the little kids were required to memorise passages of Mo letters and recite them on demand in order to qualify for their evening meal. No children were allowed outside until after 3:30 p.m. in case the neighbours reported us to the authorities and forced us into systemite school.

I was initially given a top bunk in a bedroom upstairs, sharing a room with a group of teen and pre-teen girls and a couple of single women. I knew not to get too attached to my bed, though, because it was certain I would get moved. Nowhere was private and soon after I moved in, Ralph, a married teen who lived in the house, began to grope me when we found ourselves together. A couple of times he came into my bed at night. He came even when I had a high fever and was quarantined in a loft room at the top of the house, pouring with sweat. Fortunately, he seemed to be able to source condoms, which were contraband within the Family (I had never known a man to use one), so I didn't get pregnant. I was not attracted to him, but there was some comfort in the attention and the interest of another human being, so I never shouted out.

My relentless chores defined the shape of the days for the eighteen months I spent in the north London home. The rota was punishing and I was used as a workhorse. I did piles of laundry (the clothes of the twenty adults and thirty children in the house). I was also expected to prepare and clear away breakfast (a huge vat of porridge made with water and evaporated milk) and lunch for the household. Once I had done that, it was my responsibility to police 'quiet time' after lunch with the children, some of whom were very little. With some of the other grown-ups and teens, Ralph, his wife Leila and his brother Tom, we would take the children to the park at 3:30. I would then help prepare dinner and run the evening children's activity. Bedtime was at ten, when I collapsed onto my mattress. My body ached. I lived for a weekly lie-in on a Sunday and for the relative release of Saturday nights, when we would have a film night and sometimes other teens would come from other Family homes nearby.

My job, along with Leila, on those Saturday nights was to cut the hair of the boys from other homes who some-times visited. I enjoyed this and did my best to deliver the hairdos that were fashionable but forbidden in the group because they indicated a 'spirit of independence, rebellion and worldliness'. I wanted to look my best on those nights, but with clothes consisting solely of what I could forage from the large 'forsake-all' pile in the cupboard under the stairs, my options were limited. The boys didn't look much better. They would troop into the kitchen looking like a menagerie of tropical birds in their ill-fitting lurid provisioned shell suits popular in the late eighties and early nineties: purple, turquoise and yellow. We would chat, and Leila and I would trim away with our scissors, then we would all sit down, sharing a platter of whatever had been provisioned from the bakery. Saturday evening was prime time for provisioning and doughnuts that had reached their sell-by date were a favourite. The boys would always try to sneak an extra one or two.

The films on the 'approved cult leadership' list for our entertainment on these nights were shockingly heretical, I thought. I wondered why the grown-ups had failed to see the parallels between the plot lines and our reality as children within the Family? They must be blind, or self-absorbed, or both, I decided. To their own minds, we were all rebels who had broken free of the system, with all its restrictions, and were forging a new way. Certainly not my way, I thought. But still . . . We watched *Yentl*, about a young orthodox Jewish woman, played by Barbara Streisand, who disguised herself as a man because she was desperate to study and learn. I loved this film and remembered the time some of the kids had found an old 1950s volume of a *Encyclopaedia Britannica* in one of the cupboards in the house whilst doing chores. A few of the kids crowded around it, fascinated. Aunty Libby soon caught them, confiscated it and rebuked them for being 'curious about the world and systemite books'. We also watched *Dead Poets' Society*, and *Heaven Help Us*, set in a New York school run by cruel Catholic brothers. These stories of rigid authoritarian institutions resonated with me. I began to have fantasies of escaping.

My daydreams were given fresh inspiration when an Australian couple who had been staying in the home for a few weeks, and who had their own camper van, took flight in the middle of the night, and reappeared a week later in the *Daily Mail*, in a double-page exposé of life inside the Family. I heard this second-hand, of course, because systemite newspapers were not allowed in the house. The adults were outraged by the betrayal. They convened an emergency meeting to discuss the backsliders, worrying we were at risk of a raid by the authorities.

Not long after the Australians left, Jack, whom I had shared with in India and had dobbed us in, showed up with a posse of others at the house. He was visiting with some other Family members who were just back from the mission fields. I was so happy to see him. We hugged in the hallway, and checking there was no one around, I said to him:

'So, what are you up to, Jack? How've you been?'

'Oh, you know,' he said with a sardonic smile. 'Changing nappies and waiting for Jesus to come back.'

I chuckled and nodded knowingly. It was so depressing yet so true, that answer. 'Shall we get out of here, together, shall we run away?' I said.

He looked at me as if he didn't understand. 'Don't be crazy, Faith, that would mean going against everything our parents have taught us. Where would we go, anyway? You've always been crazy.'

I made him swear not to tell on me, as he had told on me once before, but a seed was planted within me then. I had said it aloud. It was a seed that grew as I began to question my faith more and more. A Mo letter emerged which recommended some 'strong meat', a new form of worship which I thought was utterly revolting. It was particularly hard to accept and I could tell that even some of the grown-ups were struggling to come to terms with it. We were instructed to masturbate whilst fantasising about Jesus – this was a particularly powerful way to experience the 'love of the Lord', according to Grandpa. We were encouraged to practise, and I attempted to put myself in the frame of mind where I could imagine such a thing. It was impossible; I lasted only seconds and felt so upset, so violated by the idea of it, that I abandoned it immediately. I'll wrap it up into a little bundle of faith and put it on the back burner, I thought, like Mum had with the intergenerational sharing.

I started having out-of-body experiences and disturbing visions in my dreams of the severed head of a black-eyed Jesus. I knew this wasn't my Jesus, but theirs. I would know a vision was coming when I closed my eyes and felt a hissing noise take over my ears. Sometimes I would travel outside of my body. It was very frightening. I kept these experiences to myself and told no one. 'They will try to exorcise me and put me in spiritual quarantine.' Of that I had no doubt.

More and more, I was put on the rota to do witnessing, which meant I got to escape my chores. I was sent out on a number of occasions with a zealous African American uncle, Demetrius. One Saturday, out in west London selling our tapes, I caught a glimpse of Freddie Mercury performing in his skin-tight jeans and vest; it was on the TV in the background in a shop we had wandered into. He was singing 'Another One Bites the Dust'. I was mesmerised. Systemite music was strictly forbidden and I had rarely heard anything like it. I was transfixed by his passion and his camp charisma.

'Disgusting homo, what a pervert,' Demetrius spat, sensing my reaction. 'Let's get out of here.'

I remember that particular occasion for another reason. It had been a long day, wandering up and down Kensington High Street trying to sell our posters and tapes. We had had very few takers. I knew, though, at the end of the day, that Demetrius would provision us a good dinner.

He would always pick a restaurant at the end of our witnessing days, and explain to the manager that we were missionaries, in need of food. Despite the embarrassment, I could usually slope in after him and I always enjoyed the meal. This time, though, having selected an almost empty Indian restaurant and asked for the manager, an extremely good-looking British Indian man introduced himself.

'Faith has something to ask you,' Demetrius said, pushing me forward.

I froze, my cheeks burning up, and my tongue suddenly bloated, stupid in my mouth. Eventually, I mumbled something about being missionaries who help raise funds for children in orphanages and for those in old people's homes. That this was the end of our day of fundraising in the local area. 'Would you be able to donate something for us to eat?' I asked, feeling the prickles of shame crawl up from my chest to my cheeks and to the top of my ears. The manager looked straight at me. I could see he had taken pity on me, and he said: 'Be my guest, Faith. Both of you. Order whatever you like.'

His kindness and understanding of my predicament, a fellow young person, seeing my mortification for what it was, felt remarkable to me. He was a systemite stranger. It was another indication that perhaps at least some people in the outside world were kind after all.

At this time, letters appeared in the house from Grandpa enthusing about a new mission field opening up in Eastern

Europe. The fall of the Berlin Wall and revolution in Romania meant people there were ripe for witnessing. There would be new 'missile teams' (an acronym for something I can no longer remember). Each house was to volunteer a team. I was overjoyed to be picked – I felt like Cinderella, desperate to escape the drudgery of my life in London. I learnt I was to go with Uncle Stewart and Aunty Mila, a British–Dutch couple who did most of the driving, along with Ajit, (who had changed his name to Peter, his new 'bible' name) a British Pakistani guy in his early twenties, so full of enthusiasm for our mission, it was infectious. There was also a Spanish man, Miguel, who was very withdrawn and, I later realised, conflicted about his sexuality (homosexuality, especially for men, being strictly forbidden within the Family). We made up a motley crew in our converted van, stuffed with brightly coloured Family posters to distribute. It made a change that we were instructed to give the posters away and not to have to ask for donations. We drove through France and Belgium, then through Luxembourg and Germany and into Austria. I would stand with one foot balanced on the sink, and another on the edge of the top bunk, half of my body sticking out of the van's skylight, drinking in the scenery as we drove. We slept like sardines in a can until we reached the Family home in Austria.

Worn out from the trip, I was looking forward to a hot meal, and a bed for the night. I was happy to see my friend India, whom I had last seen three years ago in Greece and then in India, but was shocked to find she had a baby on her hip. We stopped to chat, but as I cooed over the baby and we caught up, I saw a stern forty-something man approaching. He looked angry, full of righteous indignation. Her husband's father. He spoke to her as if she were five. 'Your attitude this morning was totally out of the Spirit!' he said, in front of everyone in the room. 'You are to receive correction from your elders without justifying yourself. You set a terrible example to the other teens and pre-teens in the room. I want you to ask for forgiveness at devotions, tomorrow. Amen?'

I could see the humiliation on her blushing face. 'Amen,' she meekly replied.

At sixteen, India was a year younger than me. After apologising to her father-in-law, she told me she was married to Andre, an older boy of eighteen. This fact, imparted with a brittle pride in her voice, made me feel far removed from her. Within the Family, marriage was the only way teens could move to a higher-status eche-lon of EA, 'experimental adult', which meant they were allowed to move to a married room and drink a little more wine. Her new status gave her an air of superiority. But I wasn't fooled; I saw how they treated her. At that moment, I made a promise to myself that I wouldn't fall into that trap. I wouldn't become a baby factory.

We didn't stay long in Austria and were quickly on the road again, headed to our final destination and our designated mission field, Romania, six months after its revolution. I had no idea of what to expect, although I knew a wave of rebellion was in the air. When we arrived, Bucharest was chaotic and frightening. The infrastructure had broken down. I remember all the toilets were broken, overflowing with shit everywhere we went; I was disgusted and astounded to see smudged fingerprints all over the walls, there was not an inch of clean space left on the floor, even in the Grand Hotel in the centre of the city where the journalists were staying. I had never witnessed such filth, even in India when the sewers overflowed. There were gangs of revolutionaries and soldiers patrolling and we heard constant gunfire from where we slept in our van in the car park of the Grand Hotel. We realised it was too dangerous for us in the city, so we drove out into the countryside where the villagers were happy to see us and seemed entranced by the rainbow colours on our posters. We got mobbed and ran out of our merchandise just before our three-month mission timetable was finished.

On one occasion, as I distributed posters on the high street of a mountain village, a striking-looking man approached me. His hair was black and he had very dark skin. He was tall and his eyes were bright green. He wore a leather hat and his white shirt was unbuttoned. 'You. Me,' he said. 'Hotel.' He grinned, showing a row of gold teeth. A jolt of fear went through my body. I shook my head, frantically scanning the high street for the others. I spotted them and hotfooted my way over to join them.

Back in Holloway, I was given a room with single mother, Ruth, the American disciple in her late twenties with her two children, Zachariah, aged nine, whose Israeli father was long gone, and a six-year-old boy Akio, conceived with a Japanese 'fish' she had met in the mission field. Ruth seemed detached from her children and was keen to make them my responsibility. It was hard work caring for them and the other little kids in the home. I tried to teach them what little I knew myself – using flash cards with the names of flowers on them: Michaelmas daisies, lily of the valley, tea rose. Mostly, I taught them the Family songs I had learnt myself as a young child. The Family protocol for the care of children involved a daily routine which included 'quiet time' every day after lunch. The most difficult times for me were when I was shut in a room with the children, trying to enforce 'quiet time'. At times they would be restless, not willing or capable of silence.

A month or so in, there was one afternoon when Ruth's children were particularly restless. Akio was misbehaving. I could hear he was whining and being dis-obedient although I was in the room beneath his, doing chores. Ruth appeared at the door: 'Faith, can you give Akio a spanking? I can't deal with it anymore.'

I obediently went upstairs, pulled down his trousers, bent him over my knee and I spanked him, hard. He begged me not to: 'No, no, no,' but I ignored him and carried on. He wriggled and kicked just as I had when I got my spankings as a little girl in Costa Rica. I felt a sense of power and righteousness swelling within me. I was in control; it was intoxicating. So much of what was pent up within me I vented on him that day. I will never forget the look of fear in his huge eyes. Afterwards, I hugged him and asked him to pray with me, as was the ritual in the Family after every spanking: 'Jesus, help me to be a good boy. Help me not to be disobedient to my mummy, in Jesus's name, Amen.' He managed the words between sobs. Immediately afterwards, I felt disgusted with myself. By my violence. I saw his bruised body the next day and felt deeply ashamed. But I was also frightened for myself, worried about those feelings of power and righteousness. I knew those feelings were wrong and that they were cowardly. I realised it was a sign that I was becoming one of *them*. I had to get out.

Epilogue: Healing

I began to write this book just as the Covid-19 virus was declared a pandemic and we went into lockdown. Like many of us, I found myself with time and space to inhabit my memories and relive my past. There were many sleepless nights, but also laugh-out-loud moments, as I recalled some of the crazy situations I have found myself in. I have wondered, what would my life have been like had my parents not joined a cult? Would I be the same person? Without hesitation I can say that I do not regret my experiences. They have made me who I am.

Although I have never had formal therapy, I have continuously looked for ways in which I could help myself to overcome the traumas of my childhood. Experimenting with psychedelics was the first step for me. They catapulted me out of my depression and a hopelessly nihilistic view of life and allowed me to see things from a completely different perspective. Then, I began to visit church on and off. There, I opened myself up to accepting love, and prayers offered up on my behalf, and I cried. A lot.

One day, at the age of thirty-six, I discovered yoga. I learned to notice my thoughts, my breathing and my body with gratitude and without judgment. I also found 'tapping', an alternative therapy for trauma, extremely helpful. In 2011, one of my sisters introduced me to a woman who was training to be an Emotional Freedom Technique (EFT) therapist, and she offered me a few free sessions as part of her training. At first, it sounded bonkers, but I was open to trying it for myself. I was to call to mind negative and traumatic experiences and say the line, 'I deeply love, accept and forgive myself,' whilst tapping acupressure points on my face and chest. I found interesting evidence for its benefits in treating PTSD in war veterans and survivors of abuse. As I moved through the process, I learned to question my desires and beliefs, and I made a promise that I would allow myself to change my mind based on new knowledge gained as I go through life.

I worked through the most acute of my painful memories in turn, using the mantra and EFT. I practiced tapping on my own, using videos on YouTube for guidance. Nathanael's beatings, the humiliations and betrayals, the rapes, being shouted down by the teens and adults in the Philippines, spanking Akio in the house in London . . . 'I deeply love, accept and forgive myself.' Sometimes, during these very intense sessions, I felt a similar version of the sensation I had felt with the pastor, when the 'demons' had made their way out of me. I wondered if the experience I'd had with the pastor was just another way of tapping into a deeper part of myself. Could it be that when we have traumatic experiences, something gets stuck? Then, when we're ready, the original trauma can be released in a range of ways, ecstatic experiences being one of them?

I felt lighter and freer the more I used the EFT technique. I taught my boys how to tap too. I showed them an acupressure point on their hand that they could surreptitiously tap, telling them that it would help them to stay calm during stressful situations at school or in the playground. Theo used to have trouble sleeping at night, so we would sometimes tap before bed. We would recall whatever events of the day were causing him to feel anxious, and it would invariably work, helping him to relax his mind and body. I was grateful that I had found a tool that could help me to help my boys, instead of looking on helplessly whilst they navigated the often cruel world of childhood friendships and school.

By tuning into myself in this way, with the tapping and mindfulness, I became aware of a punishing inner voice. My inner critic. When I began to analyse my thoughts, I wondered if it was my mother and father's voice I was hearing. I began to notice that, for all my outward confidence, inside I was insecure and did not truly love or value myself. I understood and accepted that in order to truly love and value others, I would have to start with me.

I was overly hard on myself and would mercilessly berate and hate myself in moments of sadness and pain at the memory of horrible events. 'Pull yourself together!' the voice would shout. 'Stop being so self-indulgent and self-pitying, you got off lightly, many people suffered much worse than you.'

This harsh, unmerciful voice was hard at work a lot of the time, trying to run things. The tapping helped me to recognise it for what it truly was. Not my voice, but a recording of other people's voices. Gradually, I have grown better at zoning it out and tuning in to my own instincts. I am learning how to put that voice back in its box, the little dictator that it is, full of bad advice and destructive criticism. It can stay there, I've decided, along with the letters, yellowing journals and those newspaper and magazine clippings of the indignant, angry girl who spoke out.

I am proud of that girl, for her bravery and ferocity, for her willingness to call out evil. I realise now, though, with the passage of time, that my rebellion has been a quieter, more private one: taking responsibility for myself by facing up to the voices of the past, so that I can live and love in peace.

Acknowledgements

I would like to give my heartfelt thanks to Rupert Younger, my dear friend and mentor. This book would never have been written without his encouragement, support, and introductions.

On a summer's dinner and drinks do in 2019, I blurted out to him that I had been born in a cult and that I had escaped when I was 18. It hadn't been long since my youngest son had discovered the old box with papers from my past. This event shook me, and the entire saga was at the forefront of my mind. Rupert looked at me intrigued and asked me how I had escaped. I told him. 'You must write a book!' he said. 'Oh, no' I said. 'I'm not a writer, and besides, no one will want to publish it'.

Rupert encouraged me otherwise, and some weeks later, he introduced me to my wonderful agent, Katie Fulford. Thank you, Katie, for working tirelessly on my behalf and for your unwavering belief in me. One morning I found myself sitting with these two lovely, decent people telling them my weird story over a cup of coffee. As I began to tell it, I could barely believe what was coming out of my own mouth. Did all this really happen to me? Yes, it had happened to me. And it is an extraordinary story. Perhaps it might be worth telling after all, I thought.

Katie introduced me to my publisher, Briony Gowlett, senior editor at Hodder and Stoughton and to the brilliant and highly skilled ghost writer, Zoe McDonald. Thank you Briony for jumping in with us on this project and my thanks to you, Zoe, for helping me to sculpt and shape this book. You have generously given me your expert advice and I deeply appreciate your kindness, sensitivity, and patience. It has been a joy to work with you!

I would like to thank my siblings for being my friends and confidants. I love you all so very dearly. Despite our many squabbles over the years, we always kiss and make up. Blood is thicker than water, no matter what they tried to tell us, and we have stuck together like glue, despite the cult's best efforts to tear us apart.

My thanks to Eli Stone for giving me permission to include his beautiful song, and a big thank you to Vicky, my dear friend and party partner for still being in my life.

A very special thanks is reserved for my two sons. It is an honour and a privilege to be your mother and I love you with all of my heart. And last but not least, a huge thanks to my husband and best friend for being my rock. Never a dull moment with you, my love. Never a dull moment!